THE STORY OF BABY P

Setting the record straight

Ray Jones

First published in Great Britain in 2014 by

Policy Press
University of Bristol
6th Floor
Howard House
Queen's Avenue
Bristol BS8 1SD
UK
Tel +44 (0)117 331 5020
Fax +44 (0)117 331 5367
e-mail tpp-info@bristol.ac.uk
www.policypress.co.uk

North American office:
The Policy Press
c/o The University of Chicago Press
1427 East 60th Street
Chicago, IL 60637, USA
t: +1 773 702 7700
f: +1 773-702-9756
e:sales@press.uchicago.edu
www.press.uchicago.edu

British Library Cataloguing in Publication Data
A catalogue record for this book is available from the British Library

Library of Congress Cataloging-in-Publication Data
A catalog record for this book has been requested

ISBN 978 1 44731 622 0 paperback

The right of Ray Jones to be identified as author of this work has been asserted by him in accordance with the 1988 Copyright, Designs and Patents Act.

Cover design by Chris Hamilton-Emery
Front cover: photograph kindly supplied by
Nicola Margaret/istockphoto
Printed and bound in Great Britain by Hobbs, Southampton
Policy Press uses environmentally responsible print partners

FSC
www.fsc.org
MIX
Paper from
responsible sources
FSC® C020438

Contents

List of photo credits

p 25   Upper image courtesy of Paul Grover; map courtesy of Rachel Pistol
and OpenStreetMap.org

pp 49 & 51 Images courtesy of the London Metropolitan Police

p 65   Image courtesy of Dafydd Jones

pp 83, 85, 99, 108, 137, 173, 182, 211, 212, 239, 244, 254, 308
With thanks to the University of Cambridge Library

p 180 Images courtesy of BSkyB

p 242 Left image courtesy of National Images; right image courtesy of
the Press Association

p 246 Image courtesy of the Press Association

The author would also like to thank Rachel Pistol for undertaking the picture
research for the book.

Foreword

Patrick Butler, Society, Health and Education Editor, *The Guardian*

It is hard to look back at the Baby P story, five years down the line, and not feel vaguely bewildered by the collective madness it unleashed. At the heart of the tale is the desperately sad death of a 17-month-old boy, Peter Connelly, at the hands of his mother, her lover and his brother in Haringey, North London, in 2007. But this local tragedy spun out of control, following the conviction of Peter's killers just over a year later, becoming a full-blown national outbreak of public hysteria, and a media witch hunt. A tabloid narrative of Baby P became quickly established, supposedly telling us important truths about ourselves, but they were not the truths we first thought. It seemed initially to be a straightforward narrative with clear-cut heroes and villains; now it presents as a peculiarly grotesque fable of vicious media exploitation, and political opportunism.

Over time, the story has turned on its head. Characters in the narrative who initially seemed honourable and decisive have been revealed as opportunistic and cowardly; some who were portrayed as bunglers and incompetents have been shown to be unjustly scapegoated. What started as a simple tale of almost unimaginable cruelty and an earnest desire for justice now stands as a guide to a complex, murky world of political brutality, administrative cynicism and media greed. We were supposed to believe the response to the tragedy – the crude sacking of Haringey's Director of Children's Services, Sharon Shoesmith, above all – was about political boldness; we now know that what happened in the wake of the trial of Peter's killers was driven as much by official panic, fear and blame avoidance. The sad irony is that the public may have believed that the vast resources of time, money and political capital expended in the wake of Baby P may have made another such tragedy less likely. The truth is that it hasn't. This was ostensibly a story about child protection, but really, it was about media power, political calculation and bureaucratic back-covering on a grand scale.

This is not to forget Peter. The circumstances of his death, recounted initially through reports of the criminal trial of his killers,

—

are genuinely disturbing. I recall reading court reports and feeling shock and repulsion, and inchoate anger towards the perpetrators. A child death of this nature is relatively rare, and press accounts naturally triggered profound soul-searching and shock. How could such a horrific killing happen? How can we try to ensure it does not happen again? The singular barbarity of the killing led many to wonder if our child protection services were as good as they could be. There was a natural interest in finding out what had happened in Haringey, and whether errors had been made.

Like most people, I imagine, I followed the campaign against Shoesmith and Haringey Council orchestrated by *The Sun* newspaper, in November 2008, with slightly detached fascination (at that point I was not involved in *The Guardian*'s coverage of the story). I watched the then Children's Secretary Ed Balls' sacking of Shoesmith delivered live on TV with appalled awe. I thought Shoesmith's treatment had been harsh but believed – naively it turned out – that it must have been surely warranted. It was not until I read the Balls-commissioned joint area review into Haringey later that afternoon that alarm bells rang. The summary dismissal of Shoesmith led me to expect she had been guilty of grave personal errors – gross misconduct at the very least. The absurdly-hyped report, however, was oddly bland and hardly exceptionally critical; if a director of children's services gets vilified and sacked without compensation on live TV for this, I thought, there will be many others fearing the chop. Something, I felt, was not quite right.

A few weeks later I met Shoesmith for the first of a series of regular meetings. We'd sit in a cafe near King's Cross and talk at length about the case. I wanted to hear her side of the story, which, after all, had not been aired publicly. She painstakingly took me through the case, what had really happened, and how she had been scapegoated. It was complex, and took me a while to piece together. At the same time I wasn't sure I believed her version of events, and equally she needed to decide whether she could trust me. At this time she was pursued and harassed constantly by tabloid photographers and reporters. Articles about her appeared in *The Sun* almost daily. As I sat patiently hearing her story, it was hard initially to overcome the established narrative about Shoesmith – arrogant, incompetent, untroubled by contrition. But the more we spoke, the more I realised the official version of events was inconsistent and partial. I went over her story again and again. This was far more complicated than anyone had so far been prepared to say. In early 2009 I interviewed Shoesmith in *The Guardian*: it resulted in a front-page story, in which she memorably accused Balls of 'breathtaking recklessness' in his handling of the Baby Peter aftermath. She subsequently went to court to overturn her sacking, launching a judicial review against Balls, Ofsted and Haringey. This, I thought, was hugely risky.

But Shoesmith, I had to come to realise, was made of granite (I knew nothing then of the extent of the private stress she was experiencing). Going to court was, for her, about honour, truth and justice – not values obviously associated with her at the time. The political establishment wanted closure; it crushed her and expected her to disappear quietly. Instead Shoesmith got back off the floor, and against the odds and at great personal cost, and after two seemingly interminable court cases over the next two years, she won – and the real story of Baby P slowly emerged.

Professor Ray Jones tells the real story of the Peter Connelly case and its aftermath in this compelling account. Jones was one of the few authoritative voices who openly voiced scepticism of the original Baby P narrative, and was prepared to warn of the unintended negative consequences of the management of the fiasco for child protection and social work. As he makes clear in the following pages, few in the media (or politics, or the children's services profession) were prepared to challenge openly the official version of events (*The Guardian*, happily, and Tim Donovan of BBC London being almost alone in going against the grain). But why was the media so supine? Why was the social work profession so timid, and politicians so spineless? Why did *The Sun* pursue Shoesmith and Haringey with such hostility and hatred? Why were the Metropolitan Police and Great Ormond Street Hospital, both of which played a critical part in Peter's story, so quickly airbrushed out of the picture? What were the links between politicians, police and *The Sun*'s publishers News International, and how did these connections come to affect the way the story was told and presented? Why were the official accounts of what happened in Haringey (such as a second serious case review) so shoddy and partial?

Jones not only challenges the prevailing Baby P myths, and re-tells the story in its proper complexity, but also spells out the overwhelmingly negative consequences of the entire episode for social workers and the families they work with (consequences which continue to reverberate after all this time). Some of our most powerful and ostensibly talented politicians play central roles in the sorry saga of Baby P, showing varying degrees of poor judgement and cynical opportunism (although none, I'm sure, would profess regret). One of the ironies of this story is that Shoesmith – who at the start became the most vilified woman in the country – emerges at the end as a battered, if unlikely, hero. For the British political class, however, it was a shameful episode, and one that Jones recounts brilliantly.

Introduction

Peter Connelly was a little boy who died, aged 17 months, in 2007, because of the horrific abuse inflicted on him by those who were his carers. Accounts of his life and of the neglect and ill treatment that led to his death have been widely reported.

During the criminal trials of those who were to be found guilty of causing or allowing his death, the press and other media were not allowed to give Peter's name, so he was called 'Baby P'. 'Baby P', if not Peter Connelly, became a name widely recognised by the public across the UK and internationally. This is exceptional. Fifty to seventy children, although thankfully a small number (but still too many), die in the UK from abuse or neglect each year. The media may never report their deaths, or if they do report them, only very rarely do they receive any continuing coverage and comment. The deaths are briefly news, but then the media move on. But not so with the 'Baby P story'.

One tabloid newspaper and its editor in particular, *The Sun* and Rebekah Brooks, turned the death of 'Baby P' into a campaign. The core of the campaign was not about more severe punishment for those who were involved and implicated in killing Peter. It was not about improving the child protection services and system in England. Instead, it was a campaign of vengeance and vilification directed at those who gave their professional lives to assisting and protecting children and who had sought to assist and protect Peter.

It was a campaign that was heavily targeted at social workers, their managers and the council where they were employed, with, for example, *The Sun* initiating a petition demanding the sacking of the social workers and their managers. Others who had roles in assisting and protecting children, such as those within the health services and the police, largely stayed on the margins of the story.

It was a campaign that had intense implications for those who were targeted, and also more generally for child protection services, and therefore for children and families, throughout England and beyond. Social workers, their managers and their own children were threatened and placed in danger. Reporters and paparazzi photographers harassed them, not for days or weeks, but for months and years. They lost their jobs and subsequently their careers, not able to continue with their commitment to care for and to protect children. They have become unemployable, left stranded and destitute.

For the child protection system more generally, it is now creaking at the seams, and at or near the point of collapse. Workloads have rocketed. Less time, in some places very little time, is available for social workers and others to get to know children and families and to make the difficult decisions about when courts need to be asked to order that a child be taken from its family. The fear and threat that was now a burden on every social worker's shoulders, that they, too, could become a target of *The Sun* and others has, in part, led to more children being removed through the courts from their families. Others then, such as *The Times* and the *Mail*, castigate social workers for taking children from their parents. The media know how to have it both and every way.

This book tells the tale of the 'Baby P story', how this story was structured by *The Sun* and others and how it has been promoted and pursued year after year. Although Peter Connelly died in August 2007, it was when his mother and two men living in the family home were convicted in November 2008 for their involvement in his death that the media 'Baby P story' was launched. Five years later, at the time of writing in 2013, the story continued to be told and further fed and fuelled whenever there was another development, as when the social workers sought to challenge in tribunals and courts their sackings by Haringey Council, which itself came under intense media and political pressure.

I am a social worker who became a director of social services, and who has been involved in protecting children for over 40 years. I am now Professor of Social Work, researching, for example, services to make 'troubled families' less troubled and troublesome. I have also been the independent chair of a local safeguarding children board

(LSCB) for a major English city, and have overseen the safeguarding improvement programmes, reporting to government ministers, in five areas where the national inspectorate has rated child protection services as 'inadequate'.

During the initial frenzy of media activity about 'Baby P' in November 2008 and the following months, I was a frequent media commentator and columnist. I presented a five-minute cameo for Sky News, 'A Letter to Mr Balls', warning about destabilising England's child protection services. It was broadcast over and over again during the weekend at the end of November 2008 before the Monday at the beginning of December when Mr Balls gave his press conference. At the press conference he dismissed Sharon Shoesmith from her role as Director of Children's Services in Haringey.

On the day of the press conference the BBC located me in a television studio so that I could give an instant response to Mr Balls' comments. Immediately after, ITN and Channel Five News interviewed me on the street outside the BBC studios. When Sharon Shoesmith's initial judicial review about her sacking was concluded, the BBC arranged for me to be at the Royal Courts of Justice, and I gave interviews on the BBC News Channel, BBC Radio 4 and Radio 5, and was also interviewed by LBC Radio. Later, in a related story, which clustered along with others with the 'Baby P story', about the sentencing of two boys in Edlington who had seriously attacked and abused two other boys, I was at the Millbank Studios at Westminster and between 11:30 and 18:00 gave 14 live radio and television interviews for the BBC, ITN, ITV London, Channel Four News, Sky News, among others.

One reason why I had so much media engagement at the time the 'Baby P story' was at its height was, I was told, that other possible commentators − some of whom I had suggested to the media − who might speak about the realities of child protection and the management of child protection services were not willing to be interviewed. There were a few other voices that were heard, including some leading social work academics and spokespeople for the British Association of Social Workers (BASW), but powerful voices that might have been heard, for example those of directors of children's services, were largely silent. There is no doubt that the tabloid press, in particular, was seen as hostile and harassing, and maybe it was best to 'keep heads down'.

But the consequence for me was that I was drawn into how the 'Baby P story' was being told, was kept abreast of how the story was being shaped and developed, and became more and more aware and alert to the impact and implications of *The Sun*'s campaign and of the targeting of social workers and their managers.

This book draws heavily on my understanding of how the 'Baby P story' was created and championed by parts of the press and other media. It relies heavily, indeed largely exclusively, on what is already known within the public arena, although there is more that I have been told and more that I understand about the how the story was shaped and fed, and some of what I have been told – if true – is more shocking than what is recorded and reported in this book. But I felt it best to rely on what has already been made available to anyone who wants to track the media reporting or to seek out publicly available court and other documents.

There are, of course, others with whom I have spoken in the process of writing this book. Reporters and media commentators and columnists, people who were personally involved in the events at the time they were unfolding, some of those who were drawn into the story by the formal roles they were given as a consequence of and following the initial media telling of the 'Baby P story', and wise and informed people who have themselves tracked the impact of the story. On reflection, I thought it best to leave them all unnamed and unreferenced in this book. Although their contributions to my understanding have been considerable, not all want to be named, and naming some and not others could end up being more exposing.

This book reflects my horror at how good people who undertook distressing and difficult – and sometimes dangerous – work to protect children were attacked and abused by powerful media forces, with other powerful forces getting drawn into the process. But the greatest horror is what happened to a little child, Peter Connelly, and my concern is that the campaigning by *The Sun* and others has done nothing to make it safer for children like Peter.

ONE

The life and death of Peter Connelly

Two of the shortest sentences in this book are 'Peter was 17 months old when he died' and 'Sharon Shoesmith was scapegoated'. The first was on 3 August 2007. The second reports the Court of Appeal judgment on 27 May 2011. This book is largely about what happened between these dates in the telling of the story of 'Baby P'. But first, who was the little boy who continued to be called 'Baby P' even when his real name was known?

Peter Connelly was born on 1 March 2006 in Tottenham, North London. Few will recognise him by this name – most will know him as 'Baby P', as he was named in November 2008 when there was the first significant media coverage following the criminal trial of his mother, her boyfriend and the boyfriend's brother, each of whom were found to have been culpable for and to have contributed to his death. He was later identified as 'Baby Peter', and in the serious case reviews that were undertaken to track the involvement of public agencies and others with Peter and his family, he was anonymously named 'Child A'.

Throughout this book he will be known as Peter or as Peter Connelly, the names he was probably beginning to recognise for himself when he was killed, aged 17 months, on 3 August 2007. However, across the UK and much further afield it was the media's renaming Peter as 'Baby P' which was and is remembered, along with the iconic picture of Peter looking up from a squared-tiled kitchen floor, which was widely used across the national and international print press, television and internet. Even when I showed it in Siberia in 2010 during a presentation to 300 Russian social services directors and policy makers, it was readily recognised.

When Peter was examined following his death, his injuries included a fractured spine, eight fractured ribs on his left side, a torn frenum (the tissue that connects the tongue to the lower mouth or the gum to the cheek), bruising, marks to his head and a tooth was found in his colon.[1] In total, it was noted that he had over 50 injuries.[2] He had also been examined by a paediatrician two days before he died who had noted numerous bruises, that his weight was only at the 9th centile (ie, 91 per cent of children of his age would have been expected to be heavier), and that he had a fungal infection on his ear and scalp.[3] This was, therefore, a little boy who had experienced considerable neglect and abuse.

There had been long-standing concerns about Peter's care and there was a child protection plan in place. Indeed, his mother, Tracey Connelly, had been subject to two criminal investigations for the possible abuse of Peter, although she was informed by the police the day before Peter's death that she was not to be prosecuted.[4] But what is now known about Peter and his family, their backgrounds, and Peter's life of 17 months?

Tracey Connelly's background is described in the second serious case review commissioned by Haringey Local Safeguarding Children Board.[5] Serious case reviews have to be undertaken when children are seriously injured or die as a consequence of abuse or neglect. Tracey Connelly has been described as having 'a lifetime's experience of dealing with social workers'.[6] Born in Leicester in 1981, she lived there until her mother and stepfather separated. It is stated that there was domestic violence that was witnessed by both Tracey Connelly and her brother. In 1984 she moved with her mother to London while her brother remained in Leicester with his father. Throughout her childhood, Tracey Connelly had wrongly understood that her stepfather was her biological father.

Tracey Connelly's stepfather died in 1989 when she was eight years old, and her brother then joined her and their mother in London. He is described as having difficulties in settling into his new home, with 'challenging' behaviour, to have been violent at school and to his sister, and to have truanted from school and to have started offending.

In May 1990 the brother was placed on the London Borough of Islington's child protection register because of physical abuse. The mother is described as having drink and drug problems.[7]

A year later, Tracey Connelly's name was also added to the child protection register, because of neglect. It is stated that there were concerns about her appearance and hygiene, and that the parenting she received was inconsistent and abusive. She was referred to the child guidance service, which suggests concerns about her own behaviour and development, and in 1993 she was placed in a special residential boarding school.

The second serious case review is so heavily redacted and edited, with sections blacked out, that following the sequence and timings of Tracey Connelly's subsequent years as a young person and young adult is difficult. It is noted that she met her future husband, who was 17 years older than her,[8] in 1997, when she was 16, but nothing is known about his background from the published reports. This highlights a significant limitation of the serious case review process, which is based largely on agency records that may be incomplete and that were prepared for different purposes than trying to piece together and understand the events which led to the death of a child.

What is indicated in the serious case review report is that Tracey Connelly and her husband had two daughters between 1997 and 2001, and that she experienced post-natal depression and struggled to cope with two young children. This would not have been made any easier with their very difficult and cramped housing situation. At the time of the birth of their first child, they were living in Islington with Tracey Connelly's mother in accommodation that was described as untidy, unclean and unsuitable. The health visitor noted that Tracey Connelly did not have a close relationship with her mother, and that Tracey needed help with parenting skills; there were concerns about home safety, and she was smoking 60 cigarettes a day. However, Mr Connelly, who was then her partner before they married, was seen as supportive and was in work. Subsequently they were living with two little children in a one-bedroom council flat along with a tenant, a relative of Mr Connelly. In 2001 the council placed them in temporary Bed & Breakfast accommodation in Tottenham, and they were then rehoused on their own as a family, in their own flat in Tottenham.

In 2007 Tottenham had a population of 224,700, was growing rapidly, with an increase of 8.6 per cent since 1991, a high population turnover, and 34 per cent of its population from black and minority ethnic groups. There were a significant number of refugees and asylum-seekers. Over 160 languages were spoken in Tottenham's schools. It was the fifth most diverse borough in London, and three quarters of Haringey's almost 50,000 children and young people aged under 20 were from minority ethnic communities.

It was also the fifth most deprived London borough and the 18th most deprived area nationally. As such, Tottenham had a large number of families with considerable social and economic difficulties. It had twice the national and London rates of long-term unemployment. In the White Hart Lane ward, the area to which the Connelly family were to move in 2007, over 50 per cent of children were eligible for free school meals (the national proportion is 15 per cent).[9, 10] This combination of deprivation and diversity meant that Tottenham was both a difficult and a demanding area for all those working with children, and especially children who might be in need of protection.

In July 2003 Mr and Mrs Connelly married, and a third daughter was born. But the marriage was described as soon having serious difficulties, with Mr Connelly moving out of the family home. By 2005, however, not only were Mr and Mrs Connelly living together again as a family of five, but Tracey was pregnant, and Peter Connelly was born on 1 March 2006. The relationship between Mr and Mrs Connelly was still fraught, however. Tracey Connelly had met another man whom she initially described as 'just a friend'. Mr Connelly again moved out of the family home in the summer of 2006, this time never to return, after Tracey invited her 'male friend' to her school reunion, instead of her husband.[11] Tracey Connelly's new friend was to become a more significant part of her life, and of Peter's life. He was Steven Barker, one of the people later convicted of causing Peter's death. Steven Barker was aged 30 in the summer of 2006 and Tracey Connelly was 25. At this time, Peter Connelly was four months old. His three older sisters were also living in the family home.

Steven Barker is described as 'simple', not able to write proper text messages, and as being sadistic and fascinated with pain.[12] It is claimed he had tortured guinea pigs and tormented frogs by breaking their legs, was a collector of Nazi memorabilia and possessed a number of knives. It is also stated that he was shy and easily dominated, including by Jason Owen, his elder brother, and that Tracey Connelly increasingly left him to do the housework and to look after Peter.[13] It is stated that in 1995 he and Jason Owen had attacked their 82-year-old grandmother to try to get her to change her will in their favour; they were charged with grievous bodily harm but were not prosecuted because of lack of evidence.[14] *The Sun* newspaper claimed that Steven Barker had been sadistic as a child and, typically graphic and gruesome, described him as a '6ft 4in, 18st monster'.[15]

According to the serious case review, following Mr Connelly's departure from the family home, he initially saw his children two or three times a week. Tracey Connelly was being treated for depression, and had been referred in July 2005 by her then general practice doctor (GP) to a primary care mental health worker as she was irritable and crying. She was prescribed medication for anxiety and depression. In the summer of 2006, her concerns were said to be related to her separation from her husband, to her mother's drinking and to the impact this had had on her mother's care of her grandchildren. It was Tracey Connelly's mother who had been actively involved in looking after the children, and it is noted that most of the time she had also taken the older children to school.[16] This takes on a significance later.

In summary, the first phase of a few months in the summer of 2006 of Peter Connelly's short life was probably the most stable period he ever knew. His mother and father were living with him, along with his three older sisters (two at infant school; one at pre-school). Even then, however, his experiences as a baby were not all harmony and security. There were tensions between his parents, his mother had a new 'male friend', she was depressed, with a history of anxiety and irritability, and in a family health needs assessment completed by a health visitor, it was noted that there had been a discussion with Tracey Connelly about hygiene, smoking and health and safety, and with the home being very untidy. Tracey Connelly's behaviour was volatile, and there were concerns at the school attended by Peter's two oldest sisters about her bad language, intimidation of other parents and her shouting and complaining vociferously within the school. The school was also concerned whether she was taking the necessary action to tackle her children's head lice.

None of this might be surprising when it is recalled how bad were Tracey Connelly's own experiences of parenting from a mother who drank heavily, where it has been described how sexual boundaries seem to have been confused,[17] who had not cared well for her own children, and now, as Peter's maternal grandmother, was still involved in the care of the Connelly children. The poor competence and capacity in parenting – both of Tracey Connelly's mother and of Tracey Connelly herself – was likely to be having an impact on the children, and one of Peter's older sisters had already been referred to a child development centre because of concerns about her development and behaviour.[18] But while Peter's parents were living together there was no information or evidence about assaults or abuse of any of the children. Indeed, the health visitor had noted that the parents appeared loving towards the children. All of this was about to change for Peter over the coming months after Peter's parents separated in the summer.

In September 2006 Tracey Connelly took Peter to see the GP because of a cough and a nappy rash. What, in retrospect, may be seen to have more significance is that Tracey Connelly commented to the GP that Peter bruised easily, and that she was afraid she might be accused of hurting him. The second serious case review report notes that the GP might have seen some significance, although this is not recalled by the GP, that a mother was expressing concerns that a baby of only six months old and who was not yet mobile should be seen to bruise easily. However, the SCR report might also, but did not, comment that this was a mother who was known to get very anxious, and who herself had had experiences of child protection allegations and procedures when she was a child.

One of the hindrances and limitations of serious case reviews is that everything which happened is interpreted and evaluated from the perspective of now knowing that terrible events will occur in the future.

A month later, Peter was again taken by his mother to see the GP. This time it is stated in the serious case review report that Tracey Connelly was concerned that Peter, who was still only seven months old, had fallen down the stairs. He had a bruise to his left breast and to his left forehead. The GP advised installing a stair gate. At this time Peter and his sisters were primarily in the care of their mother, although it is uncertain how much time Tracey Connelly was spending with her new friend, Steven Barker. Tracey Connelly's mother was also in contact with her daughter and with her grandchildren, and Mr Connelly was in contact with his children.

There are now, therefore, two records which in retrospect have been given particular significance as signs of potential abuse of Peter, but it might also be noted that it was Tracey Connelly who had taken Peter to the GP on each occasion and who was expressing concerns for Peter and his health and welfare. It is only as the story and history builds up over the coming months that the significance of the September and October visits to the GP becomes clearer.

And this is where the next phase of Peter's 17-month life might be seen to start, a phase that begins with the first recognition of child protection concerns for Peter, and with an escalation of the injuries that Peter is known to have had. It marks the first involvement of social workers and police officers. The second serious case review report, not surprisingly, covers the events in December 2006, when Peter was nine months old, in some detail:

> On the 11 December 2006 [Mrs Connelly] telephoned the surgery and spoke to the GP. She told him that [Peter] has a swelling on the head and asked what she should do. He invited her in, explaining that there was nothing he could do until he examined the child. He recalled that when she arrived she was in an excited mood and talking very fast. She did not know how it had happened but she found him in the back seat of the car. He had been in the care of her mother [his grandmother]. When [Peter] was examined, [the GP] found a frontal haematoma

with a discolouration of the nose and bruises over the body which suggested to him they were probably non-accidental. He told [Tracey Connelly] that he was going to refer [Peter] to the hospital, wrote a referral letter and gave it to her to take to the hospital. He telephoned the hospital to let them know they were coming. There is no record in the patient log of a telephone call to Whittington Hospital. An hour or two later, [Tracey Connelly] telephoned the GP to ask him to phone the hospital to tell them that she was a good mother and that she would not harm her child.

At the Whittington [Peter] was seen initially by a registrar who subsequently consulted [a consultant paediatrician], the named doctor [for child protection] at the hospital. A number of bruises were seen on his body and documented on a body map. [Tracey Connelly] said that she did not know when or how the swelling on [Peter's] forehead had occurred. She attributed the other bruises to him climbing and falling and bruising easily, as well as her slapping his body in play.

The body map at the time shows extensive bruising to his buttocks and other bruises to his face and chest, including the swelling to his forehead which had triggered the referral from the GP. There were also some minor scratches which [Tracey Connelly] said were caused by one of their two dogs. [Peter] was admitted for assessment.... [*The serious case review text is redacted here: why, when it presumably relates to a type of test?*] Tests were done in order to assess whether [Peter] did bruise easily. The tests indicated that he was not suffering with any condition which would mean that he would be susceptible to bruising easily. A referral form was faxed to Haringey Children and Young People's Services social workers the same day as the [hospital] referral.[19]

By any understanding, here was a nine-month-old child with an array of injuries, injuries that in their range and location could not have been the outcome of just one action or incident. A swollen forehead, bruised face, bruised chest, bruised buttocks and scratch marks. At nine months Peter may have been crawling, but he would not have been mobile enough to have gathered this range of injuries by himself. An initial skeletal survey, an X-ray examination of Peter's bones, showed what may have been an old fracture of the right tibia, but a later more detailed bone scan showed no abnormality.

Peter stayed in hospital overnight, and the following day, 12 December, a meeting was held which was attended by a social worker and a detective constable (and presumably by doctors at the hospital although this was not made clear in the SCR report). It was decided that Peter could not return home until child protection and police criminal investigations had been undertaken. The following account is based on the second serious case review report.

When Peter was in hospital, Tracey Connelly was interviewed by a detective constable but did not provide the police with any clear or consistent explanation for Peter's injuries. Instead she conjectured that the injuries may have been a consequence of her not being gentle with the children, but that she never hit them, that Peter had fallen from a settee or that he had thrown himself against the bars of his cot, that the dogs (there were two dogs at this time in the Connelly home) had caused him to fall or that the injuries were caused when playing with the other children.

On 19 December the police arrested and bailed Tracey Connelly and her mother as the investigation into the causes of Peter's injuries was to continue. Peter's sisters were separately interviewed at their school, and gave no indication that their mother hit them. The police were aware that Tracey Connelly had a male friend, but understood that he was only a friend, did not stay at the house and did not look after the children.[20] They apparently made no further inquiries about this friend (this would usually have been a crucial part of the investigation to check who had had access to the child). The school also gave no indication to the police that they had any concerns about the children. The health visitor informed the social worker of Tracey Connelly's past history of post-natal depression, but that she had no concerns about the care of any of the children, and that Peter was brought to the clinic to be weighed, although his immunisations were not up to date. The health visitor had not been informed of the GP's previous contacts with Peter in September and October. The social worker also received information from Islington Council that Tracey Connelly and her brother had each, as children, been the subject of child protection plans, and that Tracey Connelly's mother, Peter's grandmother, had received a caution for physically assaulting her son.[21]

The general thrust of the understanding at this time seems to have been that the injuries to Peter may have been caused by his grandmother, and Tracey Connelly stated that she would not allow her mother to babysit Peter again. However, Tracey Connelly was told that while the child protection and criminal investigations were continuing, Peter would not be allowed to return home from hospital. A possible foster placement was identified, but Peter's parents were allowed to identify alternative arrangements. Mr Connelly offered to take time off from work to look after Peter, but when Tracey Connelly objected, it was instead agreed that Peter would stay with a family friend. A written agreement was prepared about these arrangements, including that the family friend would supervise any contact between Peter and his mother and grandmother.

So, at this time, just before Christmas 2006, when Peter was nine months old, what was the understanding of what Peter's life was like, and what was happening within his family and his home? The following picture is based on the information within the second serious case review report,[22] and many of the contributors to building this picture – the social worker and managers, the hospital paediatrician, the detective constable – had only started to have knowledge of and contact with Tracey Connelly and her family over the previous two weeks. It was the school headteacher, the health visitor and the primary care mental health worker who had known the Connelly family for longer (as well as the GP, who did not attend the child protection conference).

Those who had had more contact with the Connelly family expressed little serious concern about Peter's care. The health visitor reported that Peter seemed fine and happy and that she had no concerns about the parenting he received. The mental health worker described Tracey Connelly as having good insight into her difficulties, and that she requested anti-depressants when she needed them. She said that she had seen Peter with his mother, and he was calm and smiling and looked like a happy child. Previously, she noted, there had been heavy binge drinking by Mr and Mrs Connelly, but that it had decreased recently, presumably referring to Tracey Connelly as Mr Connelly was no longer in the family home and not in contact with the mental health worker. The headteacher had not raised any serious concerns. The social worker, although newly in contact with Tracey Connelly, found her to be cooperative, and noted that she had herself asked for help from the mental health worker and also from HARTS (Haringey Tenancy Support for Families), an advice, advocacy and support agency.

The view which flows from those workers who had known Peter and his family for some time was hardly, therefore, a picture of a family in crisis or of significant concerns about parenting and childcare. This was reflected in the assessment of Peter's sisters when they were assessed as part of the inquiries now being made following the injuries to Peter. It was reported that there were no concerns about parenting, although when Peter's sisters were seen at the child development centre, they were wearing dirty clothing and were described as being dirty, evidence of some neglect, but not of any immediate danger to the children.

Tracey Connelly contributed comments herself to the child protection conference, which she attended with a solicitor. Workers who may know the family attend case conferences to share information and to decide on what action should be taken. Parents are also usually invited to attend and to contribute. Tracey Connelly said that Peter liked to 'rough and tumble', that she had a good relationship with him, that he liked to smile and was happy. She also said Peter had a good relationship with his father, and indeed this was observed when Peter was taken for his bone scan as part of the investigation into his injuries and only his father was able to calm his distress. She reported that she had no difficulty with the housework, but some trouble with doing the laundry. She agreed to get rid of her two dogs and also to provide more supervision for Peter and his youngest sister. She is also reported as having said that she had relied on her mother to babysit to give her some respite and time for shopping.

There was little reference at the child protection case conference to a male friend. He was, however, mentioned in the paediatrician's report to the child protection conference, and also by the mental health worker. The school knew that Tracey Connelly had referred to a boyfriend when speaking to a nursery nurse, but this was considered by the school as not reliable and so was not reported to the child protection conference. There was little information, therefore, about Steven Barker, and little significance attached to his possible participation at this time in Peter's life, although the mental health worker had noted that Tracey Connelly had support from a boyfriend.

What was reported to the conference was that the police had information about Tracey Connelly's mother but the police had not been able to access it. The Haringey social worker had, however, obtained information from children's services in Islington from the time when Tracey Connelly, as a child, was living there. It noted that she had herself been named on the child protection register, having been beaten (but by whom is blanked out in the serious case review report). She had also only recently learned last year of the true identity of her birth father, having grown up thinking that her stepfather was her biological father.

Three pictures emerge from this story so far.

Picture one, based on the views of those who had known Tracey Connelly and her family for the longest, is that there were no significant concerns about her parenting of her children, including Peter. From what was previously known, as noted earlier, if there were concerns, they were about hygiene, not anticipating dangers for the children, and about supervision arrangements that were made by Tracey Connelly with her mother, whose own behaviour and track record as a parent had been far from positive.

Picture two is of a nine-month child, Peter, who had a wide range of injuries located around his body, injuries that it would be very hard to understand could be anything but caused by others. There were no adequate or believable explanations for these injuries. Tracey Connelly claimed not to know how they had occurred. Her conjecturing was unconvincing, especially as she should have been aware of the injuries soon after they occurred if they were accidental as Peter was in her care, but she had also indicated that Peter had at times been in the care of her mother, Peter's grandmother, so this was another potential source of Peter's injuries.

Picture three, however, takes on more significance with all the benefits of hindsight. Who was this man who was providing some support for Tracey Connelly and who was variously known as her friend and her boyfriend? His significance only came to be understood later, and at the time, Peter's older sisters did not mention him when assessed at the child development centre.

It is not difficult, with the information known at the time and shared at the child protection conference, to understand that here was a household where there were signs of neglect, where the children may not have been well supervised, which, with two dogs and four young children must have been quite crowded, and where, regardless of any intent, there were dangers for a baby of nine months old. The risks for Peter were compounded by the mother's own poor parenting experience, that the grandmother who had not cared well for her own children was sometimes caring on her own for Peter and his sisters, that Tracey Connelly was volatile and now on her own with four children, without the support of her husband who had had a positive relationship with Peter, and where, from time to time she was depressed with an anxiety state.

Three possible scenarios at this time. One of a mother who was coping and caring, as described by those who had known her longest. One of a mother who lacked capacity and competence and where the children were neglected, and one where possibly the children were being left in danger or, at worse, were being assaulted and abused.

The outcome of the child protection conference was that child protection plans were put in place for Peter and his youngest sister. For Peter, the child protection plan was because of concerns about neglect and physical injuries. His sister was made subject to a child protection plan because she, too, was very young and vulnerable.

The child protection plan included the requirement for the completion of a core assessment on the children. A core assessment is defined by the Department of Health as 'an in-depth assessment which addresses the central or most important aspects of the needs of a child and the capacity of the parents or caregivers to respond appropriately to these needs within the wider family and community context'.[23] Haringey Council's solicitors were to be contacted if any of the children suffered further injuries. HARTS was to seek to help with housing issues because of the overcrowding in the Connelly's current accommodation. The mental health worker would also continue to support and assist Tracey Connelly with psychotherapy to be considered. There was also to be an assessment of Tracey Connelly's mother's role with the children, and the social worker was to undertake fortnightly announced and unannounced visits to the family.

One area of reported disagreement at the time of the conference was about whether Peter should be taken into the care of the council, preferably with Tracey Connelly's agreement, but presumably by seeking a court order if she did not agree, and placed with foster carers (who were known to be available) or placed with Peter's father or with a family friend. The father was excluded as an option when Tracey Connelly objected. This left the foster carer or the family friend, and Peter was placed with the family friend.

There are significant criticisms in the second serious case review report of the decision that Peter should be living with a family friend while the further inquiries by the police, and further assessments by the social worker, were being undertaken following the child protection conference. In particular, this decision was seen as not confronting Tracey Connelly with the seriousness of the concerns about Peter's injuries. It was argued that the overall approach was not authoritative enough in making clear what the concerns were for the Connelly children, and with explicit requirements and expectations about what was and would now happen to follow up further on the concerns. The family friend now had very serious responsibilities placed on her to care for Peter and, importantly, to personally supervise any contact Peter had with his family, including his mother and grandmother. All of this was to be initially managed over the Christmas and New Year holiday period, when oversight and availability from the agencies would be limited because of the extended holiday period.

But it could be that the Christmas dimension also played into the decision-making in a different way. What underlying views might there have been about separating nine-month-old Peter from his mother and sisters at the time of his first Christmas, placing him with strangers some distance away? Would an in-between arrangement where he was in the care of someone else who he already knew and where there could be easy but supervised access to his family be more desirable than a foster placement? It is not hard to see how this thinking may have had some influence on what was decided and actioned, and if the later outcome for Peter had not been so terribly tragic, it might even, in retrospect, have been commented on as appropriate management of risk and as being in Peter's best interest.

It may be timely here to recall the comments made 40 years before in the Minority Report by Olive Stevenson, one of the three members of the Maria Colwell Inquiry and at the time a Reader in Applied Social Studies at the University of Oxford. Maria Colwell was a seven-year-old who was killed by her stepfather. At the conclusion of the Maria Colwell Inquiry, Stevenson commented that:

> … there are few, if any, situations of the kind in which Maria was involved which are 'black and white'. The harsh lesson which social workers in child care services have to learn is that … there are very few situations in which choices are clear cut and predictable.[24]

So, on 23 December 2006 Peter left hospital and moved to the care of the family friend. Tracey Connelly saw Peter three times on Christmas Day, and the social worker saw him on Christmas Eve and on 27 and 29 December. This was not a case or concern which was lost from view by the social worker.

Although not clear from the serious case review report that this was required from the child protection conference and child protection plan, there was also discussion within the council with solicitors about initiating care proceedings in court to provide greater powers either to care for Peter apart from his mother and family, or to supervise the arrangements if Peter was not in the council's care. It was decided, however, not to pursue legal proceedings. The serious case review report gives no information whether this was based on the legal view and advice about there not being grounds for care proceedings, and that these proceedings were unlikely to be successful if the evidence then available were presented to the court, or whether the social worker and her managers took a view in opposition to any legal advice about the appropriateness of care proceedings at this time.

However, with no determination as to how Peter's injuries were caused, with the police investigation continuing and incomplete, and with Tracey Connelly's care of her children having been seen by those who had known her for the longest as affectionate and adequate, even in retrospect it seems borderline and uncertain that any application to a court would have been successful in removing Peter from his mother's care. There is always then the difficulty and danger that the outcome of a failed application to a court in care proceedings may be limited and less access being allowed by a family to their children.

The published second serious case review report now raises more questions than it answers. This is especially because a large number of dates were deleted from the report. Why have so many key dates been redacted (the terminology used for blacking out information in the published report), making the report less readable and also removing information about when events happened and time intervals and sequences? If it were because of the criminal proceedings that were in train when this second serious case review report was prepared it could possibly be understandable as the events and dates on which they occurred may have been significant in the criminal trials. But this serious case review report was published after the findings from the criminal trial that three adults had 'caused or allowed' Peter's death.

What can be read in the report, although with specific but significant dates omitted, is that Peter stayed in the care of the family friend into the New Year, although she was asking if Peter could have unsupervised time with Tracey Connelly. The conditions within Peter's family home, however, were not good. A worker from the Family Welfare Association (FWA) had visited and found the home smelling, dirty and disorganised. The dogs were still there and had not been removed as agreed by Tracey Connelly at the child protection conference several weeks before. Tracey Connelly failed to keep her appointment with the mental health worker. The health visitor contacted her and asked that the family friend bring Peter to the clinic, but it is not known from the serious case review report whether Peter was actually taken to the clinic.

While these contacts with the family were taking place, the police were engaged with the Crown Prosecution Service, which was asking for further medical evidence on Peter's injuries before considering prosecution (and presumably, who to prosecute).

On 10 January 2007, three weeks after the initial child protection conference on 22 December, the first core group meeting was held. A core group is composed of the different workers from different agencies working with a family. It is an opportunity for them to keep each other up to date with what is known about the family, and to track that the actions decided at the child protection case conference are being followed up. The serious case review report does not state who were within this core group or note all who attended the meeting, but Tracey Connelly did attend, along with Peter. It is not unusual for the parent(s) to attend the core group meetings – it was and is generally seen as good practice to keep parents engaged and involved in taking the actions needed to improve the care of children. However, there is always the limitation that it may hinder workers from speaking openly with each other.

The second serious case review report notes what was decided at this meeting:

> The FWA remit was for practical help including improving conditions in the home. The remit was changed to include direct work to address [Tracey Connelly's] relationship with [one of Peter's sisters]. Visiting frequency was reduced from weekly to fortnightly to monthly. The school did not attend although they provided a report. There were minutes of the meeting. Peter was to attend the health clinic once a month, to have a one-year developmental check, and [Tracey Connelly] was referred to 'Mellow Parenting',[25] a health facility to improve parent/child relationships

through group work.* The child Mellow Parenting would focus on was [one of Peter's sisters], as Peter was too young to fit the criteria for the programme – although it is not clear the Core Group understood this – but it was agreed he could accompany them and [it was] hoped that the improvements in parenting skills would transfer to the other children.[26]

At the time of the core group meeting, the family friend was still caring for Peter, and Tracey Connelly expressed her anger about this to the mental health worker. Peter was returned to his mother's care on 26 January following a review strategy meeting attended by the police and social workers. A condition, which was not actioned, was that the dogs should be removed from the house before Peter's return.

Soon afterwards, Peter was seen by the GP with impetigo in both groins, again reflecting concerns about his basic care and hygiene. On the same day, Tracey Connelly met the mental health worker and was happy that Peter had returned home to her care, said that she was finding her male friend helpful, but was angry about being told what to do by others. At about this time a housing association made an offer to Tracey Connelly of long-term temporary accommodation, and the family moved to a four-bedroom home on 19 February.

In summary, what must life have been like for Peter and the other Connelly children at this time? First, they had previously been living in cramped, dirty, untidy accommodation with health and safety hazards compounded by the two dogs. Second, their mother was known to be volatile and her boyfriend may by now have been living in the family home, and as known later, this would have presented further risk to the children. Third, the older children may, through normal boisterous behaviour, have presented potential risks to a very young child that would not have been minimised because of

---

* In a 2009 Care Quality Commission review of NHS services in Haringey it was stated that 'Mellow Parenting sessions are designed to help families with relationship problems with their infants and young children, including families where there are child protection concerns' (Care Quality Commission, 2009, *Review of the involvement and action taken by health bodies in relation to the case of Baby P*, p 11).

poor supervision from their mother. Fourth, the grandmother was still presumably caring at times for the children, and her parenting was known not to have been good. So, it was likely that this was a threatening household for a 10-month-old child who was likely to be crawling, may have been starting to stand and possibly beginning to take those first unsteady steps. It is also possible that the mother was focused on her boyfriend and less on the children, and it has been stated that she spent much time on the internet, using social media.[27]

Not all of this picture was available to the workers in January and February 2007, and there was still little knowledge about the boyfriend despite the assumed continuation of the police criminal investigation into Peter's injuries in December, a criminal investigation where it would have been crucial and critical to have concentrated on who had had access to Peter at the time he was injured. But it later became known that the police investigation had drifted and then been unallocated and discontinued for a time when the detective constable undertaking the investigations took on a new role. A crucial opportunity to identify and find out about the boyfriend seems not to have been followed up.

What was being focused on instead was attempting to improve the conditions in the family home through better housing, improving Tracey Connelly's home-making skills, and concentrating on her care of her children. Bearing in mind the poor parenting she had herself experienced, and with only poor models of parenting to draw on, helping her to respond to the needs of her children, and the concerns about hygiene and safety, was an understandable goal for those working with the family.

However, among other families who were in contact with social workers, health visitors, doctors and the police in this area, and indeed in many areas nationwide, the Connelly family, with what was known at the time, may not have stood out as of exceptional concern. Other homes were no doubt dirty, grubby and unhygienic. But there was still the number and range of injuries that Peter had when nine months old in December that would, or should, have made this family stand out. The plans that were made were not, therefore, just about seeking to make Tracey Connelly's parenting and home-making skills stronger; they were also about regular monitoring and observation of Peter by a range of professionals, including the health visitor, social worker and other workers from the FWA, Mellow Parenting and the mental health worker. Explicitly, as Peter now approached his first birthday, there was to be a 12-month developmental check. And the police were presumed still to be conducting their criminal and forensic investigations into Peter's earlier injuries.

But whatever was already known, and what had been planned, was significantly disrupted in late February and into March. The Connelly family moved to their new larger and better accommodation. This should have been and probably was positive, but it also led to changes in who was in contact with the family. As shown in the map below, the new family home was further away from the primary school attended by Peter's two older sisters. It was also further away from where Peter's father was living and from the GP practice. All, however, remained within walking distance, and the new family home, very near the Tottenham Football Club stadium and underground station, was also only a short walk away from the North Middlesex Hospital, with its Accident and Emergency (A&E) department and its NHS walk-in centre. Indeed, all the key locations within the story of Peter's short life were within a very small radius and little more than 15–20 minutes walking distance of the two homes in which he lived, with the exception of Whittington Hospital (where Peter was seen in December 2006), which would have required at least one if not two bus journeys.

The move of home in February 2007 resulted in a change of health visitor. Although the family remained with the same GP, all the children are reported to have been seen by a different doctor in the GP primary healthcare practice at about this time. There was also a change of social worker as the case moved from the initial assessment stage to a team that undertook longer-term work with children and families with child protection concerns. And, as noted above, the police officer leading the investigation into Peter's injuries in December moved to other duties, and the criminal investigation stalled and was only later picked up again, but by a different police officer. A new health visitor, new social worker and no police officer.

The Connelly family home, from February 2007, at Penhurst Road

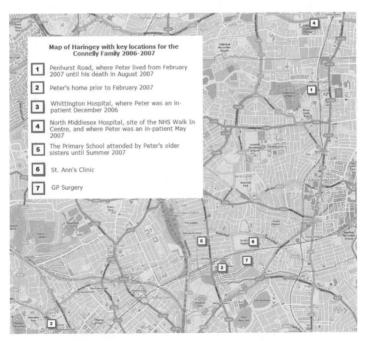

Map of Haringey with key locations for the Connelly family, 2006–07

It is not hard to see the difficulties and dangers that the disruption of key workers now presented. Although briefed by their colleagues previously working with the Connelly family, they were starting largely from scratch in establishing their own working relationships with Tracey Connelly and the children, and were having to form their own judgements about the family and about the care and development of the children. In one sense this provided fresh opportunities to reflect on what was happening for the children and what their lives were like. But it was also unlikely that in the absence of any new information or evidence of concerns they would be giving the Connelly family greater attention than many other families where they knew directly about immediate and worrying issues of children with severe injuries, wide-ranging and frequent complaints of severe neglect or emotional abuse, allegations of serious sexual abuse, or of families with repeated reports of domestic violence or of parents incapacitated by drug or alcohol misuse. None of these acute and immediate alarms or anxieties related to what was then known about the Connelly family.

And a mixed picture is recorded in the serious case review report about what the new and continuing workers were now seeing. The new social worker at the end of February saw all the children with their mother, and noted that she was affectionate towards them. However, when visiting the family soon after, the social worker saw Peter headbutting the floor, which is unusual for a child approaching their first birthday. She once again, however, observed a good relationship between Tracey Connelly and Peter, observations that were repeated in March when she visited at the same time as the new health visitor. Tracey Connelly was, however, arguing that she should keep the two dogs now that she had a larger home, a home in which Peter was to have his first birthday on 1 March 2007.

From the school, new concerns were being observed. First, in early March the school nurse telephoned the social worker as the nurse had seen Tracey Connelly shouting loudly at one of Peter's sisters, and slapping her cheek. Second, a mysterious event was noted in the serious case review report about 'an incident with a cooker' that Tracey Connelly had reported to the school but had not told the social worker. Why this incident with the cooker is blacked out and not made explicit in the serious case review is a mystery, but as it is referred to in the report, it is clearly seen as significant. The slapping of Peter's sister's face was discussed by the social worker with her manager, and the social worker saw the child alone, who confirmed that her mother hitting her was apparently provoked by the child having kicked out at Tracey Connelly's friend's son. The social worker followed this up in discussion with Tracey Connelly but it was decided that as she was already about to attend a parenting programme, no other action was necessary. On 8 March Tracey Connelly was interviewed for the NHS Mellow Parenting course, and during the interview she said she had no partner. On the same day she was visited again by the social worker, and stated that she was intending to keep the two dogs.

On 13 March the new social worker met Mr Connelly. He had not been seen since December when he had offered to care for Peter when he was discharged from hospital. He told the social worker he wanted more contact with his children. He also told the social worker that Tracey Connelly had a boyfriend whom he had seen at the family home. He also gave his view that Tracey Connelly would not hit the children (although she had very recently been seen to have done so outside the school). When the social worker shortly afterwards confronted Tracey Connelly and asked if she had a boyfriend, she became angry and denied it, but went on to say that she would like to date her male friend (later to be known to be Steven Barker).

A further child protection review conference was held on 16 March. The police did not attend (indeed, in the serious case review report, they seem to have vanished from view). At the conference Peter's sister, who had been seen outside the school to be hit by her mother, was also made the subject of a child protection plan. It was decided that the social worker should increase her announced and unannounced visits to weekly, and that the health visitor should have monthly contact with the family. Peter was also to be referred by the health visitor to the NHS child development centre because he had been seen to be headbutting the floor.

The contacts with Tracey Connelly continued throughout March. She was still expressing concerns about Peter's headbutting, said to the mental health worker that she was coping but feeling low on the day of the contact with the worker, and was angry that the social workers were visiting her so often which prevented her relaxing and enjoying the children.

On 29 March another core group meeting was held. It was noted that the health visitor had the task of referring Peter to the child development centre. At about this time a children's services manager, who is described in the serious case review report as the social worker's team manager, had a brief-focused therapy session with Tracey Connelly as part of the manager's training in brief-focused therapy, also known as 'solution-focused therapy' (an approach that focuses on parental strengths and what the client wants to achieve rather than problems in the past; it may be a positive approach in improving parental esteem and confidence, but can undermine a focus on concerns about a child's safety).

The session that was videoed for the training was then later shown in a BBC *Panorama* programme (see Chapter Three). It showed a compliant and cooperative mother (in retrospect, might have been seen as manipulative and misleading) who demonstrated concern and commitment for her children. She hardly appeared as the ogre she was presented as later in the media. It draws a stark contrast (as does the video also shown in the *Panorama* programme of Tracey Connelly and Steven Barker playing with Peter in a park) between what workers at the time might have been seeing of Tracey and what later became known about her neglect and abuse of Peter and/or the very serious failure to protect him from the abuse of someone else or others.

There was then another significant and dramatic event in the story of Peter's life. Tracey Connelly took Peter to the nearby A&E department at North Middlesex Hospital. The second serious case review notes that:

> At 4.40 pm on 9 April, [Tracey Connelly] took [Peter] to accident and emergency at the North Middlesex Hospital. The triage nurse noted a large boggy swelling to the left side of his head. [Tracey Connelly's] account was that four days before, he had been pushed by another child his age against a marble fire place. Apart from

being grizzly over the next two days he had seemed fine and then he had woken that morning with neck pain, holding his head to the left side. He had a small, round bruise on his right cheek, and obvious head lice, as did his siblings. He was also noted to have petechial spots [a rash of small blood spots] on the back of both arms. Tests were done for meningitis because of the rash and neck stiffness, although this was eventually ruled out. His throat was noted to be slightly red. Another report said he had multiple bruising. Body maps indicated bruises and scratches on his face, head and body.

[Tracey Connelly] said that she had a friend in the waiting room who had witnessed the fall, and she was fearful that [Peter] would be taken into care because he was on the child protection register. The friend is now thought to have been [Steven Barker].[28]

What seems surprising is that this was apparently not considered within the hospital to be evidence of child abuse. A hospital nurse told the social worker that it was viewed as an accidental injury and the mother had stated that another child had caused the injury. Over the two days that Peter was observed in hospital, with his mother staying with him throughout, and with someone assumed to be Peter's father (possibly Steven Barker) visiting each evening, the serious case review report noted that the usual shift transfer arrangements were not in place in the hospital. No account is given for this in the serious case review, and it seems not to have been followed up in the review. The consequence was that the final team of doctors who assessed Peter seem to have lost track of Peter's story and speculated that his symptoms were due to an allergic reaction. It was agreed with the social worker, who had consulted her manager, that Peter should go home.

The comments in the serious case review report about these events in early April are critical:

> The [serious case review] panel take the view that the threshold of concern in the child protection system at the

time was too high. Both the hospital and the social work staff were too willing to believe the plausible accounts the mother was offering to explain [Peter's] injuries. In the more holistic context of the case the explanations offered by [Tracey Connelly] should have been questioned. A different assessment of [Tracey Connelly's] parenting and her motivation to protect and care for her son should have been considered.[29]

It was noted in the serious case review report that there was an 'over-reliance on medical opinion'. The serious case review process might also have sought explanations from the workers involved at this time about how they were understanding the information they had, and how and why they came to the decisions that were taken – although if it did so it is not in the report. It would also be helpful in understanding what was decided at this time to have further information about the context for the workers. What else was happening within their workloads? Were holidays having an impact on their work, with March being the end of the local authority leave year and with bank and school holidays around Easter? What was it that led to the disruption of the usual shift handover arrangements at the hospital? Were the child protection named doctor or nurse at the hospital involved in discussions about Peter at this time? How were interagency working arrangements and relationships in April 2007, including with the police? Was anyone intrigued about the man who was at the hospital with Tracey Connelly and Peter? Did anyone speak with him (and if not, why not, especially when he was assumed to be Peter's father)? So many questions, and even with all the attention and cost that must have been applied to this second serious case review process, with the first belatedly having been determined as inadequate, these questions still seemed not to be been asked or answered.

What it exposes is that within the second serious case review, even when there was the considerable deployment of time and task focused on only one case and one child, and where it was now known that terrible events had occurred, a coherent and comprehensive story is still not told. How much more difficult, however, for the workers at the time, each of whom will have had some but not all of the information later collected and collated, each with many families requiring their attention and where there may have been even more urgent concerns about some of these other families, to piece it all together. Undoubtedly the jigsaw of information should have been put together better at this time, but the serious case review does not tell why this did not happen. It is a significant limitation of the serious case review process. It tells of events but is weak on explanation. It details issues, but is lacking in inquiry. It relies heavily on case files and case recording, but is lacking in getting the views from the workers who were involved. It is overly focused on case and ignores context. It suggests hubris, but lacks humility.

After Peter's discharge home on 11 April there was the continuing activity of delivering on previous child protection plans. The health visitor visited the home and had also referred Peter, as decided at the earlier child protection review conference, to the child development centre because of concerns about headbutting. This referral was, however, rejected as it did not contain enough information. The FWA worker telephoned Tracey Connelly to arrange to visit, and Tracey Connelly asked for a copy of the Ofsted report for the school her older children would be attending (which, among all the concerns about her care for her children, seems somewhat unusual and an indication of care, not neglect), and she was also asking the health visitor to help to get milk tokens. Tracey Connelly was also informed at about this time of the first meeting of the Mellow Parenting programme.

However, the visit by the FWA worker was cancelled (the serious case review report states that it was not clear – presumably to the serious case review report's author – who cancelled the appointment, or why), and Tracey Connelly did not attend the first meeting of Mellow Parenting as the taxi did not arrive to collect her. Before the social worker visited the Connelly home on 24 April, she had had the hospital discharge report. It noted that Peter had had a trivial head injury caused by playing with siblings a few days before the hospital admission. When the social worker visited, she found Peter unsteady on his feet, and discussed this with Tracey Connelly but again the account and trail is left hanging in the air in the serious case review report.

On 2 May another core group meeting was held, three weeks after Peter's discharge from hospital. It is noted in the second serious case review report that the social worker, health visitor, headteacher and FWA worker attended the meeting. The school was concerned about Tracey Connelly sending the children to school too early. Actions decided at the meeting were that the social worker was to make an appointment for one of Peter's sisters to be seen at the child and adolescent mental health service, but the reason for this is not commented on; the health visitor was to visit the family again; Tracey Connelly was to take the dogs to the RSPCA to ask them to do a risk assessment (it is not specified about what type of risk); the social worker was to arrange the money for a fireguard to be purchased; and it was noted that someone who is described as Tracey's maternal grandfather from Leicester was to visit for a week and the family was to go to the seaside.

Shortly after the meeting, Tracey Connelly started attending the NHS Mellow Parenting programme with one of her children. Two of Peter's sisters were seen for child health assessments. The health visitor visited the home and noted that Peter was a lively and active toddler, and was clean and appropriately dressed. Another child was also seen, and was talkative and playing happily. There was still no fireguard, but there were no concerns arising from this visit about Peter or his sisters.

What would not have been understood at this time was that Peter may have been experiencing deliberate physical and emotional harm in the home and may have been targeted for abuse for the gratuitous satisfaction and pleasure of others. His life may have been full of danger, threat, pain and humiliation. His sisters may have been having similar experiences or at least have been aware of and intimidated by what was happening to Peter. And this was soon to get worse. However, even now, with all the investigations and reviews that have since taken place, it is not clear when the severe abuse of Peter started, whether it was long-standing, or whether it was more confined to the immediate weeks before his death.

In May there were reports from the FWA worker that when she visited the home she saw Peter and one of the other children playing happily, and the social worker noted she saw all the children and they were well and playing happily. But there was also continuing contact with doctors, with Peter taken by his mother to the GP because of urticaria (hives), a skin rash. On the same day as the GP visit, Tracey Connelly took one of Peter's siblings to North Middlesex University Hospital A&E department, but the information is blanked out in the serious case review report as to which child was taken to hospital and why. The GP also does not recall receiving any information from the hospital about this visit to the accident and emergency department. There was, therefore, considerable continuing activity by agencies in working with the family and in seeing the children, and some of this was initiated by Tracey Connelly herself in taking children to the GP and to hospital. This was not a family that was ignored or that had gone out of sight, but with one exception, the incomplete criminal investigation.

In May, as noted in the first serious case review, the police realised that, because of changes of staff, the original criminal investigation of Peter's injuries in December, six months before, had not been followed through and completed. The investigation was resurrected as a matter of urgency, although much of what would have been potential evidence in December and January may not now have been available, or trails would have gone cold. As noted in a later chapter, it is surprising that this did not receive more subsequent attention, either in the second serious case review report or in the future media coverage. Concerns and recommendations about police (in)actions were noted, however, in the first serious case review,[30] which was rejected by the government as inadequate (see Chapter Four).

It is a significant omission that the first criminal investigation had drifted and not been completed. If it had been, it may have clarified who might have caused Peter's injuries in December, and more might have been known about Steven Barker's involvement with the family. As it was, Steven Barker was still a shadowy and largely unknown figure to the key workers with the Connelly family.

The referral that had been made by the health visitor to the NHS child development centre at St Ann's Clinic bounced back again.

This time the view expressed to the health visitor was that Peter might be more appropriately referred to the child and adolescent mental health service, but that the child development centre would reconsider a referral if further information was provided. It is hard to see, however, that the child and adolescent mental health service might be the most appropriate service to provide an assessment for a 14-month-old child compared to the paediatricians focused on child development. The social worker, however, then wrote to St Ann's Clinic requesting a paediatric assessment of Peter before the next child protection review conference on 8 June. In the referral Peter is described as a 'happy, sociable boy who smiles and likes to engage with his mother and siblings. He seems to be interested in his environment and shows a healthy, inquisitive nature.'[31] There were concerns, however, about his headbutting people and furniture, and his mother's reports that he had a high pain threshold. It is questioned in the referral to the clinic whether there might be an organic reason for his behaviour. It is explicitly stated that he was subject to a child protection plan and the social worker's manager also, unsuccessfully, contacted the child development centre to try to get an appointment for Peter before the next child protection review conference.

On 1 June the social worker made an unannounced visit to the family home and saw a bruise under Peter's chin. There are now two accounts of what then happened. In the first serious case review report it is stated that 'the social worker informed the police, arranged a paediatric assessment and attended with [Tracey Connelly] and [Peter]'.[32] The second serious case review states that, 'the social worker requests that [Tracey Connelly] take [Peter] to the GP. [Peter] was taken to the accident and emergency department at North Middlesex University Hospital who were aware that he was on the child protection register. The social worker acknowledged to the police that [Peter] was clumsy and he does fight with his other siblings. At the hospital a history is taken.'[33]

Peter was found to have multiple bruises and scratches of different ages, but it was noted that they could be explained by rough play. Indeed, at the hospital, Peter was very active and banged his head once and fell twice onto his bottom. He was observed to play happily in the presence of his mother. However, he was also seen to have grab mark bruising on his lower right leg which concerned the doctors. Tracey Connelly's explanation was that she had grabbed Peter to prevent him falling off a sofa. The police were informed but decided not to attend the hospital, and would wait for the medical assessment about the nature of the injuries. It was subsequently decided by the social worker and her manager that Peter could go home as a friend would be staying with the family over the weekend.

When Peter was at home the health visitor visited. She had not been aware of the visit to the hospital but was told about it by Tracey. The health visitor tried unsuccessfully to contact the social worker and then contacted the hospital. She was told that Peter had also had an infected finger, but that Tracey Connelly was observed to have 'bonded well' with Peter.

The second serious case review report states that the police were convinced that Peter's recent injuries were non-accidental, and requested a child protection strategy meeting that was quickly held on 4 June. At the strategy meeting which, according to the serious case review report, was attended by the police, the social work team manager and the senior social work team manager (but not the social worker who was away), the police officer(s) are reported to have argued, against the views of the social work managers, that there were no grounds to seek an emergency protection order from the courts to remove Peter from his family.

At the child protection strategy meeting, however, an agreement was reached to:

> Undertake Section 47 inquiries [*under Section 47 – of the
> 1989 Children Act – inquiries are undertaken when a child is
> suffering, or is likely to suffer, significant harm*]; hold an urgent
> legal planning meeting to consider care proceedings; fast
> track a paediatric assessment; make arrangements for Peter
> to be supervised at the family home by the family friend;
> draw up a contract with Tracey Connelly; identify a child
> minder to assist with the care of the children during the
> day; and continue an ongoing joint investigation by the
> police and children's social care. The original plan by
> the children and young people's service was that Peter

and [one of his siblings] would stay at the home of the family friend, but [Tracey Connelly] objected, pointing out that the friend did not have sufficient accommodation. The arrangements were then made that the friend would stay with the family. Tracey Connelly was arrested when she reported for the original bail condition [*presumably dating back to December 2006, seven months earlier*]. She was interviewed and she offered a variety of possible causes for the injuries and no admissions were made. When the child development centre were contacted the same day for an urgent appointment for Peter whom they were told was on the child protection register, they thought they might be able to see him in July or August [*it was now 4 June*].[34]

So, at this time, in June 2007, when Peter was 15 months old, there was a heightening of concern and of action. The police had become more engaged. Measures were also put in place to seek to ensure that Peter was cared for and seen by others (both through a friend, who received payment from the council, and through Peter having day care for four days each week with a childminder). And stronger and clearer consideration was being given to care proceedings being initiated in the court, with the possible outcome of Peter being cared for by the council, away from his mother. There was, however, a delay with Haringey Council's legal services department in arranging the requested legal planning meeting. Indeed, the first serious case review report notes concerns about capacity within, and the service provided by, the legal services.[35]

Three reasons, as noted in the serious case reviews, might be seen to have led to this more assertive plan. First, the police were more active, with another detective constable and a detective inspector now engaged with the investigations about the possible abuse of Peter. Second, the pattern of Peter's injuries was being recognised as sporadic and intermittent, whereas it was argued that if they had been due to the rough and tumble of boisterous play in and outside the home, or Peter's alleged rough behaviour, they might possibly be more continuous. Third, and significantly, there were injuries to one of Peter's sisters that were not all explained by the account

—

given by Tracey Connelly. These included bruising of different ages and with injuries to the lower back, chest, face, ear and chin. Tracey Connelly was arrested and bailed by the police who were now also investigating these injuries as well as, presumably, still investigating the injuries to Peter in December.

There is a strange style within the serious case review report, where the social worker, social work managers, health visitor and so on are individually identified, whereas individual police officers largely remain anonymous as they are only referred to as 'the police'. This has the limitation of not tracking the police investigations and involvement so clearly. Indeed, there is little account of the police investigations in the second serious case review report, although these should have been of considerable significance in building a fuller account of the life of Peter and his sisters, potentially leading to action to provide protection for the children. Instead, the overwhelming attention is on the action of the social workers and the other health, education and care workers. The police are on the margins throughout, and especially so in the second serious case review report, in which, for periods, the police disappear from view.

A child protection review conference was held on 8 June. This was a time when meetings were frequently being held about Peter, with a strategy meeting, a core group meeting and a further core group meeting planned. There was much activity across agencies and workers related to this one family. It would be of interest and relevance to know, but it is not reported, how many other children and families each worker was also working with as the commitment of time and attention to the Connelly family had been considerable for several months and was now increasing further.

At the conference there was new concern for Peter. It was reported that Peter's weight had reduced from the 75th centile for a child his age to between the 25th and 50th centiles. This is a significant change. It could have suggested an organic disorder, but it could also have been due to neglect. The appointment for a paediatric assessment was still being sought.

At the time of the core group meeting in late June, Peter and his youngest sister had been seen earlier in the day at the childminder's home. Both children interacted well with the three other children being cared for by the childminder, and the childminder is reported as not conveying any concerns about the Connelly children for whom she was caring. There were still delays in holding the legal planning meeting, and still no date had been given for Peter to be seen for the paediatric assessment at the child development centre. The police criminal investigations into Peter's injuries in December, and at the beginning of June, had not been concluded. There was, in essence, little new information for this core group meeting, with action and advice from the legal services, the child development centre and the police still being awaited.

It might be timely at this point, before the story and the abuse of Peter escalates towards its conclusion, to recall and summarise what actions had been taken with, for, and to, the Connelly family since the first significant concerns arose seven months before, in December 2006, when Peter was admitted to hospital with a range of bruises and scratches:

- The two older Connelly children were attending and monitored at school.
- Tracey Connelly continued to meet with the primary care mental health worker and received medication when necessary when depressed or anxious.
- The family was rehoused into larger, four-bedroom accommodation.
- HARTS (Haringey Tenancy Support for Families) had provided housing advice, advocacy and assistance.
- A Family Welfare Association worker had been visiting the Connelly family home to seek to improve Tracey Connelly's home-making and parenting skills.
- Tracey Connelly had been attending the NHS Mellow Parenting programme to improve her parenting skills and her awareness of the needs of her children.
- The health visitor continued to monitor the children, especially Peter, to give advice to Tracey Connelly.
- The social worker had also visited regularly to monitor the children and to follow up on actions that were agreed with Tracey Connelly and others.

- A family friend more recently had received funding from the council to share Peter's care.
- The GP had seen Tracey Connelly and Peter, as well as his sisters, when health concerns had been identified, including by Tracey Connelly.
- Peter had attended the clinic and his immunisations were now up to date.
- Peter had been seen at the hospital and assessed by paediatricians following two occasions in the first six months of 2007 when bruising had been observed.
- Arrangements were now in place for Peter and his pre-school sister to have day care four days a week with a childminder, arranged and paid for by the council.
- Regular, and frequent, child protection review conferences, strategy meetings and core group meetings had been held to up-date information and assessments between workers and agencies and to review and revise action plans.
- There had been contact with Mr Connelly, and he was still in contact with his children,[36] as was the maternal grandmother.

This indicates considerable time and attention being given to the Connelly family, with assistance put in place to seek to improve the parenting and home conditions, with monitoring of what was happening for the children and how they were, and with the children being seen by other family members.

There were, however, three outstanding actions at the beginning of July 2007:

- The criminal investigation started in December 2006, seven months earlier, when there were the first concerns about injuries to Peter, still needed to be completed, as did the new investigation into Peter's bruising which was observed at the beginning of June.
- The child development centre still needed to arrange to see and assess Peter, with the first request having been made in April 2007.
- The legal planning meeting with a solicitor from the council to consider court care proceedings still had to be held, with it noted as 'urgent' at the child protection strategy meeting held on 4 June.

However, although there may have been much activity, there was less evidence of assertiveness and what the serious case review report calls 'authoritative practice', setting, demanding and enforcing with Tracey Connelly behaviours and actions that she had to demonstrate and deliver. Professor Harry Ferguson echoed this as a concern in his references to 'Baby P' in his 2011 book, *Child protection practice*.[37]

The only enforcement that may have been possible, however, was likely to have been taking action to remove some or all the children from Tracey Connelly's care. Even now, with all the disparate information collated through the serious case review processes, and with all the benefit of hindsight and knowing that something terrible was about to happen, it is not clear that an application to the court to remove Peter from his mother's care would have been successful. With what was known at the time, it would have been difficult to prove that the children were experiencing significant harm. The consequence of unsuccessful care proceedings would have been to leave the workers disempowered in their future contacts with Tracey Connelly and weakened in actions seeking to improve her parenting and to monitor the children.

The real world options are often less clear-cut than in the script which is created by more distant observers whose accounts rarely cover the 'what ifs'. What if care proceedings were initiated, but the context was that the criminal investigation by the police found no substantial evidence that any of the children had been assaulted or abused, or the awaited assessment of Peter at the child development centre provided no evidence that the care he was receiving was a major factor in any developmental or behavioural problems which might be found? What if Tracey Connelly then withdrew her cooperation, which to date she was seen to have largely given, from the social worker, health visitor and others, refusing them access to her, her children or to her home, and what if she stopped taking the children to the GP or hospital when they had an injury or illness? And did the Connelly family and children really stand out at this time from the many other families where there was low-level pervasive neglect, occasional bruising seen to the children and explained and possibly understood as being caused by the children's boisterous behaviour or a parent not anticipating dangers for their children in a chaotic, dirty and untidy household?

But these comments are based on what was known at the time in July 2007. What subsequently became understood as particularly significant in the horrific tale which is about to unfold, about who was living in the Connelly household, was apparently not known to the police who were undertaking two criminal investigations about Peter's injuries, nor to the social worker or health visitor who were visiting the household, and nor to the school, the childminder, the Mellow Parenting programme workers or the GP who were seeing Tracey Connelly and the children outside the family home. If it was known to family friends, to Tracey Connelly's mother, to Mr Connelly, to neighbours or to others, it was not apparently shared with the police or with other key workers concerned about the Connelly children. Maybe even if family, friends and neighbours knew of the changes taking place in the Connelly household they did not see them as significant or of concern. Unknown to the workers and agencies, Steven Barker was now living in the Connelly home, and had been there for several months. But there were, as will be recounted below, now additional occupants as well, and it may be that this is what really turned the story from one of chronic neglect to one of horrific abuse.

But back to the narrative. What was happening with and for the Connelly family in July 2007? From 29 June until 5 July the school records show the Connelly children were away from school. Tracey Connelly had left a message for the social worker saying that as it was her birthday she was going away with the children. The school and the Mellow Parenting programme workers, however, were told by Tracey Connelly that she had gone to look after a sick uncle. The childminder left a message for the social worker stating that Tracey Connelly and the children had gone away (as did the school nurse when she became aware of it). It will be noted later that it is now understood that this is the week that Jason Owen, Steven Barker's brother, with his 15-year-old girlfriend and three of his pre-school-age children, moved into the Connelly home, but none of the workers, including the police, knew this until after Peter's death.

The social worker made several attempts to contact Tracey Connelly, and on 2 July managed to contact her (presumably by mobile phone). Tracey Connelly then said she was in Cricklewood (less than 10 miles away, in north London) looking after a sick uncle, and would be back in Tottenham at her home on either 4 or 9 July; 2 July was a Monday, so Tracey Connelly was saying she would either be returning on the Wednesday or on Sunday, 8th. The social worker, with her manager, decided that Tracey Connelly should be contacted again by the social worker and asked to return to Tottenham with all the children. The second serious case review report does not note when Tracey Connelly returned to Tottenham, but she was back by 4 July and attended the Mellow Parenting programme; on 9 July she was contacted by the social worker when she was at the NHS walk-in clinic in Haringey with Peter, who was seen to have an ear infection, and with one of Peter's sisters who had a cold.

This is conjecture as it is not clarified in the serious case review report, but what may be more likely is that Tracey Connelly had never gone to Cricklewood, but was making herself and her home unavailable to visitors as Steven Barker's brother, girlfriend and children had now moved into her home. Their continuing presence was apparently not welcomed by Tracey Connelly, and it is claimed she was frightened of Jason Owen and that he refused to move out of the home when she asked him to.[38]

In the serious case review report a considerable amount of contact between workers and agencies, and contacts and attempted contacts with Tracey Connelly, are noted at this time. The housing association tried to contact Tracey Connelly as her current home was only supposed to be temporary. Little is noted in the serious case review report about housing issues for the Connelly family, so it is not clear how uncertain and anxiety-provoking the housing issues were for her. The headteacher of the school the two older children had been attending was in contact with the deputy headteacher of the new school. The new school was much closer than the school they had been attending after the move in February to their larger family home. It is stated that the headteacher of the former school gave information about the children and family, the contact details for the social worker and that two of the children had child protection plans, although this information was not noted at the new school. The deputy headteacher of the new school did not recall being told about the child protection plans, and the teachers at the new school were not told about the child protection plans. The school nurse sent a letter to Tracey Connelly to make appointments to see the children. And the police were asking the social worker to contact the GP, which she did, for a report for their criminal investigations into possible abuse.

At about this time the police concluded their investigations into Peter's injuries from December 2006, and supported the findings of the original medical opinion that they, as recorded in the serious case review report, 'suggested' non-accidental injury,[39] but with no further evidence available. There is still no account, however, of how the police investigated the injuries, who undertook the investigation and what was done after it was realised within the police that the investigation had not been pursued and completed and when it was then belatedly resurrected. In particular, there is no account in the serious case review reports of any attempt by police officers to find out about the mother's male friend who was visiting Peter in hospital in December 2006.

On 9 July Tracey Connelly is reported to have taken Peter to the NHS walk-in centre where he was provided with cream for head scabs and antibiotics for an ear infection. When seen by the health visitor at the clinic nine days later, on 18 July, his left ear was red on the outside and his ear lobe appeared infected. Tracey Connelly stated that she had caused the bruising to the ear while she had been trying to clean it. Peter's weight had reduced to the 25th percentile and he also had a small bruise under his chin. A further appointment was made to discuss diet and nutrition. One of Peter's sisters was seen at the same clinic, and had bruising under the right eye that was explained by Tracey Connelly as resulting from falling out of bed and landing on a toy. The health visitor spoke with the social worker about the injuries to the two children and Peter's ear infection, and the social worker and team manager agreed that the social worker would discuss these new concerns with Tracey Connelly. The health visitor had also advised Tracey Connelly to go again to the NHS walk-in clinic at North Middlesex University Hospital, which she did on the following day.

Peter was taken to the walk-in clinic late on the afternoon of 19 July. When contacted by the social worker earlier in the day to check that Peter had been taken to the clinic, which was no more than 10 minutes walk from the family home, Tracey Connelly said she had been to the clinic with Peter but the queue was so long she would go back later (which she did). When Peter was seen at the walk-in clinic on the North Middlesex Hospital site, he was referred to the A&E department. His inflamed ear was diagnosed as a sudden onset ear infection. Peter was noted to be well groomed and nourished, and alert and looking around, although there is a later comment in the second serious case review report about the same hospital visit that Peter looked grubby. In addition to what was seen as an ear infection, Peter had an infected scalp with bloody scabs, lice and there was blood around his left ear where he had apparently been scratching. He also had an infected nail bed on the middle finger of his right hand. It was noted that Peter was on the child protection register and the council's social services emergency duty team, the out-of-office hours emergency social work service, were informed by the hospital that Peter had been seen and had now left the hospital. The hospital were clearly concerned about Peter but not concerned enough to keep him at the hospital. No information is given in the serious case review report about what response was given by the emergency duty team. It may be that they received the information and relayed it to the social worker's office the following day.

On 23 July the childminder contacted the social worker stating that she could no longer care for Peter and his pre-school-age sister as the parents of the other children for whom she cared were complaining about the head lice. She would take the children back when the head lice had been cleared. The childminder also said that Peter's ear infection appeared to be getting worse. The social worker contacted Tracey Connelly and asked her to take Peter to the GP as the ear infection was not getting better. Later that day the social worker contacted Tracey Connelly again to check if Peter had been taken to the GP, and was told that he had, and that the GP was unable to prescribe more antibiotics, was not concerned, and that Peter might be having an allergic reaction to the head lice treatment.

Tracey Connelly was seen at different times with her children in mid and late July, and she was described as having a good relationship with one of her children when she attended the school for the child's health review. She also went to the school when contacted to attend because one of her children had a splinter from an accident in the playground and teachers were not allowed to remove it. Tracey Connelly was observed to be gentle, caring and reassuring when removing the splinter.

Tracey Connelly's extensive contacts with her children with agencies and workers, sometimes initiated by herself as when she took children to the GP, NHS walk-in clinic or hospital, would have taken much time and were frequent events. This was not a mother who was hiding herself from agencies, although she was hiding the terrible reality of what was happening to her children and especially Peter, and managing what was known to others. The children were also not unseen. They were seen by the social worker, health visitor, teachers, childminder, FWA worker, NHS Mellow Parenting workers, GP and hospital and walk-in clinic nurses and doctors. They were also seen by relatives, including Peter's father and grandmother, family friends and by neighbours. I have heard comments made, for example, that one of the failings for Peter was that he was not seen by the social worker and that she did not seek to see him. This is not true. Peter was seen by the social worker and many others, including on his own, as when in the care of the childminder. But what was not seen or understood by the social worker or other workers, and only became known after Peter's death, was what was happening and who was living in the Connelly home.

On 26 July Tracey Connelly was again seen with Peter by the GP. The second serious case review report notes that 'the GP has said subsequently that he had considerable misgivings about Peter's appearance and demeanor at that appointment. He felt that Peter was in a "sorry state". However, he did not take action to alert others to his concern. He assumed that others would have similar concerns and would be in a better position to take action. He knew that Peter had an appointment [for the paediatric assessment] at the child development centre in a few days.'[40] However, the second serious case review report also notes that at the end of July Peter 'stayed overnight with his father', spent a day at the crèche at Mellow Parenting, and was seen at a case conference with his mother and father. No one expressed concern about his safety. It can only be assumed that he was as well as he appeared to be at those times. The serious injuries were to come later.[41] Peter was also seen with his mother by chance by the FWA worker when they met out on a street.

Towards the end of July, the day before the GP contact with Peter noted above, there were arrangements for the long-awaited legal planning meeting in the council. It was scheduled for 25 July, having been sought since early June. Arrangements were now also being made for Peter's long-awaited assessment at the child development clinic, with an appointment for 1 August, with this assessment having been sought since March, five months earlier.

The belated arrangements for the legal planning meeting, the police criminal investigations and the NHS child development centre assessment had not only been delayed for some time, but they were to come too late for Peter. However, the outcome of each would not have stopped the horrific events that were now only days away:

- The *legal planning meeting* on 25 July was attended by the social worker, her team manager and a lawyer. The serious case review report notes that the solicitor was inexperienced in advising about care proceedings. She was also acting without the assurance of experienced supervision and oversight. The outcome of this meeting was that the lawyer did not feel able to advise that the threshold for care proceedings had been met. The limitations of Haringey Council's legal services received little later attention or coverage in how the 'Baby P story' was shaped and told.
- The *child development centre paediatric assessment* appointment was on 1 August but the assessment did not take place. Tracey attended for the appointment with Peter, along with her friend who had cared for him. But Peter had a high temperature, was miserable and had a runny nose, and it was decided by the consultant paediatrician that he was too unwell to be examined and assessed, and that he probably had a viral infection. It was also noted, however, that

he had numerous bruises, a fungal infection on his ear and scalp (which was being treated by antibiotics) and that his weight was now only at the 9th centile (he was now in the least heavy 10 per cent of boys his age). The doctor knew that it was reported he had a history of headbanging, headbutting, aggression and hyperactivity, with a history of recurrent bruising and infections. But the doctor had no record or reports about Peter from Whittington or North Middlesex University Hospitals, or from Peter's many other numerous contacts with health professionals. However, she did have the letter from the social worker that noted that Peter was subject to a child protection plan. The doctor thought that Peter should be in hospital and advised Tracey to take Peter to his GP or to the A&E department if he did not get better, although she did not refer Peter directly to any hospital or seek his admission. What she did do was to make a new appointment for three weeks' time for Peter's assessment.

• The *outcome of the police investigations* was that, following consultation with the Crown Prosecution Service, no further action was to be taken. The police informed Tracey Connelly on 2 August, a date which takes on particular significance as the next day's events unfolded, that neither of the potential prosecutions, relating to the injuries in December and in May, would be pursued.

The final entry in the narrative chronology in the second serious case review report notes:

> On 3 August the London Ambulance Service responded to a 999 call at 11.35 am. The caller was [Tracey Connelly] who reported a 17 month old child, taking antibiotics, now not moving. She couldn't wake him up. She reported to the crew that she had last seen him at approximately 1 am and that he had been unwell recently with a fungal infection. [Tracey Connelly] travelled in the ambulance to North Middlesex University Hospital with Peter. He was pronounced dead at 12.19 pm.[42]

Peter was 17 months old when he died.

—

The second serious case review report ends at this point. It gives no information about what was found to have caused Peter's death. It does not record all the injuries Peter was found to have sustained. It gives no account at this time of the other children living in the Connelly household. It gives no information or consideration about what was soon to become known about who had been living in the Connelly home with Peter. It is incomplete in the story it tells. It is even less complete and comprehensive in the conclusions drawn and the recommendations made. This will be commented on later in Chapter Three where there are further reflections on the two serious case review reports that were prepared following Peter's death.

Sharon Shoesmith, Haringey's then Director of Children's Services, recalls the social workers being told by the police that Tracey had been charged with Peter's murder:

> The day before he died, police [Sharon Shoesmith said] "saw the mother with the social worker and said there was no evidence to press any charges". They told the social worker to go ahead and organize a short holiday for her. "I was in the room when the police came to tell some of those staff that [Tracey Connelly] had been charged with murder and I'll remember the scene for ever because they simply could not believe it."[43]

After his death on 3 August 2007, and as reported by the pathologist, Peter was found to have had 22 injuries, including:

- fractured tibia some months before his death
- loss of tissue on the right middle finger
- up to two weeks before his death, seven rib fractures
- loss of a finger nail
- loss of a toe nail
- injuries to his legs and feet
- about three to four days before his death, a broken spinal cord
- three bruises to the left side of his face
- an infected raw area in front of the left ear

- about 10 bruises between his shoulder blades
- a tooth that had been knocked out and which he had swallowed.

A photograph released by the police to
the press of Peter's bloodstained t-shirts.

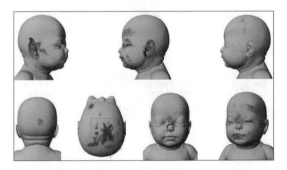

The pictures above show Peter's blood-stained clothing and a body map of Peter's head injuries, pictures that the police gave to the media. They tell a story of a 17-month-old child who had been assaulted and abused repeatedly with the abuse escalating and leading to his death. Indeed, with the loss of a toe nail and the loss of a finger nail, which it was noted in the judge's comments was likely to have been removed deliberately, it is hard not to see that Peter was tortured before he died. The judge's comments note that:

> 2nd August: the forceful knocking into his mouth of a tooth which he ingested. That forceful knocking could have caused the injury to his upper spine to re-bleed and in turn could have affected his respiratory and cardiac functions. It could well have been the immediate cause of his death.[44]

It would have been a very, very frightening and horrific time for Peter, with adults with power deliberately injuring him, and with no adult in the home stopping him being injured. He was powerless amidst the powerful. And it would seem very unlikely that the other children in the home would have been untouched by the fear and threat within the home.

The criminal investigations that followed Peter's death led to the arrest of Tracey Connelly, Steven Barker and his brother, Jason Owen. All were now found to have been living in the Connelly household, along with Jason Owen's 15-year-old girlfriend and three of his young children. It might now be assumed that the girlfriend was the young girl who had been seen at the school with Tracey in late July.

So, who was living in the Connelly home between December 2006 and August 2007?

Who was living in the Connelly household?

Pre-December 2006	Tracey Connelly
	Three girls
	Peter Connelly
	Two dogs
	Total: one adult /four children/two dogs
Plus, by Spring 2007	Steven Barker
	Total: two adults/four children/two dogs
Plus, by July 2007	Jason Owen
	15-year-old girlfriend
	Jason Owen's three children
	Total: three adults/one 15-year-old/seven children/three dogs

---

At the criminal trial it became known that in addition to Tracey Connelly, Peter, and his three sisters, Steven Barker had also been living in the family home possibly earlier, in 2007. His brother had moved into the family home towards the end of June, along with his 15-year-old girlfriend and three of his young children. So, between December and the end of June, it is likely there were six people in the home (two adults and four children). From the end of June until Peter's death in August, there were 11 people in the home (three adults, a 15-year-old girl and seven young children). There were also three dogs in the house, reported to be a Rottweiler, an Alsatian and a Staffordshire bull terrier, and it is stated that Jason Owen also brought a snake.[45] Despite the move in February 2007 to a bigger, four-bedroom house, the house would now again have been crowded and chaotic.[46]

Following Peter's death Tracey Connelly was arrested and held in custody, but Steven Barker and Jason Owen, with his 15-year-old girlfriend, tried to hide at a campsite in Epping Forest and were arrested when they failed to pay the site charges and the site manager contacted the police.

Three concurrent actions were then under way. First, the Metropolitan Police with the Crown Prosecution Service undertook the criminal investigation into Peter's death and prepared the prosecution evidence. This would have included interviewing those arrested, other witnesses including the workers who had been in contact with the family, collating the evidence from Peter's autopsy and other medical evidence from before Peter's death, and also

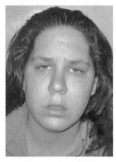

Tracey Connelly   Steven Barker   Jason Owen

seeking other expert evidence, such as further medical opinions about Peter's injuries. Inquiries would have also been undertaken on behalf of the coroner.

Second, Haringey LSCB would have initiated a serious case review (undertaken when a child dies, or when a child is seriously harmed and there are concerns about how organisations or professionals worked together to safeguard the child). This would have included case files being secured and made available to the report writers in each of the agencies that had had contact with Peter and his family. These report writers would each have produced an individual management report, relying primarily on the case records and files. They should each have had no prior involvement with the case or direct management responsibility for the workers involved with the family. An independent person, independent of the agencies, was then appointed to produce an overview report drawing primarily on the information and opinion in each of the individual management reviews.

All of this was overseen by a serious case review panel appointed by the LSCB, and the overview report and its recommendations were received by the Board which then determined an action plan. Each agency would also have produced its own action plan that was reported to the Board. In 2008, the executive summaries of serious case review reports were published, but not the full report. This has now changed, and the government has determined that the full reports should be published including, in retrospect, previous reports that it considered particularly significant. However, serious case review reports, including the report in relation to Peter and his family, are usually not published until the completion of any criminal prosecutions so as not to interfere with the criminal trial.

Third, Haringey Council would have initiated care proceedings in the civil family court to secure the safety of and care for Peter's sisters. They would have drawn on similar evidence to the criminal trial, but with a different and lesser test of proof to be applied compared to the criminal court. Peter's sisters would, therefore, have been in the care of Haringey Council.

At the beginning of the criminal trial on 9 September 2008, just over a year after Peter died, Tracey Connelly pleaded guilty to causing or allowing the death of Peter, and on 11 November Steven Barker and Jason Owen were also each found guilty of the same offence, with the judge noting it could not be determined who had caused the fatal injury which killed Peter. Steven Barker was, later and separately, convicted of raping another child, who was two-and-a-half years old at the time, sometime between the beginning of February and 3 August 2007.[47]

Steven Barker was sentenced for the rape to a life sentence minimum term of 20 years, with 10 years before he could be considered for parole, but with the judge noting that the end of the minimum sentence did not mean that he would be released. He was also sentenced to 12 years imprisonment for causing or allowing the death of Peter, to run concurrently with the sentence for rape.

Tracey Connelly was sentenced for causing or allowing the death of Peter to an indeterminate period of imprisonment with a minimum term of five years, but again noting that this did not mean that she would be automatically released after five years (as noted in Chapter Five, Tracey Connelly was released from prison in 2013). There was some mitigation allowed because of her guilty plea.

Jason Owen was similarly convicted with an indeterminate sentence of imprisonment with a minimum period of three years. In August 2011 (see Chapter Five) he was released from prison with conditions limiting his contact with children and where he could live.

The judge, in his sentencing remarks, also made comments about each of the defendants. He noted that Steven Barker, who at the time of sentencing in May 2009 was aged 32, had no previous convictions, cautions or reprimands, had had what was described as a difficult childhood and upbringing, and had mental health problems and mental limitations. Although acquitted of murder and manslaughter, it was stated that he had played a major role in the events for Peter between December 2006 (when Peter was first taken to hospital because of his injuries) and Peter's death. The judge commented that 'the offences of which you have been convicted are very grave and your culpability is particularly high'.

Tracey Connelly was described in the judge's sentencing remarks as being 27 years old at the time of sentencing, having no previous convictions, and having had a difficult childhood and upbringing.

The judge noted in mitigation that unprompted she had taken Peter to hospital in December 2006 and June 2007. The pre-sentence report described her as 'a vocal and not unintelligent young woman who is fairly articulate', although the judge himself stated that she was 'a manipulative and self-centred person, with a calculating side as well as a temper.... Your conduct over the months prevented Peter from being seen by social services. You actively deceived the authorities.... You acted selfishly because your priority was your relationship with [Steven Barker]. You too abused the position of trust you held towards your son and in a situation where, living in the same household, there were other young children who are likely to be damaged psychologically by what they have lived through.' The judge commented: 'I completely accept what the writer of the pre-sentence report says ... that taking into account the nature and seriousness of the offence, the pattern of neglect and chastisement to children demonstrated by you, your potential to obstruct those seeking to protect and care for your children, your lack of insight into your behaviour coupled with a failing to do much to moderate the risk you pose, and the other matters concerning your personality set out [in the pre-sentence report] that you ... present a high risk of causing harm to children in [your] care through potential neglect.'[48]

The judge's comments in relation to Jason Owen, who was aged 37 years at the time of sentencing, noted that the period he was living in the Connelly home coincided with an escalation in the injuries to Peter, that Jason Owen had himself had a difficult childhood and upbringing, that he had previous convictions for arson and burglary, and that he had a long-standing depressive illness. The judge commented that he had been 'more concerned about your own situation, about being discovered, and about the horror of what was happening to Peter being discovered, than taking steps to protect him', and agreed with comments in the pre-sentence report that Jason Owen had 'the potential to commit further serious specified offences at random, even in the imminent future'.

In summary, it was an explosive combination that came together for Peter and his siblings during 2007. Until then there had been no major concerns about the care of the children by Tracey Connelly, even when she was caring for the children on her own after the children's father left the family home six months before. But when Steven Barker was more involved with and then moved in with the Connelly family, the injuries to Peter, the judge noted, 'steadily mounted in seriousness' until Peter died eight months later, in August 2007. Tracey Connelly was willing to give priority to her relationship with Steven Barker rather than to her care and responsibilities for her children, with Peter in particular becoming the target of horrific abuse. Her behaviour was later seen as manipulative. She was now exposed as lying about, and on occasions seeking to hide, Peter's injuries, including smearing his bruised face with chocolate to avoid the bruising being seen.[49]

The only critical comment about the agencies and workers in the judge's sentencing remarks related not to social services, where it was noted that Tracey Connelly had prevented them from seeing Peter, but that 'I do note that the health professionals who saw Peter shortly before he died seem at least to have missed the import of the injuries to him'. All the more intriguing, therefore, how the media coverage to follow was shaped.

Notes

[1] Haringey Local Safeguarding Children Board (LSCB) (2009) *Serious case review 'Child A'*, full report published 26 October 2010, London: Department for Education, p 66.

[2] *The Guardian* (2010) 'Fresh Baby P case findings to be revealed', 26 October (http://www.theguardian.com/society/2010/oct/26/fresh-bab-p-findings-revealed).

[3] Haringey LSCB (2009) op cit, p 66.

[4] Haringey LSCB (2009) op cit, p 67.

[5] Haringey LSCB (2009) op cit, pp 16-17.

[6] *The Guardian* (2008) 'The death of Baby P: The guilty three', 12 November (http://www.theguardian.com/society/2008/nov/12/child-protection-crime-baby-p1).

[7] *The Guardian* (2008) op cit.

[8] BBC (2009) 'Baby Peter: Trio who caused his death', 11 August (http://news.bbc.co.uk/1/hi/england/7727641.stm).

[9] Care Quality Commission (2009) *Review of the involvement and action taken by health bodies in relation to the case of Baby P*, May, London: Care Quality Commission, p 6.

—

[10] Ofsted, Healthcare Commission and Her Majesty's Inspectorate of Constabulary (2008) *Joint area review: Haringey Children's Services Authority Area*, November, p 15.

[11] *The Guardian* (2008) op cit.

[12] BBC (2009) op cit.

[13] *The Guardian* (2008) op cit.

[14] *The Independent* (2009) 'Baby P's killers: The untold story', 11 August (http://www.independent.co.uk/news/uk/crime/baby-ps-killers-the-untold-story-1770263.html).

[15] *The Sun* (2011) 'Addicted to torture', 12 January (www.thesun.co.uk/sol/homepage/news/2580959/Baby-Ps-stepfather-Steven-Barker-Addicted-to-torture.html).

[16] Haringey LSCB (2009) op cit, p 21.

[17] McShane, J. (2009) *It must never happen again: The lessons learned from the short life and terrible death of Baby P*, London: John Blake, pp 8-9.

[18] Haringey LSCB (2009) op cit, p 19.

[19] Haringey LSCB (2009) op cit, pp 23-4.

[20] Haringey LSCB (2009) op cit, p 25.

[21] Haringey LSCB (2009) op cit, p16.

[22] Haringey LSCB (2009) op cit, pp 27-31.

[23] Department of Health (2000) *Framework for the assessment of children in need and their families*, London: Department of Health, p 45.

[24] Department of Health and Social Security (1974) *Report of the Inquiry into the care and supervision provided in relation to Maria Colwell*, London: HMSO, p 316.

[25] Department for Education (undated) 'Mellow Parenting' (http://education.gov.uk/commissioning-toolkit/Programme/Detail/44).

[26] Haringey LSCB (2009) op cit, p 41.

[27] BBC (2009) op cit.

[28] Haringey LSCB (2009) op cit, p 45.

[29] Haringey LSCB (2009) op cit, p 47.

[30] Haringey LSCB (2008) *Serious case review 'Child A'*, November, London: Department for Education, p 115.

[31] Haringey LSCB (2009) op cit, p 48.

[32] Haringey LSCB (2008) op cit, p 41.

[33] Haringey LSCB (2009) op cit, p 49.

[34] Haringey LSCB (2009) op cit, p 50.

[35] Haringey LSCB (2008) op cit, p 115.

[36] Lakhani, N. and Johnson, A. (2008) 'Nasty, brutish and short: The horrific life of Baby P', *The Independent*, 16 November (www.independent.co.uk/news/uk/home-news/nasty-brutish-and-short-the-horrific-life-of-baby-p-1020487.html).

[37] Ferguson, H. (2011) *Child protection practice*, Basingstoke: Palgrave Macmillan.

[38] Lakhani and Johnson (2008) op cit.

[39] Haringey LSCB (2009) op cit, p 58.

[40] Haringey LSCB (2009) op cit, p 64.

[41] Haringey LSCB (2009) op cit, p 65.

[42] Haringey LSCB (2009) op cit, p 67.

[43] Edemariam, A. (2009) 'When a dead child is known to us, that's the biggest horror. We knew the size of that', *The Guardian*, 6 February (www.theguardian.com/society/2009/feb/06/sharon-shoesmith-haringey-interview).

[44] Sentencing Remarks (2009) *The Queen v (B) (The boyfriend of Baby Peter's mother), (C) (Baby Peter's mother), and Jason Owen*, 22 May, p 4.

[45] Lakhani and Johnson (2008) op cit.

[46] McShane (2009) op cit, p 52.

[47] Hughes, M. (2009) 'Fury as Baby P stepfather is guilty of raping girl aged two', *The Independent*, 2 May (www.independent.co.uk/news/uk/crime/fury-as-baby-p-stepfather-is-guilty-of-raping-girl-aged-two-1677641.html).

[48] Sentencing Remarks (2009) op cit, p 15.

[49] Jones, S. (2008) 'Baby P death: "They rubbed chocolate on his face to hide the bruises"', *The Guardian*, 11 November (www.theguardian.com/society/2008/nov/11/childprotection-ukcrime2).

TWO

The 'Baby P story' takes hold

The story of 'Baby P' was told through many routes. First, it was told through the media. This included the local, national and international print press of newspapers. It included radio and television, with 24-hour news channels both repeating the story-telling but also continuously looking for new angles and 'breaking news'. And it included the newer media of web feeds, blogs and Twitter.

Second, the story was told through inquiries and reviews which informed media comment and provided material for media coverage, with new inquiry and review reports re-energising and feeding the continuing story over many years. The inquiries and reviews were also conducted in the context of the previous and present media coverage, which may have had an impact on the inquiries and reviews.

Third, the story was told through the tribunal and court proceedings that in different ways were related or contributed to the 'Baby P story'. These tribunal and court hearings included, as shown in Chapter One, the criminal trial of the adults convicted of causing or allowing the death of Peter Connelly. They also later included the employment tribunals and the High Court hearings in relation to the workers who had been dismissed following Peter's death and the demands of *The Sun* and others. There were also the hearings by professional bodies that considered the competence and conduct of the professionals who were referred to them following the initial media coverage and the subsequent dismissals.

Fourth, one book was quickly prepared and published in 2009,[1] capturing and repeating how the story was then being structured and told within the media, and especially by *The Sun*. A further book has been printed in the US, but with no date or publisher noted in the book.[2] Although there was a dominant story line largely set by *The Sun*, over time other media beyond the tabloid press came to tell more differentiated stories of the complexities of child protection work and also to re-frame and re-balance the overwhelming focus of *The Sun* and other tabloid newspapers on social workers, Sharon Shoesmith and Haringey Council.[3]

Fifth, the story was not so much told but analysed and interpreted through academic papers and publications[4,5,6,7] that reflected on how the story was told and the impact of its telling. One of the outcomes of the 'Baby P story' was argued to be that:

> … the London borough of Haringey's case of Baby Peter opened up spaces for a more progressive debate about social work for children and families. First, attention began to be focused on Ofsted, which had previously approved of services there. It had relied too much on quantitative data, on how many forms had been filled in within the specified timescale, and not enough on the underlying quality of service provision. Second, there was an increased public awareness about the electronic recording system social workers were forced to use, including the inordinate amount of time social workers spent on computers…. Third, there was a more sensible debate about what could and could not be achieved by social workers, namely that, although generally the child protection system works well, risk and child deaths cannot be *totally* eliminated. Fourth, attention was focused on how neo-liberal policies, reflected in unfilled vacancies, agency staff and high turnover, were impacting on the ability of social workers to deliver effective services.[8]

And finally, the story was told through word-of-mouth. It became a topic of discussion and debate among people in the home, office, train and pub. I can recall hearing 'Baby P' being talked about in all of these venues. What I also recall was how limited some of the information and knowledge underlying the conversations was about what had happened to and with Peter Connelly. But this should not be surprising. In the midst of the media coverage in June 2009 I led an informal seminar at the university where I work. Anyone within the university could attend. It was to reflect on what was then known about the 'Baby P story' and the impact it was having on those working with very vulnerable children. It was attended by students and staff with particular interests in social work, early years and teaching, law, the media and journalism, and in the social sciences. About 60 people attended. We started by trying to work out from what information was then in the public arena through the media who was living in Peter Connelly's home when he was so horrifically abused and died in the summer of 2007. Many people knew about and recalled the mother, two men and Peter. Others added the young girlfriend of one of the men. Some knew that Peter had siblings, but none were sure how many or of what age or sex. No one knew that there might also have been children of one of the men also living in the home. So, even on the basic facts of who was within Peter's household, there was confusion and partial and incomplete information. It was this incompleteness of information that characterised then in 2008, and still characterises later, much of the comment and conversation about the 'Baby P story'.

But why did the 'Baby P story' get so much telling? In the period April 2007 to March 2009, 268 serious case reviews were conducted because children had suffered serious harm or died as a result of neglect or ill treatment.[9] So at the time that Peter died and in the subsequent 18 months there were about two or three children every week identified as having died or having been seriously harmed through neglect or ill treatment. It is the government's *Working together to safeguard children* statutory guidance which requires that serious case reviews be undertaken when this happens. It states:

> When a child dies (including death by suspected suicide) and abuse or neglect is known or suspected to be a factor in the death, the Local Safeguarding Children Board should always conduct a Serious Case Review into the involvement of organisations and professionals in the lives of the child and family ... and [where] the case gives rise

to concerns about the way in which local professionals and services worked together to safeguard and promote the welfare of children.[10]

There is appropriately and understandably great concern and distress whenever a child is killed or seriously harmed, and every day health workers, police, social workers and others in every area are working to protect children and to promote their welfare. In 2007 in England, for example, when Peter died, there were 27,900 children with child protection plans because they were seen as being especially in danger of abuse and neglect,[11] there had been 545,000 referrals of children to social workers in the past 12 months[12] and 60,000 children were in local authority care, usually living in foster homes or children's homes.[13]

These are large numbers, each one telling a tale of distress and of children in difficulty and maybe danger. They are numbers, as will be seen later in Chapter Five, which have increased further since Peter died. But in some ways they reflect not failure, but success. Every child who dies or is harmed is a terrible tragedy, but it has been reported by Pritchard and Williams that in the UK there is greater success in protecting children than in other countries where there is comparable information available about child deaths:

> The results tell a relative 'success story' for England and Wales, whose violent child-abuse-related-deaths (CARD) rates of children have never been lower since records began and who have made significantly greater progress in reducing violent possible CARD than the majority of other major developed countries.[14]

International comparisons are fraught with difficulties in measuring like with like,[15] but as Pritchard and Williams note:

> The death of Baby Peter was tragic and criminal and has become as iconic as Maria Colwell and Victoria Climbié [commented on later in this book], attracting considerable media furore.... Yet, a reasonable question, does the child

protection service make any difference in reducing
extreme consequences of abuse – the death of a child?[16]

This is a question that, throughout the structuring and telling of
the 'Baby P story', has largely remained unasked and unanswered.
Does this matter? It matters because there is the very real danger of
destabilising, disrupting and destroying what is generally working well,
albeit needing continuous reflection and refinement in response to
infrequent and exceptional but terrible events. The same applies, for
example, when there is the thankfully rare shooting of police officers,
with politicians and the police having to resist the call and clamour
that all police officers should therefore be armed with guns.[17]

So, among 130 children a year known to have suffered abuse or
neglect causing them serious harm or death, what is it that leads to
some becoming a cause of national concern? It is not that every
one of these awful stories gets told by the media with coverage
nationally (and internationally) as well as locally in newspapers
and on the radio and television. It is very rare for any one of these
tragedies to become a national front-page story or the leading item
in a news bulletin or broadcast. And it is even rarer for a child's death
to become a continuing issue of media interest over months or, as
with Peter's death, years.

And the coverage and comment about Peter's death was
exceptional. In the year from 1 November 2008 to 1 November 2009,
the year following the criminal trial findings that Tracey Connelly,
Steven Barker and Jason Owen had 'caused or allowed' Peter's death,
it is reported that there were 2,832 pieces in UK newspapers which
referred to 'Baby P'.[18] That is an average of almost eight pieces every
day. In *The Sun* newspaper alone, a tabloid newspaper that majored
on the 'Baby P story', it is stated that there were 848 articles referring
to 'Baby P' in this one year, an average of 2.32 stories every day for
a year. And among all the newspapers across the UK, it was *The Sun*
that provided 30 per cent of the stories in that year that referred to
'Baby P'.

So how was the 'Baby P story' told? How was it sustained over such a long time? And did the story change? How was it initiated, and how and why was it captured and driven in particular by *The Sun*?

Rather like what we now know about Peter Connelly and his life and death, what is now known about *The Sun* newspaper in late 2008, when the 'Baby P story' was first being told, was not then known. Through investigative reporting by *The Guardian*, hearings before select committees of Members of Parliament, the Leveson Inquiry into the British media, and criminal proceedings initiated in 2012, we now know about the network of relationships between members of the Murdoch family and their employees with senior politicians and with the Metropolitan Police. We now know of concerns about News International newspapers owned by Rupert Murdoch and News International journalists regarding phone and email hacking, corrupting public officials, interfering with criminal investigations, intimidating and threatening politicians and others, and perverting the course of justice. We know now about the close relationships between senior officers in the Metropolitan Police and senior managers and journalists of Rupert Murdoch's newspapers, and of the hesitation and failure of the Metropolitan Police to initially investigate serious allegations about the News International papers, editors and reporters. We now know about the social intertwining of the current Prime Minister, Mr Cameron, who was himself a significant player in the early shaping of the 'Baby P story', with Rebekah Brooks, editor of *The Sun* in 2008, and who was promoted to an even more senior role within News International. Mr Cameron also appointed and employed Andy Coulson, formerly editor of News International's *News of the World*, as his Director of Communications. Rupert Murdoch closed down the *News of the World* when evidence of illegal phone hacking by its reporters became increasingly known. Both Andy Coulson and Rebekah Brooks had had senior management responsibilities for the *News of the World*.

In relation to children who had been killed or kidnapped, Rebekah Brooks in particular, but News International newspapers more generally, were now found to have had significant but embarrassing associations. It was when it became public knowledge in July 2011 that reporters from the *News of the World* had hacked into the mobile phone of Milly Dowler, whose phone number they had obtained by contacting Milly's school friends, disrupting and misleading the police investigation into her disappearance and besieging Milly's family, that there was a general public outrage about the intrusion and illegality of the behaviour of *News of the World* employees.

Mr Cameron with Mrs Brooks

Milly Dowler was a 13-year-old schoolgirl who was murdered in 2002. It was only in 2011 that Levi Bellfield, a nightclub bouncer who had abducted Milly on her way home from school, was convicted of her murder. It is alleged that in 2002, when the Surrey Police were trying to trace Milly, that the *News of the World* conspired to hack into her phone messages, disrupting the police search for Milly, listening to distressed messages left by Milly's parents, and giving false hope to her parents that she was still alive. Parliament's House of Commons' Culture, Media and Sports Select Committee concluded in its report in 2012 that 'for those actions, and the culture which permitted them, the editor should take responsibility'.[19] The editor was Rebekah Brooks.

It was also in 2002 that the *News of the World* and its editor, Rebekah Brooks, reported the story of the disappearance in Soham,

Cambridgeshire, of Jessica Chapman and Holly Wells, two 10-year-old girls who, it was subsequently found, had been murdered by their primary school caretaker, Ian Huntley. Again, it is alleged there had been phone hacking of family members on behalf of the *News of the World* as the paper sought new information and story lines about the girls, their families and the girls' disappearance.

Two years earlier, in 2000, Rupert Murdoch had promoted Rebekah Brooks from deputy editor of *The Sun* to editor of the *News of the World*. One of her first actions as editor was to major on the abduction and murder of eight-year-old Sarah Payne in West Sussex. She launched a 'For Sarah' campaign for parents to be given information by the police about people locally who had been convicted of sexual offences against children. Part of the campaign was the *News of the World* publication of 49 pictures of paedophiles with the promise that the paper would publish information about 110,000 child sex offenders.

The campaign created concerns for the police that those convicted of sexual offences against children would seek to disappear and their locations become unknown to the police and other criminal justice and child protection agencies, exposing more children to danger. There was also mob violence. In Newport in Wales the home of a paediatrician was attacked because local vigilantes did not understand the difference between a paediatrician working to care for and protect children and paedophiles. In Portsmouth over 100 people gathered over several nights and marched to the home of a taxi driver named in the paper and made threats to kill paedophiles. In Portsmouth, Plymouth and Manchester innocent people with no association with sexual offences against children were attacked after being mistakenly identified locally as paedophiles. The circulation of the *News of the World* increased by 95,000 in the two weeks of the paper's campaign[20] before the identification of paedophiles in the paper was abandoned following the public disorder that had occurred.

But this was also a story with a later sting in its tale. Rebekah Brooks and other *News of the World* executives had apparently, over many years, befriended Sara Payne, the mother of Sarah Payne, following her daughter's murder. There had been a common interest in promoting 'Sarah's Law', which would allow parents to be informed about those living locally who had sexually abused children. But in 2010, as part of the inquiries into phone hacking committed by or on behalf of journalists at the *News of the World*, it became known that Sara Payne's mobile phone had been hacked, a phone that it was stated was given to her by Rebekah Brooks. Sara Payne was reported to be devastated, and it is stated that she subsequently received a payment for undisclosed damages from News Group Newspapers.[21]

Although these accounts of the interest and coverage of News International into the terrible killings of children and the tragedies of families are historic, going back to the early 2000s, at the time of and following the death of Peter Connelly in the late 2000s similar coverage of his death and of stories concerning other children were evident in the *News of the World*, *The Sun* and other papers. It was Rebekah Brooks (then Rebekah Wade) who, as editor of *News of the World* in the early 2000s, had shaped the coverage and story lines then, and had the senior management responsibility for the actions of her reporters. It was Rebekah Brooks who, as editor of *The Sun* in the late 2000s, had the same responsibilities for shaping story lines and for reporters' actions and behaviour.

In a 2012 book entitled *The Fall of the House of Murdoch* Peter Jukes, himself a journalist, writes about how:

> the tabloids have carried on pursuing these stories [of missing and murdered children] long after many of the victims are buried and the perpetrators apprehended and imprisoned. Lacking hue and cry, most of the subsequent coverage then concentrates on those peripheral to the crime, particularly the bereaved families who become – through infamy rather than fame – celebrity victims.... This tabloid obsession with child murder, especially as it began to lead the coverage of mainstream broadcasters like BBC and Sky News, felt uncomfortable at the time, an intrusion into private grief which over stepped a moral boundary. We now know it overstepped several legal boundaries as well.

Peter Jukes continued with specific reference to Rebekah Brooks:

> All tabloids, but the *News of the World* in particular, found ways to keep the photos of the victims on their front pages. For many years any headline including the words Soham, Sarah Payne or Madeleine McCann usually resulted in increased circulation. Rebekah Brooks personally led a campaign to name and shame sex offenders which she called 'Sarah's Law' (much like Megan's Law in the US) after Sarah Payne. At various lunches and press events, the editor of the *News of the World* stood side by side with the dead girl's mother, Sara Payne. Brooks became her friend and provided her with a mobile phone. It was later revealed that her phone number was on Glenn Mulcaire's list. [*Glenn Mulcaire was a private investigator with a year's payment of over £100,000 from the* News of the World *and who had been imprisoned for phone hacking.*[22]]

> The tabloid fascination with child murder has killed privacy by invading the privacy of death. But what did *The Sun*, Britain's biggest selling tabloid have to say about these shock-horror revelations about its sister paper to the *News of the World*? *The Sun* led with a headline about some spurious IVF lottery to win a baby and a photo of Victoria Beckham heavily pregnant in red dress, with the leaden pun 'Victoria Becktum'. Again, News International was mute when it came to news about itself.[23]

In 2008 Rebekah Brooks had moved on from editing the *News of the World* to editing *The Sun*. It was *The Sun* in November 2008, in the midst of the beginning of the considerable coverage about 'Baby P', that also majored, along with other papers,[24, 25, 26] on the story of Shannon Matthews and the criminal trial of her mother and kidnappers.[27] Shannon was a nine-year-old girl in Dewsbury, West Yorkshire, who was missing from home for 25 days in February

2008. Her mother had rung the police emergency number saying that her daughter had not returned from school. A massive police search, aided by the local community, took place at a cost of £3.2 million.[28] But, in effect, the police and the media were hoodwinked by Karen Matthews, Shannon's mother, and the mother's boyfriend and his uncle. They had created a potential scam where they would hide Shannon away and then 'find her' to claim a reward.

They must have thought their scam was working. A reward was offered. It was *The Sun* that, while reporting the terrible distress of Karen Matthews about her lost daughter, put up an award of £50,000. In this instance, despite the considerable deployment of media and police resources, an abusive parent and her accomplices sustained a lie that was reported extensively. In the end, it was information from the wider family and neighbours that led to Shannon being found by police officers hidden under the bed in her mother's boyfriend's uncle's flat a mile away from Shannon's home.

The story of Shannon Matthews at the time of the publication of the serious case review about her and her family[29] became a story of two distinct headlines. For *The Guardian* and the *Metro* it was:

> Social workers cleared, but inquiry warns patterns in Shannon Matthews case not rare.[30]

> Social workers 'clear of blame' in Shannon case.[31]

But for *The Sun* and *Daily Mail* there was a different story to be told:

SHANNON SCANDAL Council ruled out taking her into care 5yrs before kidnapping

- Matthews left kids open to sex abuse
- They endured neglect and squalor
- But a year on social workers ruled:

'SHANNON IS NOT AT RISK'.[32]

Neglectful. Filthy. And living with a paedophile. So why did social workers decide that little Shannon Matthews' mother was ... **Not such a bad parent!**[33]

Same story. Same serious case review. But two dramatically different story lines.

At the same time as the initial telling and shaping in November 2008 of the 'Baby P story', and when the Shannon Matthews story was also high profile, there was also reporting about a father who, while living in Lincolnshire and Sheffield, had 'made his daughters pregnant 19 times during almost 30 years of repeated rape and physical abuse'.[34] The terrible abuse and the abuser was compared to the 'Fritzl case' in Germany where a father had held his daughter hostage in an underground cellar and had repeatedly raped her over many years, fathering two children.[35] *The Sun* Editorial, when the serious case review about the Sheffield/Lincolnshire family was published in March 2011, referred to 'Baby P' and was consistent with the paper's primary targeting of social workers and councils:

> **SHAMELESS Yet again officials line up to apologise for a child abuse scandal that should never have happened.** And yet again, nobody has been sacked. Or disciplined. Or had the decency to resign.... We saw the same ducking with Baby P. We have filled our town halls with highly-paid child protection officials, yet complacency and incompetence are still widespread. **The least we are entitled to expect is that those who have failed so disgracefully should pay the price.**[36]

A similar story line and headline appeared within the *Daily Mail*. The full headline, in **bold**, read:

> **100 care workers, 28 agencies, 16 case conferences, countless complaints of abuse, 18 pregnancies,**

7 children. Yet no one is blamed for failing to stop the evil father from raping his daughters.[37]

There were comments quoted from relatives of the abused girls that 'social services are a waste of space as far as I am concerned' and 'they've still got their jobs or their pensions so I doubt if they will be losing any sleep about this [serious case review] report'. In the middle of the *Daily Mail*'s article of 21 column inches there is one very brief comment that 'proper action by just one of the workers or other officials including police who knew about the family could have ended the horror'. Overwhelmingly, however, the focus and blame is directed at social services and social workers.

It was no different in how the 'Baby P story' was told, but why was it that among all the children who were seriously abused and died in 2007 his life and death became such a focus, and a focus that was sustained while other children were being abused and killed? And how did the story of Peter Connelly's death come to be told as it was? The answers to these two questions may well be linked.

There are three possible explanations as to why Peter Connelly's death attracted such considerable media coverage and subsequent public interest. First, it was a story of violent abuse of a little child. However, the horror of Peter's life and the assaults and torture that culminated in his death and that became known during the criminal trial were extreme but they were not wholly exceptional. There were other children, including very young children, who died following extreme abuse in the year that Peter died and in the following years when it was Peter's story that continued to attract attention. The experiences and tragedies of these other children were not given the same media attention, and their names remain unknown to most of us.

Second, Peter Connelly died in Haringey. There was already an established narrative about Haringey by the press, politicians and public. It was in Haringey in February 2000 that Victoria Climbié had died shortly after being admitted to North Middlesex Hospital. She had been in the care of her aunt, Marie Therese Kouao, and the aunt's boyfriend, Carl Manning. They lived only hundreds of yards from where Peter Connelly later lived and died in the same area, near the football ground in Tottenham. Victoria had been tied in a black plastic bin bag in a bath, had 128 injuries and was covered in filth. Her abuse and neglect had continued for some time. The then Labour government initiated a public inquiry led by Lord Laming, a former probation officer, then Director of Social Services, and before his retirement he was Chief Inspector of Social Services in the Department of Health.

There was considerable media coverage of the Climbié inquiry, much of which came to focus on Haringey Council's social services department where it was found that good practice would have been very difficult:

> There was evidence of profound organisational malaise and an absence of leadership as exemplified by senior managers' apparent indifference to children's services, which were underfunded and neglected. Local child protection procedures were way out of date. This was compounded by major staffing problems and low morale amongst staff who were invariably overworked and 'burning out'. Frontline workers got little support or quality supervision and were uncertain about their role in child protection. Extremely poor administrative systems existed for tracking referrals and case information.... The [Laming] report connects up well the experiences of frontline workers with poor management and a lack of accountability right up to the highest levels. We are left in no doubt that the workers involved were overworked and under-supported.[38]

Despite the then organisational failings of Haringey Council, the spotlight largely fell on Victoria's young and recently qualified social worker, Lisa Arthurworrey. She lost her job and her professional registration was suspended. Workers and managers in other agencies including the police and health service were also noted to have fallen short of good and necessary practice, but went largely unchallenged, unnamed and unknown to the public at large.

Lord Laming features again later, in Chapter Four, as the government used his report as a lever for changes they were already moving towards in children's services and which might now be seen to have contributed to the child protection context in which Peter Connelly died. Lord Laming was also asked by the government after Peter's death to review the progress made in implementing the changes that followed his report from six years before.

The death of Victoria Climbié, and the major inquiry by Lord Laming, meant that Haringey Council was a remembered cause of concern about child protection. Haringey Council had, however, long before the death of Victoria Climbié been characterised by *The Sun*, along with other north London councils with a majority of Labour councillors, as the 'looney left', with 'scam stories' created and published to attack the councils' reputations. *The Sun*'s reported stories included that:

> Bernie Grant's Haringey was planning to spend £500,000 on providing twenty-four 'super-loos' for travellers and had instructed council workers to demonstrate solidarity by drinking only Nicaraguan coffee – a story headed in *The Sun* as 'BARMY BERNIE IS GOING COFFEE-POTTY – STAFF MUST DRINK MARXIST BREW'. Pegged on the latest scam story that Bernie Grant was personally planning Creole language lessons in the borough's schools, *The Sun* made a national connection: 'Don't imagine that Bernie's antics will afflict only one suffering part of London.... Remember he is a Parliamentary candidate for Labour at the next Election.... Labour is now the Official Barmy Party!'[39]

Haringey Council had, therefore, a history of being a target, and a politically motivated target, for *The Sun*.

But there is a third possible explanation why Peter's death and the 'Baby P story' had so much sustained telling and attention, and how the story was shaped as it was. As noted above, whenever a child is seriously abused or neglected, and especially when a child dies of neglect or abuse, there is a requirement that a serious case review is undertaken. At the conclusion of the serious case review the executive summary and recommendations had to be published (this has now been changed to require that the full serious case review report is published). The expected and normal practice would be that the agencies involved with the child and within the serious case review process would work together in contributing to the serious case review and in presenting together the findings to the media through a press release, media briefing and maybe a media conference. This would usually be after the conclusion of any criminal trial, or when there have been findings of guilt, in relation to the neglect or abuse of the child. This would allow the serious case review to take into account any new facts that might emerge through the criminal trial, and also so that the serious case review's publication did not interfere with the proper process of the trial by placing information into the public arena as yet not declared at the trial.

But what happened in November 2008 immediately following the findings of guilt in relation to Tracey Connelly, Steven Barker and Jason Owen, and prior to the sentencing hearing that took place many months later, was that the Metropolitan Police briefed the media ahead of the participation of the other child protection agencies such as the council and the health services. The briefing and police comments were led by Detective Superintendent Caroline Bates, a senior officer responsible for child protection in London's Metropolitan Police.

Detective Superintendent Bates' statements to the media had several themes. First, as reported by Sky News on the afternoon of the court decision, there was an acknowledgement by Detective Superintendent Bates that 'police errors were made which caused a delay at the start of the abuse inquiry' but second, 'these had not been significant to the outcome'.[40] Third, there was an explanation that it was the mother who 'was lying and trying to subvert agencies involved with the family' who had thwarted the police investigations before Peter's death. Fourth, there was a description of the adults, with Tracey Connelly described by an (unnamed) detective as 'a slob, completely divorced from reality. She was living in a dream world and put her lover before her child' and that the boyfriend was 'sadistic – fascinated with pain'.[41]

Detective Superintendent Bates is quoted in the Metropolitan Police press release on 11 November 2008 as saying:

> There is no doubt that this child's death was a tragedy and that he suffered terribly at the hands of his carers during the last months of his short life. The child's mother consistently lied in an attempt to conceal the ill treatment of him and avoided the assistance she was offered by the professionals to help protect him from harm. She repeatedly chose to mislead professionals in order to enable the continued abuse of her son.[42]

But there was also a fifth theme in the statements made by Detective Superintendent Bates on behalf of the Metropolitan Police, and this was that Haringey Council had not taken the actions necessary, despite the police strongly arguing for the action to be taken, to seek to remove Peter from his mother's care.

The Metropolitan Police press release is surprisingly headed, 'Baby death: Man found guilty', with the focus on Steven Barker. The findings of the criminal trial, however, were that Tracey Connelly, Steven Barker and Jason Owen had each 'caused or allowed' Peter Connelly's death. There was terrible and horrific abuse taking place within the Connelly household, but the police were unable to determine or prove who was committing the abuse, although Detective Superintendent Bates noted in the press release that 'detectives from the Child Abuse Investigation Command Major Investigation team conducted a thorough investigation into the child's murder to ensure today's successful prosecution of those responsible for his death'.

There is, however, nothing within the Metropolitan Police pre-prepared press statement about any errors or failings within the criminal investigations before Peter's death. There is also no actual or implied criticism of any other agency. Indeed, the repeated attention is on a mother determined to mislead:

> The child's mother contrived to evade the best efforts of agencies who were trying to help her and her son, she

lied to prevent them knowing the truth about her having a personal relationship with this man [Steven Barker] and the risks he posed. This is a case where the mother appeared to cooperate with agencies and to accept offers of help to safeguard her family, whilst constantly misleading professionals about the reasons for her son's injuries and presenting false, but potentially plausible explanations, for his ill health.

Detective Superintendent Bates concluded:

> We cannot guarantee that a child will not be the victim of abuse by his carers, but we continue to investigate allegations of child abuse and to assess the risks to children based on information available to us. Together with our partner agencies, we work to protect children and it is a matter of great distress when a child has suffered unnecessary cruelty at the hands of his supposed carers.

So, from the press release issued by the Metropolitan Police on 11 November 2008 a picture is given of agencies working in a positive partnership and of the agencies being deliberately misled by a devious mother. The latter may be true; the former is rather more contentious. It is the reported comments made by Detective Superintendent Bates outside the court on 11 November at the time the adults were found guilty that highlight possible strains within the partnership, with the police seemingly feeding and fuelling the story line that the errors in the criminal investigations before Peter Connelly died were not important in relation to his death but that the police wanted Peter removed from his family:

> Outside court today, Detective Superintendent Caroline Bates said police errors were made which caused a delay at the start of the abuse inquiry, but these had not been significant to the outcome.... In June, "police officers felt very strongly that [Baby P] should not be returned"

to his mother, and a police inspector asked twice if the threshold had been reached to start care proceedings.[43]

This theme of police officers wanting Peter Connelly to be removed from his family was stated even more strongly in a report timed at 12.40pm on 11 November in the *Haringey Independent*, headed 'Police speak out on baby P':

> Police detectives involved in Baby P's murder investigation have admitted the decision to return the abused toddler to his mother was made against their wishes. The toddler's mother was arrested for the first time in December 2006 when she brought Baby P into the hospital with suspicious injuries. She was bailed while an investigation was carried out but on January 26, 2007, the child was returned to his Haringey home despite police advice.[44]

This is now the focus of the story on the day of the findings of guilt and just before the serious case review media conference that afternoon which the Metropolitan Police did not attend. It is only at the end of the report in the *Haringey Independent* that it is noted:

> Ch Supt Bates admits more could have been done during the investigation. She said: "There were delays in that investigation and it could have been done better. The officer involved has been provided with that feedback and it was not representative of her general work".

The police officer who could have 'done better' was not named. There were no subsequent calls in the press for her dismissal or for disciplinary proceedings. She had received feedback and that was seen as adequate and accepted by the press. It was not a reflection of her general work, and Detective Superintendent Bates said it was 'these three adults who killed that child and it is very important that everyone remembers that'.

So the ground for the story of 'Baby P' is now partly set, with the Metropolitan Police minimising the impact of errors in the police criminal investigations into Peter's injuries before he died, but stating that they had wanted Peter removed from the care of his mother, and with the obvious corollary that this was not agreed or actioned through a court application by Haringey Council and its social workers.

The first significant national reporting of the story was on the afternoon of Tuesday, 11 November 2008. And initially it was concerns about the actions of the police and of the paediatrician at St Ann's Clinic that attracted attention. The 24-hour rolling news media had the story first. The BBC website carried the headline of 'A short life of misery and pain' and gave information about Peter's injuries and an account of the involvement of agencies with Peter and his family. The report began by stating:

> Two men have been found guilty of causing or allowing the death of a 17-month-old-boy. The child's mother had already admitted allowing or causing the child's death. The trial highlighted the missed opportunities to save his life and the case has chilling echoes of the death of Victoria Climbié. On 2 August 2007 police announced they were dropping an investigation into allegations of child abuse they had launched the previous December. Baby P's mother was elated and told social workers she would go home to hug her son and bake cakes. The next morning he was dead.[45]

Sky News led their report about the findings of guilt at the criminal trial with the statement that:

> Two men have been found guilty of causing the death of a toddler who was used as a 'punchbag' for months. The 17-month-old – known only as Baby P – suffered injuries similar to the 'force of a car crash'. Just two days before the boy was found dead in his blood-spattered cot, a doctor failed to spot his broken spine. And police

told the mother she would not be prosecuted after being arrested twice for suspected child cruelty.[46]

The Sky News report also noted that:

> Detective Superintendent Caroline Bates said police errors were made which caused a delay at the start of the abuse inquiry, but these had not been significant to the outcome. She said, "With hindsight, having the benefit of a major investigation, we know quite clearly that the mother was lying and trying to subvert agencies involved with the family".

Was this then to be the story, how a police investigation had failed to identify the perpetrators of the abuse experienced by Peter, and how the day before he died they had informed his mother that they were not investigating any further and that she was not to be prosecuted?

But the Sky and BBC reports also drew explicit parallels with the death of Victoria Climbié:

> The tragedy has echoes of the Victoria Climbié murder in 2000, when eight-year-old Victoria died after care workers and police in Haringey failed to save her.[47]

> This is not the first time Haringey social services has come under the spotlight. In February 2000 eight-year-old Victoria Climbié was killed in Tottenham after a number of failings by Haringey social services and other agencies. The public inquiry which followed, headed by Lord Laming, criticised the lack of communication between the different agencies and suggested an overhaul of child protection guidelines.[48]

The BBC report continues by quoting Mor Dioum, Director of the Victoria Climbié Foundation, as saying:

> I strongly believe this case is worse than Victoria Climbié.
> Personally I do feel betrayed by the agencies. Given the
> government's extensive reforms of the child protection
> system I never thought I'd live to see another case so
> similar to Victoria Climbié. For the sake of public interest
> we ought to have a wider inquiry into this case to identify
> the mistakes made.

As will be discussed in Chapters Four and Five, not everyone was
or is convinced that the reforms introduced by the government in
2004 were sensible or appropriate in improving child protection.

The same day, Mr Dioum was quoted in the *Haringey Independent*
as 'once again laying the blame at the feet of Haringey Council',
and saying that 'we are looking at both operational and systemic
failures in this case. I am just hoping Haringey Council will not just
say it was a mistake and that is as far as it goes.'[49] But what was not
quoted in the *Haringey Independent* is Mr Dioum's view that 'I do
not think we can scapegoat an individual in this case. We must look
at the system as a whole.'[50]

However, what was about to happen was that individuals were
about to be 'scapegoated', and the individuals were almost exclusively
within Haringey Council. This became evident when, on Wednesday,
12 November, the day after the findings of guilt in the criminal
case and the publication of the first serious case review executive
summary, Mr Cameron sought to ask Mr Brown* about the death
of 'Baby P' at Prime Minister's Question Time,[51] although it became
evident that Mr Cameron was not well briefed. Mr Cameron started
by asking Mr Brown:

---

*   It is claimed in a biography of David Cameron that there was animosity
between Mr Cameron and Mr Brown which was 'not just political, but
personal', and that 'aside from Brown himself, Ed Balls attracts particular
vitriol from the Tory leadership. Balls is an exact Oxford contemporary of
Cameron and also read PPE [Politics, Philosophy and Economics] – Balls
got a higher first-class degree, something that matters to both of them'
(Elliot, F. and Hanning, J. [2009] *Cameron: The rise of the New Conservative*,
London: Harper, p 318).

I want to ask about the tragic death of Baby P. This happened in the same children's services department [*and he could have said the same Metropolitan Police Force and the same NHS, but he didn't*] that was responsible for Victoria Climbié and yet again nobody is taking responsibility, nobody has resigned.

He went on:

Let's be honest. This is a story about a 17 year old [*it wasn't. Tracey Connelly was not a teenage mother. She was aged 27*] who had no idea how to bring up a child. It's about a boyfriend who couldn't read, but could beat up a child and it's about a Social Services Department [*it was a children's services department with social services departments effectively abolished by the 2004 Children Act*] that gets £100 million a year and can't look after children [*Haringey Council in 2007 was looking after 455 children in care and was protecting 156 children who had child protection plans*].

When Mr Brown tried to explain that the process now to be followed was that a report would be received by Mr Balls, Secretary of State for Children, who would then decide what actions should be taken, Mr Cameron apparently became angrier and angrier:

I don't expect an answer now, you never get one – but will the Prime Minister at least consider whether the time has come to take over this failing department and put someone in charge who can run it properly for our children.

There was considerable concern about how the death of Peter Connelly became a subject within the political debate and the territory of political points scoring within Prime Minister's Question Time, with headlines such as 'Spat was shameful'[52] and 'Shame, they cried. And they were right'.[53]

—

81

However, the concern about Mr Cameron using a political arena and opportunity to raise the death of 'Baby P' was not a concern shared by *The Sun*. Indeed, there was a considerable symmetry between the stance taken by Mr Cameron and *The Sun*, with *The Sun* feeding off the opportunity created by Mr Cameron at Prime Minister's Question Time to promote its coverage and story line. On the same day as Mr Cameron raised the death of 'Baby P', *The Sun* prepared an editorial based on Mr Cameron's comments:

> SHAMEFUL, disgusting, cowardly and disgraceful. There are no words strong enough to express *Sun* readers' anger at the buck-passing and blame-dodging over the horrific death of Baby P. The scandal is down to Haringey council. The same one that let little Victoria Climbié be tortured to death eight years ago.

It then referred directly to the clash Mr Cameron had generated with Mr Brown:

> Time and again in the House of Commons the Prime Minister refused to join David Cameron in condemning Haringey's social services. Instead, Mr Brown fell back on jibes about Mr Cameron using the baby's death to score party political points. Mr Brown's instincts failed him. He was badly briefed and looked out of touch with public opinion while Mr Cameron was in tune with it.

The Sun editorial ended with a promise that, however inappropriately, it kept:

> Baby P will **NOT** be forgotten by *The Sun*. **A price must be paid for his little life, and we will not rest until that price has been paid by those responsible.**
> [original emphasis]

A price to be paid by those responsible? No, not Tracey Connelly, Steven Barker and Jason Owen, but:

Heads must roll. Nothing else will do. Sharon Shoesmith, the smug Haringey director of children's services, must be fired. So must Baby P's social workers Maria Ward and Sylvia Henry. And their boss Gillie Christou. Paediatrician Dr Sabah Al-Zayyat, who failed to spot Baby P's broken back, must be struck off. And if the head of Haringey council won't act, the Government must put in a new boss.

There can hardly ever have been such an instance as this when an editorial in a tabloid, or any other paper, demands sackings and specific actions which within weeks were to be implemented exactly as demanded.

The Sun's demand for sackings

In *The Sun* on the same day, which was the day it also first launched its petition campaign that there should be sackings, Mr Cameron had a column that was presumably prepared before or immediately after Prime Minister's Question Time. It was headlined 'Excuses won't do'. He went on to write (or allowed someone else to write in his name):

> Less than ten years after Victoria Climbié's death, another
> child slips though Haringey Council's safety net. We've
> heard countless excuses but no apology. The killers will
> pay the price in prison. The professionals who let Baby P
> down must pay the price with their jobs.[54]

Here was Mr Cameron explicitly entwined within *The Sun*, with its
story line of targeting Haringey Council exclusively and calling for
the dismissal of those involved in protecting children and who had
sought to protect Peter Connelly. There is no concern for proper
process here. No concern that Mr Cameron may not have had the
necessary information and evidence before calling for sackings. And
what was evident when Mr Cameron sought to ask Mr Brown about
the death of 'Baby P' at Prime Minister's Question Time was that
Mr Cameron did not have a grasp of the story that *The Sun* and
Rebekah Brooks were promoting.

What is now known is that Mr Cameron, as well as being a
Cotswold neighbour, was also a close personal friend of Rebekah
Brooks (whose husband was at school at Eton with Mr Cameron and
with Mr Cameron's brother). In 2008 she was the editor of *The Sun*
and was leading the 'Baby P campaign for justice'. The relationship
between Mr Cameron and Mrs Brooks is reflected in the slightly
surreal story of Mr Cameron riding on a police horse loaned to Mr
and Mrs Brooks by the Metropolitan Police.[55] Here was a symbolic
'coming together' through a horse of the Prime Minister, the editor
of *The Sun* and the Metropolitan Police, all of whom were central to
how the 'Baby P story' was shaped, but each of whom were found
to be remarkably close and networked with each other through
the evidence heard at the Leveson Inquiry into the media. It is also
now known through the Leveson Inquiry[56] that Mr Cameron and
Mrs Brooks were in frequent contact and communication, including
meeting with each other socially for 'country suppers', and with
Mr Cameron also texting Mrs Brooks and ending his texts 'LOL'
(which she said he mistakenly thought meant 'lots of love').

Alongside the reporting on 11 November 2008 of the findings
of guilt at the criminal trial, a photograph of Peter's blood-stained
clothing and a body map of his injuries, which had been given to

the media by the Metropolitan Police, were also being shown (see Chapter One). The first picture of Peter himself was published on the internet by *The Sun* on 14 November. It was the now iconic picture of 'Baby P' looking up, with the background of the chequered floor covering. *The Sun* reported that:

> This is Baby P. A gorgeous, blond-haired, blue-eyed tot with a heart-melting smile. *The Sun* is today publishing the first picture ever of the little boy who died in the most tragic circumstances. In the heart-wrenching photo he gazes up at his photographer in search of the love and affection he was so cruelly denied. The photo was taken by a child minder as Baby P happily toddled around her kitchen. But the baby found lying in his cot by police [*it was the ambulance workers who found Peter in his cot and rushed him to hospital*] last August [*not last August but August of the year before*] bore little resemblance to the little boy in this photo ... taken at the home of [the child minder - whose name was given in *The Sun*] who was employed by Haringey Social Services to look after the tot.[57]

The Sun launches its 'Campaign for justice'

The following day, a Saturday, the picture of 'Baby P' was the full front page of *The Sun* with the caption of 'Campaign for justice' and pages 4, 5 and 6 also devoted fully to the story.

The Sun's 'Campaign for justice' was not primarily about the sentencing and punishment of Tracey Connelly, Steven Barker and Jason Owen, the three people found guilty in the criminal court for Peter's death. Nor was it about the failures in the police investigations before Peter died of his abuse. Instead, *The Sun* turned its attention to those working within Haringey Council to protect children:

> At every turn this heart-rending story reveals the arrogance of people who think they are a law unto themselves. Gordon Brown vows he will do everything in his power to stop another tragedy. *That must mean the sacking of Sharon Shoesmith and every social worker and official involved.* **Look at that face on Page One today, and then – if you haven't already – please fill in our petition on this page or online at thesun.co.uk/news.** [original emphasis][58]

The Sun also made the story explicitly political:

> The Haringey scandal gets worse. We now learn that **FOUR** Labour ministers were sent letters by a whistleblower warning them the council's children's service was a shambolic failure. The warning came from courageous Haringey social worker Nevres Kemal. She had **ALREADY** confronted Haringey children's services director Sharon Shoesmith with her fears – and was ignored. Her warning letter to the government could not have been clearer. 'Child abusers are not being tackled', she told the-then health secretary Patricia Hewitt, health ministers Rosie Winterton and Ivan Lewis, and local MP David Lammy, then a culture minister ... but in typical Whitehall fashion the letters were shuffled between officials and sank without trace.[59]

In one editorial *The Sun* had turned the horrific death of Peter Connelly into an attack on the Labour government, on the civil service and on social workers. The petition it launched demanded the dismissal of Sharon Shoesmith, Director of Haringey's Children's Services, Gillie Christou, described by *The Sun* as 'head of the child protection register', Maria Ward, Peter's social worker, Sylvia Henry, the social worker for Peter in December 2006 when he was first admitted to hospital because of his injuries, and the paediatrician who had seen Peter two days before he died. Their pictures were also shown under the heading of '5 WHO HAVE NO SHAME'.

The Sun had no picture of Sylvia Henry, who was captioned as 'SOCIAL worker SYLVIA HENRY took part in the decision to send Baby P back to his mother'. She was also accused of 'lying after the shocking murder of Victoria Climbié eight years ago'. Rather belatedly, on 10 June 2011, two-and-a-half years later, *The Sun* published an apology to Sylvia Henry, and also paid her damages. The apology compared to the five pages on the 'Baby P story' targeting Haringey social workers in November 2008 is rather short, so here it is in full:

> In our campaign to highlight the failings of authorities to protect Baby P from his killers, we identified staff at Haringey Social Services including one of the social workers Sylvia Henry. It is now clear that Ms Henry was not at fault or to blame in any way for decisions contributing to Baby P's tragic death and should not have been a target of our campaign. She did her best for Baby P. It was also untrue to suggest that she was lazy and uncaring in her work and deserved to be sacked.
>
> Our articles referred to Ms Henry's involvement in the tragic case of Victoria Climbié, a young girl who had been abused and killed by her carers in Haringey some 8 years previously. We accept that Ms Henry's evidence to the Laming Inquiry was truthful, and withdraw any suggestion that she lied to avoid criticism. We sincerely apologise to Ms Henry for these allegations and we have agreed to pay her compensation.[60]

Accused of being partly to blame for Peter Connelly's death. Described as lazy and uncaring. Accused of lying to protect herself at the Laming Inquiry. All very serious. All attacking the professional identity of a social worker by claiming she contributed to a child's death, was not caring and lacked integrity. All wrong. All made up by *The Sun*. And it took 31 months and legal action to extract an apology. The erroneous description of the social worker – lacking integrity, lazy, lying – might be applied to the journalists who conjured up this portrait of a social worker who had worked for many years to protect children, a task which, for all social workers, was to be made harder by *The Sun*'s campaign vilifying social workers, as will be shown later. However, it was reported in 2012 that 'Henry was £300,000 out of pocket despite winning her libel action'.[61]

In November 2008 *The Sun*'s petition that it asked its readers to sign, demanding the sacking of Sylvia Henry and others, read:

> The fact that Baby P died despite 60 visits from Haringey social services is a national disgrace.
>
> I believe that ALL the social workers involved in the case of Baby P, including Sharon Shoesmith, Maria Ward, Sylvia Henry and Gillie Christou should be sacked and never allowed to work with vulnerable children again.
>
> I call on the chief executive of Haringey Council, Ita O'Donovan, to ensure this.
>
> And I further demand that Beverley Hughes, the Children's Minister, and Ed Balls, the Education Secretary, should apply immediate and sustained pressure to ensure this happens.
>
> I also demand that the doctor involved with Baby P, Sabah Al-Zayyat, should also lose her job and not be allowed to treat the public again. And I ask the General Medical Council to ensure that this happens.[62]

The Sun's chosen targeting of Sharon Shoesmith, social workers and the paediatrician generated considerable public anger and hostility directed at them personally. Indeed, *The Sun* reported with no comments of caution or condemnation that 'some MY Sun [a *Sun* website] readers want to take the law into their own hands and Hendoo07 from London has a plan in store: "We pay these people to protect the vulnerable not protect the criminal. I just wish I could have ten minutes face to face with the lot of them."[63]

As with Rebekah Brooks' *News of the World*'s naming and shaming and publishing pictures of convicted paedophiles in 2000, her naming and shaming and publishing the pictures to identify Sharon Shoesmith, the social workers and the paediatrician meant that they were now in significant danger as a consequence of the anger generated by *The Sun* and from being so readily identified by the newspaper. But these were not abusers of children. They each, in different ways, had given their professional lives to the protection and care of children. This was to be ended by *The Sun*'s campaign. Indeed it was especially personalised and vindictive, with *The Sun* asking that its readers provide the newspaper with information and stories about those it was now targeting.

The consequence for those named in *The Sun* and their families was immediate:

> The first time Sharon Shoesmith realised the size and nature of what was being unleashed against her was a call from her 89-year-old mother in Belfast, who had been told by a reporter that Shoesmith was involved in the death of a child, and was immensely distressed. In order to avoid photographers outside her flat she had to leave for work at 6.30am and wait, at night, until neighbours told her the coast was clear. Both she and her youngest daughter received death threats, and her daughter had to be moved out of London. Her email inbox and voice messages filled with support but also with people calling her a child killer. She began to suffer periods of uncontrollable shaking. One man called her at 5am every morning with a different suggestion of how to kill herself. Police advised her to stay away from tube platforms, because it would be easy to push her off....
>
> Maria Ward, the social worker, [was] subject to a similar campaign ... she was eventually moved away for her

own safety. Even uninvolved Haringey social workers were reporting that they were finding it suddenly more difficult and frightening to do their jobs, because clients were refusing to co-operate, or being abusive. On 18 November *The Sun* quoted an anonymous Shoesmith family member saying they wanted her to go; she says this was completely untrue.[64]

The Sun had whipped up and unleashed harassment and hatred, creating a very real and serious threat and danger for those being targeted and for their families. As Rupert Murdoch's biographer wrote, 'soul-searching wasn't, to say the least, a part of NewsCorp. Culture',[65] and there seemed to be little soul-searching at this time at *The Sun*. Indeed, *The Sun*'s history of seeking sales trumping soul-searching is told over and over again in a book about the paper in the 1980s and 1990s.[66]

It was not only *The Sun* that covered the 'Baby P story'. Coverage in other newspapers was similar, supporting the statement that 'there ought to be a collective noun for a group of journalists gathered together, for they so often hunt in packs'.[67] Other headlines included:

TORTURED BABY P: SACK THE LOT OF THEM [*Daily Star*][68]

Boy left to die just like Victoria Climbié [*London Evening Standard*][69]

David Cameron says Baby P workers must be sacked, not suspended [*The Daily Telegraph*][70]

50 injuries, 60 visits – failures that led to the death of Baby P. [*The Guardian*][71]

Investigation into brutal death of Baby P increases the pressure on council chiefs. [*The Times*][72]

> Politicians call for action over Baby P case: Balls orders review of case as Cameron condemns "excuses but no apology". [*The Independent*][73]

However, the significance of *The Sun* in shaping the story was greater than others. The vitriol and vengefulness of *The Sun* targeted on Haringey's social workers, and increasingly specifically on Sharon Shoesmith, was exceptional, creating the fear of vigilante action.

Mr Cameron was not the only, although he was the most senior, politician to call for sackings of managers and social workers in Haringey Council. Haringey had two MPs. One, Lynne Featherstone, is a Liberal Democrat. The other, David Lammy, is a Labour member. The 'Baby P story' was a story on their political patch. How did they respond?

Lynne Featherstone is MP for Hornsey and Wood Green, a more affluent area of Haringey. Born and brought up in north London and now living in Highgate, she was elected as a councillor for Haringey Council in 1998, and until 2002 was the leader of the small Liberal Democrat group of four councillors. She stood down from the council in 2006 at a time when Labour's majority was cut from 25 to 3, and when there were 30 Labour councillors, 27 Liberal Democrats and no Conservative or other councillors. Haringey Council, therefore, was a closely fought political territory between Labour and the Liberal Democrats. From 2000 to 2005 she was also a member of the London Assembly. She became an MP in 2005 and in 2012 a member of Mr Cameron's Coalition government as a Junior Minister for Equalities in the Home Office.

Lynne Featherstone was, therefore, a councillor within Haringey when Victoria Climbié died and at the time of the Laming Inquiry and publication of its report. She referred back to the Laming Inquiry in her political blog about 'Baby P' on 21 November 2008, and demanded, as she had done in Parliament itself, that:

> Firstly those accountable must go – and the Children's Act 2004 names those key accountable posts. It came into being because of Victoria Climbié's death and Lord

Laming's subsequent report – so we should make sure the lesson learnt then is followed now.

Secondly – that Haringey be put under special measures so that we can be held safe whilst things are being resolved.

And thirdly that there would still be a need for a public inquiry.[74]

But Ms Featherstone also opened up two issues that will later be seen as of particular relevance in understanding the context in which child protection was being undertaken in Haringey:

Firstly, budgetary pressures. It became clear from the figures about how many children were taken into care in Haringey before and after Baby P's death that Haringey was reducing the numbers of children being taken into care whilst Baby P was being visited all those times. Directly after (and part of which could be a natural reaction) the figures shot up. Also John Hemming,* a Lib Dem MP colleague who specialises in this area, had also found figures on reductions because of budgetary pressures. So Haringey's decisions around budgets needs scrutiny for starters.

A second example of an area needing wider scrutiny – what part did the fragile state of the health team charged with looking after health needs of children at risk in Haringey play? After all, the paediatrician who failed to diagnose Baby P's broken back was a locum in that very department. A post deleted, the key post

---

* But Mr Hemming has argued that the threshold for taking children into care was too low, and the BBC reported that he claimed 1,000 children were 'wrongly' adopted each year (www.bbc.co.uk/news/uk-political-161571240). There was a lively debate, which took place in the same month Peter Connelly died, following the suggestion that social workers take children from families to bolster adoption statistics (Taylor, A. [2007] 'Adoption targets row: The sector responds', www.communitycare.co.uk/2007/08/01/adoption-targets-row-sector-responds).

of 'named doctor' who has particular responsibility in Child Protection cases. £400,000 of cuts required by the PCT [primary care trust]. Doctors leaving because of unhappiness with management. An unbelievably high level of sickness. A high level of bullying found by the Health Commission inspection. All in all – a service that needs looking at. Hopefully some of this will be pursued anyway by the urgent investigation team – but there are wider issues to go into.

I did go personally to see the Chair of Haringey PCT with all these concerns. I was told – this is no longer the concern or business of the PCT. They had 'outsourced' their health team to Great Ormond Street Hospital. So – in my limited research as to why such an important local service would be outsourced – this is what I have been told thus far. Great Ormond Street wanted to become a Foundation Hospital Trust. In order to do so it had to demonstrate 'community outreach'. Great Ormond Street had none and no experience in that area. Hence it negotiated with Haringey to take on that department. Well – if that's all the case, is that what should have happened?

As I said to Ed Balls – there is a wealth of information that people are contacting me about that needs to come to the inspection and that's why we need a public inquiry. And we need a new start with new faces at the top – so that everyone involved in child protection in Haringey is included with the necessary zeal and support to make that fresh start and to make our vulnerable children as safe as they can be.[75]

Lynne Featherstone was, therefore, also demanding that Sharon Shoesmith resign or be removed from her post of Director of Children's Services and for the resignation or removal of the lead councillor for children's services, both roles which, in the 2004 Children Act, are given explicit leadership and accountability responsibilities for children's services. But she was also raising issues about the context in which workers were seeking to protect children in Haringey, and especially about the context of the child protection services provided by Great Ormond Street Hospital NHS Trust. This fuse being lit in November 2008 about concerns related to the community paediatric service and its management in Haringey provided by Great Ormond Street Hospital was still burning, as will be seen in Chapter Five, in 2012. It was not leading to much attention, however, in 2008, where the focus remained almost exclusively on Haringey Council's children's services. The NHS was a marginal and off-stage issue at this time as far as the media were concerned. And the police had now become largely absent from the story altogether.

Liberal Democrat interest and comment on the 'Baby P story' went beyond Lynne Featherstone's blog, and made it an explicit political issue. For example, there is extensive coverage on the Twickenham and Richmond Liberal Democrats website of a parliamentary debate about 'Baby P' on 22 November under the heading of 'Laws, Featherstone, Harris and Hemming [all Liberal Democrat MPs] quiz Balls re "Baby P"',[76] and a blog by Iain Dale (a publisher, broadcaster and a Conservative political blogger) on 2 December 2008 draws a direct comparison between Liberal Democrat Lynne Featherstone and Labour's David Lammy:

> In a crisis some people come into their own. They ask the right questions, find the right words, keep calm, and lead from the front. Others keep their counsel for worry of getting things wrong. They appear like a rabbit caught in the headlights and wait for others to lead while they play catch up. In the Baby P case, Lib Dem MP Lynne Featherstone falls into the first category whole [sic] local Labour MP David Lammy belongs in the latter.[77]

The terrible death of 'Baby P' had, therefore, in November and December 2008 become a political, indeed party political, issue as well as, and maybe as a result of being, a media issue. *The Sun* in particular made it a party political issue. Its political editor, Trevor Kavanagh, who in 2012 described the Leveson Inquiry as a 'witch-hunt',[78] wrote a piece in November 2008 headed 'Leftie Mafia close ranks over Baby P' and with a photo of Gordon Brown captioned 'guilty conscience'. Mr Brown was described as 'a tribal chief' furious about an attack on 'The Family' of Haringey Council, which was said to be the 'last bastion of the loony Left'.[79]

The death of Peter Connelly had, therefore, become for the Conservative and Liberal Democrat parties in opposition an opportunity to seek to embarrass and criticise the Labour government and David Lammy, the local Tottenham Labour MP. David Lammy continued to be the target of Liberal Democrat bloggers, with the 'Liberal Democrat Voice'[80] accusing him in May 2009 of having initially defended Sharon Shoesmith when *The Sun*, others within the media and Lynne Featherstone had been demanding her dismissal. But the Labour government and politicians were not strong and steadfast in standing up to the media storm.

David Lammy was born in Tottenham. In 2000 he was elected to the London Assembly and also as the MP for Tottenham. He has held a number of ministerial posts, and in 2008 was a minister in the Department for Innovation, Universities and Skills. He has never been a councillor within Haringey Council.

David Lammy posted a message on his website on 14 November 2008 about 'Baby P':

> this poor child, and I am committed to ensuring that the matter is fully investigated. I have had a number of conversations with Ed Balls and Beverley Hughes [Secretary of State, and Minister of State, for Children] over the past couple of days. I have also written to both of them asking for urgent meetings as soon as the inquiry is concluded to work out the way forward for Haringey.... I await the outcomes of these reviews, but I firmly believe that if any systemic or individual deficiencies are uncovered, then questions should be raised of those in charge and they will have to be held to account.[81]

Six months later Mr Lammy* was again referring to 'Baby P' on his website:

> It is right that Haringey Council has taken responsibility, held staff accountable and is putting in place comprehensive measures to address shortcomings in child protection services.[82]

The inquiry and reviews to which Mr Lammy refers are described in the following chapters and became a focus of media and political attention, but what is now confirmed is the almost exclusive focus on Haringey Council and its children's services, and the call for workers to be held accountable and dismissed. Lynne Featherstone had put down a marker about the NHS, but any concerns about the police were now largely without comment.

The Sun continued to lead on the 'Baby P story', promoting its petition that Sharon Shoesmith, the social workers and the paediatrician should all be dismissed from their posts. In the period between the conclusion and coverage of the criminal trial and the media conference on 1 December 2008, at which Mr Balls announced the dismissal of Sharon Shoesmith from her role as Haringey's Director of Children's Services, it is known from Rebekah Brooks' evidence

---

*   But there is a somewhat strange follow-on to Mr Lammy's concerns about child protection, when he partly blamed the riots in Tottenham in summer 2011, which spread to other areas of London and nationally, on parents' inability to smack their children (Topping, A. [2012] 'Labour MP backs smacking of children', *The Guardian*, 29 January, www.guardian.co.uk/society/2012/jan/29/labour-mp-backs-smacking-children). First, in the UK, unlike some other countries, parents are allowed to hit their children. Second, it is an unclear line between physical punishment and physical abuse. Third, many who have confronted child abuse, such as the NSPCC, do not think it appropriate that physical assaults on children should be allowed or encouraged, even if the hitting of children is as a form of discipline and punishment.

at the Leveson Inquiry[83] that as editor of *The Sun* she had had conversations with Mr Balls about 'Baby P' and *The Sun*'s campaign.*

Mrs Brooks denied that she had explicitly spoken to Mr Balls about sacking Sharon Shoesmith, but said she had discussed her with Mr Balls. She was not clear what she discussed about Sharon Shoesmith with Mr Balls, but went on to say:

> I didn't tell Ed Balls to fire Sharon Shoesmith. It was very obvious from the coverage in our paper that we had launched a petition because the government were refusing to do anything about the situation. So yes, I had conversations with Ed Balls. I think I also spoke to the shadow minister, who I think at the time was Michael Gove, but I can't quite remember that. We were—I would have spoken to anybody, basically, to try to get some justice for Baby P, which was the point of the campaign.[84]

So, according to Rebekah Brooks, she had spoken more than once with Mr Balls at this time, that the intention of her contacts was to get 'justice for Baby P', and that no one could have had any misunderstandings that justice meant sacking Sharon Shoesmith and others named in *The Sun* ... 'I think he [Mr Balls] was aware we called for [Sharon Shoesmith's] resignation. It was all over the paper.'

At the Leveson Inquiry Rebekah Brooks also stated that in her contacts with Mr Balls she was asking Mr Balls for 'much more subtle information, like the contents of the review we were not allowed to see and the whitewash that Haringey had done on their own review'. So, Mrs Brooks was seeking from Mr Balls information that was confidential and not in the public arena. She had also already

---

*   Mrs Brooks' attendance at the Leveson Inquiry gave another example of coincidence and contacts (*Evening Standard*, 22 May 2012, p 16). At the Leveson Inquiry Mrs Brooks was represented by her barrister, Hugo Keith QC. Mr Keith was from the Three Raymonds Buildings Chambers, headed by Alexander Cameron, elder brother of Prime Minister David Cameron. Mrs Brooks' husband, Charlie Brooks, was at Eton College at exactly the same time as Alexander Cameron, and David Cameron was also was at Eton at the same time, albeit three years below.

The Sun's pages on its petition

drawn a conclusion, presumably communicated by her to Mr Balls, or at least he should have been aware of it from *The Sun*, that the first Haringey serious case review, although independently authored, was a whitewash, a view also taken by *The Sun* about Ofsted's independent assessment in October 2007, two months after Peter Connelly had died, and which described Haringey Council as providing 'a good service for children':

> WHITEWASH. Social Services bunglers who let tortured Baby P die were PRAISED by government inspectors weeks after his death ... even under-fire Sharon Shoesmith had a glowing assessment.[85]

However, at the Leveson Inquiry Mrs Brooks was wrong about what was known prior to Peter Connelly's death:

> I think that in the eight months that Baby P was under Haringey Social Services – Baby Peter, sorry – he was seen by Social Services and NHS officials in that time when he sustained the 50 or so injuries that he died of in the end, but also more importantly – and I am not sure the public were allowed to know this at that time,

but in the review it was revealed that Social Services had allowed the boyfriend, if you like, to live with Baby Peter, even though he was on a charge of raping a two-year-old. So there were serious failings, but it wasn't just Sharon Shoesmith.[86]

So Rebekah Brooks, four years after *The Sun* led on the 'Baby P story', was getting it wrong. As noted in Chapter One, Peter Connelly's social worker and health workers had not known that Steven Barker, 'the boyfriend', had moved into the Connelly home. Therefore they could not have 'allowed him to live with Baby P'. Nor did they know that he would later be charged with raping a child. Not only was all this not known to the social worker and health workers, it was not known to the police, albeit not mentioned by Mrs Brooks, who had conducted two criminal investigations into Peter's injuries.

But there was further information from Mrs Brooks' oral evidence to the Leveson Inquiry in 2012. First, as noted above, she had been in frequent and regular contact with Mr Cameron. Second, when *The Sun* was seeking 'justice for Baby P' and the sackings in Haringey Council and of the paediatrician, Rebekah Brooks was not only speaking about 'Baby P' with Mr Balls, Secretary of State for Children, but also to the Conservative Shadow Secretary of State, Mr Gove. This information from Mrs Brooks was not explored further at the Leveson Inquiry, but why was Rebekah Brooks also in contact with Mr Gove at that time about 'Baby P'? As noted above, the 'Baby P story' was made a political issue by *The Sun* and with Mr Cameron as leader of the Conservative opposition contributing in *The Sun* to its campaign demanding sackings.

It is now known that not only was Mr Cameron a personal friend of Mrs Brooks, but that Mr Gove was also within her social circle, and when he gave evidence to the Leveson Inquiry in May 2012,[87] he described Rupert Murdoch as 'one of the most impressive and significant figures in the last 50 years ... a force of nature, a phenomena, a great man'. Following the Conservative-led coalition coming into government, and Mr Gove being appointed as Secretary of State for what had been named the Department for Children, Schools and Families (DCSF), Mr Gove had 11 social and business meetings with

Mr Murdoch and other senior News Corporation figures, including Mrs Brooks, within the first 14 months in his new role. Mr Gove had himself been a journalist and senior executive with Mr Murdoch's *The Times*, and his wife, Sarah Vine, was also a journalist with *The Times*.

Mr Gove was an active participant in Parliament on the day when Mr Cameron clashed with Mr Brown about Peter Connelly at Prime Minister's Question Time. Later in the day, after the row at Prime Minister's Question Time, Mr Balls announced, as Mr Cameron and Ms Featherstone had in part been seeking, that there would now be an independent urgent review undertaken jointly by Ofsted, the Healthcare Commission and the Her Majesty's Inspectorate of Constabulary. This was not the 'independent public inquiry' that had been demanded, but it was welcomed by Mr Gove, the then Conservative opposition Shadow Secretary of State for Children, Schools and Families.[88]

Mr Gove also called for the full publication of the first serious case review report, and stated that 'the public are, rightly, insistent that we act swiftly and comprehensively to hold those responsible in this affair to account' and that 'the public are tired of hearing that the correct procedures have been followed when a child died in agony.... The public are astonished that a director of children's services can say, after the death of a child, that "in the light of good performance, a full scrutiny review would not be beneficial or add value to the service".'[89]

It was at this time, on 20 November 2008, that Mr Balls, in advance of the completion of the urgent review with its report to be delivered to Mr Balls on 1 December, only 18 days after he had commissioned it, had already concluded and stated in the House of Commons that, based on the first serious case review, 'there was clear evidence that agencies had failed – singly and collectively – to adhere to the statutory procedures for the proper management of child protection cases. This raised serious concerns about the wider systems and management of services safeguarding children in the borough.'[90]

However, even now, in 2013, it is not clear what this evidence was or is of failing to adhere to statutory procedures. What procedures were not followed which were seen to have contributed with any significance to the cruelty experienced by Peter Connelly? Referrals were made across agencies; information was shared; child protection case conferences, core group meetings and review conferences were held. As Mr Gove himself said four years later, when expressing concern about the Leveson Inquiry and 'the chilling atmosphere which threatens free speech' and the freedom of the press,'there was a natural temptation for politicians to "succumb" to demands for an inquiry by "establishment" figures in the wake of a major scandal'.[91] He went on in 2012 to refer to Victoria Climbié and 'Baby P':

> Mr Gove said previous inquiries into national scandals had produced reports that "give birth to quangos, commissions, and law-making creatures that actually generate over-regulation, over-prescription, and sometimes a cure that is worse than the original disease" ... he said 800 pages of guidance produced in the wake of the deaths of Victoria Climbié and Baby P was "impenetrable and has still not ensured that our children are safer today than they were two, three or five years ago".[92]

The Leveson Inquiry into the press in 2012 had clearly led to a change of mind for Mr Gove. Having been a former *Times* journalist he was now the government's Secretary of State for Education. In 2008 he was calling for the publication of the reviews and inquiries following the death of Peter Connelly. In 2012, at the time of the Leveson Inquiry, he did not think inquiries were such a good idea.

In November 2008 Mr Balls made comments supportive of professionals working with children, but with a sting in the tale and an advance warning of what was to come for those in Haringey:

> Professionals working with children in this country do a tough job, often in very difficult circumstances. They have great responsibility and they make difficult judgements every day. But where serious mistakes are made there must be accountability.[93]

It may be helpful at this point to give a summary time line of key events in November 2008, which also notes the significant actions of *The Sun* as the newspaper that especially promoted the 'Baby P story':

- 11 November: Steven Barker, Jason Owen and Tracey Connelly found guilty at the criminal trial of allowing or causing the death of Peter Connelly. Media briefing by the Metropolitan Police. Media conference with publication of first serious case review executive summary. Media coverage of criminal trial findings on 24-hours news channels. Beverley Hughes, Minister of State for Children, announced there would be a progress review by Lord Laming of child protection across England.
- 12 November: extensive media coverage with newspapers publishing photographs of Peter Connelly's blood-stained clothing and body maps of his injuries.
- 12 November: *The Sun* publishes a 'Who's who in the case that has shocked Britain'. It included 'the lodger' (with an artist impression), 'the mother', 'the boyfriend', 'the father', 'the social worker' (with a photograph of Maria Ward), 'the team leader' (with a photograph of Gillie Christou) and 'the council chief' (with a photograph of Sharon Shoesmith).
- 12 November: Mr Cameron gets into confrontation about 'Baby P' with Mr Brown at Prime Minister's Question Time.
- 12 November: later Mr Balls announces an urgent and very quick review by Ofsted, the Healthcare Commission and Her Majesty's Inspectorate of Constabulary of child protection services in Haringey.
- 13 November: Mr Cameron's column appears in *The Sun* demanding sackings.
- 14 November: *The Sun* reports that its readers are holding a 'MY Sun' inquiry into the death of 'Baby P'.
- 15 November: *The Sun* publishes in print the first picture of Peter Connelly, which had been taken by his childminder, and demands sackings of 'six key people involved in social services who failed Baby P'.[94]
- 16 November: a column in *The Sun* by Kelvin Mackenzie, a former editor of the newspaper, headlined 'Idiots who betrayed Baby P

must go now', with a photograph of Sharon Shoesmith captioned 'must go', and a text of 'once again it's down to the social workers whose job it was to detect and protect. Why didn't they learn from the Climbié case?'.[95]

- 18 November: *The Sun* reveals Peter Connelly's 'final resting place' and lays a plaque reading 'Safe at last'.

- 26 November: *The Sun* delivers a petition to the Prime Minister's residence at 10 Downing Street. The petition attracted 1.4 million signatures.

- 1 December: Mr Balls receives the report of the urgent review he had commissioned only 18 days before, and holds a media conference at which he orders that Sharon Shoesmith be removed from her post as Haringey's Director of Children's Services.

At the media conference on Monday, 1 December, Mr Balls noted that he had received the report he had commissioned on 12 November from Ofsted, the Healthcare Commission and Her Majesty's Inspectorate of Constabulary. This report was the subject of several discussions between Mr Balls' senior civil servants in the DCSF and senior managers in Ofsted.[96] It has been stated that the report initially prepared by the inspectors who had actually undertaken the quick inspection of child protection services in Haringey had been altered and amended within Ofsted 17 times before being finalised for Mr Balls.[97, 98] Many of those amendments were alleged to be the consequence of interventions by senior staff in Ofsted who had no or little experience in social work or child protection services and who, like Ofsted's chief inspector, had a background in teaching and management.

Mr Balls' statement at the media conference on Monday, 1 December 2008[99] fed off this rapid, rushed and revised re-review led by Ofsted, and although it was a review that also involved the national inspectorates for health services and the police, it was targeted very heavily at Haringey Council, on its children's services and on its children's services director.

At the media conference Mr Balls stated that:

The whole nation has been shocked and moved by the tragic and horrific death of Baby P. All of us find it impossible to comprehend how adults could commit such terrible acts of evil against this little boy. And the public is angry that nobody stepped in to prevent this tragedy from happening.

I want to say very clearly at the outset: social workers, police officers, GPs, health professionals, all the people who work to keep children safe, do a very difficult job, often in really challenging circumstances – all around the country and in particular in Haringey. They make difficult judgements every day that help to keep children safe – and many of them are unsung heroes. But they must be accountable for their decisions.

And where things go badly wrong, people are right to want to know why and what will be done about it. In the case of Baby P, things did go tragically wrong.

Mr Balls went on to note that after receiving the first serious case review report on the morning of 12 November, he 'immediately arranged for the secondment to Haringey of John Coughlan, the Director of Children's Services in Hampshire, to oversee that proper procedures for safeguarding children are in place and being followed [in Haringey]'. However, as the first serious case review had been completed some time before, and would already have been available to Ofsted and the DCSF, why did Mr Balls wait until 12 November 2008 before taking any action, albeit there was now the increasing media clamour led by *The Sun* that action be taken and workers and managers sacked?

Mr Balls also noted at his media conference on 1 December that he had 'immediately decided that Ofsted, the Healthcare Commission, and the Chief Inspector of Constabulary should carry out an urgent inspection of safeguarding in Haringey. At 6 o'clock yesterday evening, I received the final draft [*why still a draft ... albeit one of an extensive number of drafts?*] of the inspector's report. The Children's Minister [Beverley Hughes] and I studied it overnight with our experts. Her Majesty's Chief Inspector presented the final report to us at 9 o'clock this morning and to Haringey Council shortly thereafter.'

This seems a significant train of actions and events, and not at all usual practice. The national inspectorate shared a draft of an independent report with politicians and civil servants, who then poured over it on a Sunday night, and then first thing the following morning a final report was submitted to the same politicians and civil servants. It illustrates the high profile it was now being given politically, and the close engagement at this time between civil servants and the independent national inspectorate.

In his Monday afternoon media conference statement Mr Balls went on to announce that he had that morning met the Leader, Deputy Leader, Lead Member for children's services and the Chief Executive of Haringey Council to discuss the report and its findings. Following the meeting and before Mr Balls' media conference, the Council Leader and the Council's Lead Member for children's services had resigned. But what is significant here is that Mr Balls' meeting did not include Haringey's Director of Children's Services. It is also significant that she had not seen or been given an opportunity to comment on the accuracy or otherwise of the report from the national inspectorates. This is very unusual, maybe even unique. The Director of Children's Services had already, therefore, been isolated and marginalised by Ofsted, by the government and by the council.

But what is also significant is that Mr Balls only met with leading councillors and the Chief Executive in Haringey Council. He did not seek to meet with the chairs and chief executives of the local NHS organisations. He did not seek to meet with the chair of the police authority, nor the commissioner of the Metropolitan Police. Much of the media, and especially *The Sun*, had set their sights on Sharon Shoesmith, and on Haringey Council and its social workers. This was also now Mr Balls' focus.

At his media conference Mr Balls then drew on the extensive criticisms in the quick two-week review by the national inspectorates of leadership, management and practice in Haringey Council's children's services. There was now little that was good to be found or described about children's services in Haringey. This was all quite different from what the national inspectorates had found and reported before, through their previous reviews and inspections of children's services in Haringey.

In 2006 a major joint area review of Haringey's children's services had stated that 'outcomes [for children] have improved measurably in the past five years, in most cases in line with national trends, and in many cases at a faster rate than nationally and in similar authorities'.[100] Ofsted rated Haringey's children's services as 'good', with a specific comment that 'the director of children's services provides strong and dynamic leadership and is supported by many examples of good leadership and management at all levels'.[101] In 2007[102] and again in 2008,[103] Haringey's fostering services were inspected by Ofsted and also rated as 'good', and Ofsted's overall judgement of Haringey Council's children's services in 2007 was that they were 'good' and that the 'management of these services is good'.[104] It was, therefore, a dramatic, strange and unsettling reversal and inconsistency of judgement by the inspectorates in November 2008.

So what did Mr Balls now note the inspectors had found in Haringey?

> The catalogue of failures reported to me – many of which are clearly apparent in the case of Baby P – include:
>
> - a failure to identify those children and young people at immediate risk of harm and to act on evidence.
> - agencies generally working in isolation from one another and without effective co-ordination.
> - poor gathering, recording and sharing of information.
> - inconsistent quality of front-line practice and insufficient evidence of supervision by senior management.
> - insufficient management oversight of the Assistant Director by the Director of Children's Services and Chief Executive.
> - incomplete reporting of the management audit report by senior officials to elected members.

- insufficient challenge by the Local Safeguarding Children Board to its members and also to front-line staff.
- an overdependence on performance data, which was not always accurate
- and poor child protection plans.

What is noticeable in this listing is that the inspectors apparently found nothing good or even adequate in Haringey, but also that apparently, despite the involvement of the Healthcare Commission and of Her Majesty's Inspectorate of Constabulary in the fast re-review of child protection services in Haringey, the NHS and the police were of no immediate or urgent concern to the government. Two police criminal investigations into injuries to Peter Connelly that did not determine who was living in Peter's home? An NHS child development and paediatric assessment service that, along with a GP, had seen Peter only days before he died but initiated no actions in relation to the concerns about his health and well-being?

What Mr Balls did determine was urgently required was that Sharon Shoesmith be removed from her post as Haringey Council's Director of Children's Services:

> My first priority is to put in place a new leadership and management team in Haringey children's services to ensure that vulnerable children in the borough are properly protected. I have directed Haringey Council to appoint John Coughlan as Director of Children's Services. Haringey Council will now remove the current Director of Children's Services from her post with immediate effect…. My direction takes place under section 497A(4B) of the Education Act 1996. It takes immediate effect and will last until 31 December 2008. I will identify a new Director of Children's Services to take up post from 1 January 2009 – and it is my intention to direct this appointment too.

It was an exceptional action to use this clause in the amended Education Act 1996 to dismiss a director of children's services. It became the vehicle for Sharon Shoesmith to be dismissed from her post with no proper employment process to judge her competence or conduct. It followed no form of natural justice where there would be an opportunity to know in advance, and to be able to answer, any allegations. What it did enable was for Mr Balls to summarily remove, and not even only to suspend in advance of a fuller process to follow, someone from their post. It also delivered on a plate the most senior of all the heads *The Sun* had been seeking.

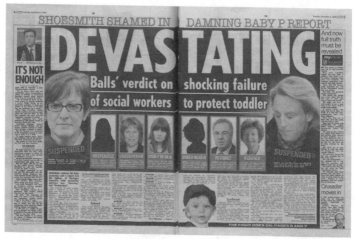

The Sun's coverage on 2 December 2008 of Mr Balls' media conference

It was a *Sun* reporter at the media conference who then got to ask the first question of Mr Balls, asking him to comment on *The Sun*'s petition demanding the sacking of Sharon Shoesmith and that she receive no compensation. Mr Balls noted the impact of the petition:

> I undoubtedly recognise the force of the petition from your newspaper, and right across the country many, many people, millions of people have been affected ... the result of my direction today to Haringey is that the [Director of Children's Services] will be removed immediately from

her post. Her employment is with Haringey and so the normal employment and legal procedures will take place; but I have to say, I think most people will look at this report, look at the clear evidence of management failures and say that this kind of failure should not be rewarded with compensation nor pay-offs.... That's a matter for Haringey. I have to say I would be astonished if elected members in Haringey chose to do that, but it's a matter for them, of course.[105]

Mr Balls had, in fact, met with Haringey's Leader and Chief Executive that morning, and it would be surprising if they had not spoken about what action was now to be taken.

Apart from responding to the force of *The Sun*'s campaigning, it is not clear why Mr Balls 'had to say' what he said, and indeed three years later in the High Court he would be found to have acted inappropriately in making these statements. He also placed Haringey Council in a very difficult position. In response to a question from a *Guardian* journalist at the press conference, Mr Balls noted that '[Sharon Shoesmith's] employment relationship ... is for Haringey, and that's something I know they will [be] considering this afternoon and immediately'.[106] They did indeed act that afternoon and dismissed Sharon Shoesmith without a notice period or compensation, and were later, along with Mr Balls, also found to have acted wrongly.

The public statement at the media conference, which Sharon Shoesmith watched on television, was the first she knew that she was being dismissed from her job as Director of Children's Services. She had not been allowed to see the inspectors' report in draft and to comment on its accuracy or conclusions. This was unusual in itself as standard practice was for reports to be seen in final draft pre-publication by the director and the council so that they could challenge and seek to have any inaccuracies amended. For workers in Haringey Council it was Mr Balls' announcement at his 2pm media conference which was also the first they knew that he had removed Sharon Shoesmith from her role.

Mr Balls' statement at the media conference went further than just targeting Sharon Shoesmith. Not only was she removed from her post, but Mr Balls also directed the council to appoint a new deputy director. As will be noted later, a whole management and practice organisational line of post holders was to be dismissed in Haringey Council, going from the top of the children's department to front-line practitioners. In effect, anyone who was to be seen to have any organisational remit in relation to Peter Connelly was to be found incompetent. It had become so toxic that reputations built on many years of successful and dedicated performance in caring for and protecting children were to be washed away by the continuing media storm. Indeed, Mr Balls was explicit in requiring that John Coughlan, his newly appointed temporary Director of Children's Services in Haringey, 'consider further staffing capability in Haringey's children's services.... I have asked Mr Coughlan and his successor to provide me with monthly reports.'

It would not be a surprise if everyone within the children's services department now felt vulnerable and if the whole service was destabilised. Good child protection services require competence, care and commitment. They also require confidence, continuity and stability. *The Sun*, and indeed Ofsted and Mr Balls, had already determined that there was a lack of competence, care and commitment in Haringey. It was now to create a crisis of confidence in Haringey and beyond, and to undermine continuity and stability.

Mr Gove also joined in the call for Sharon Shoesmith's employment and the social workers' continuing employment to be 'resolved speedily', and it was reported on 2 December that Mr Gove:

> ... [had written] to Haringey council demanding to know how long the suspended employees would remain on full pay. He also asked the local authority to make Ms Shoesmith's contract public so that the taxpayers could see how she was still employed. He wrote: 'Sharon Shoesmith has been judged unfit to continue in her role by an independent inquiry and the Secretary of State. Despite this she still continues to draw a salary in excess of £100,000. Taxpayers will want to know why. What is being done to resolve this situation as speedily as possible?'[107]

There was to be no resolution or moving on. This was a story now being set to run and run. Not only was Mr Coughlan to report to Mr Balls monthly, but Ofsted were required by Mr Balls to provide yet another report by the end of June. There was a threat here from Mr Balls. Following his receipt of the Ofsted report in six months time he would then decide 'whether I should use my statutory powers to require the Council to enter into a contractual arrangement with an external provider for delivery of some or all of its children's services'.

So, monthly reports from Mr Coughlan, the national review of child protection Mr Balls had already recently commissioned from Lord Laming, the requirement that the Healthcare Commission analyse whether health organisations were vigorously applying national child protection standards, and with the NHS Chief Executive to ask all NHS agencies to review their child protection arrangements. The picture here is of a tranche of frantic and frenetic activity, albeit focused heavily on Haringey Council and, to a much lesser extent, the health service.

But what about the police? There were no specific inspections or reviews reportedly required by Mr Balls in relation to the Metropolitan Police – these are only mentioned in Mr Balls' statement with regard to cooperating with one further initiative, with Mr Balls announcing that there was to be a new, second, serious case review into the death of Peter Connelly:

> It is unacceptable that the [first] Serious Case Review into this tragic and terrible death has been found inadequate. So I am today directing Haringey Council, under Section 7A of the Local Authority Social Services Act 1970, to appoint a new and independent chair of its Local Safeguarding Children Board. Mr Graham Badman, who last week retired as Director of Children's Services in Kent, has agreed to take up his post. He will start work this week.
>
> I have asked him immediately to begin a new Serious Case Review into the death of Baby P. He will submit the new Serious Case Review to Ofsted by the end

of February for evaluation. And he will publish the executive summary of the new Serious Case Review – which must be comprehensive and a fair summary of the full Serious Case Review – by the end of March.

This new Serious Case Review will require the commissioning of new management reports from – and the cooperation of – all the agencies involved in child protection in Haringey.

There had already been the rapid and rushed re-review within three weeks by Ofsted and the other national inspectorates of child protection in Haringey, albeit that it became heavily focused on Haringey Council. There was now to be a rapid and rushed second serious case review, with the individual management reports from each agency and then the final report to be undertaken and completed within 12 weeks, which was to include Christmas and the New Year.

This process was to be overseen and delivered by a new chair of Haringey's LSCB. For Mr Balls to be consistent the previous chair had to be replaced. It was Sharon Shoesmith. As just about everywhere else, she had chaired her LSCB as the local Director of Children's Services. The new chair was to be a former headteacher who had recently retired as a Director of Children's Services from elsewhere.

One might think that it was experience, expertise and wisdom built from a career within child protection that was most needed now within Haringey. After all, with Sharon Shoesmith's leadership, Haringey schools were doing well, and she was known to be much respected by headteachers in Haringey. It is always something of a surprise when within areas where there are apparently significant concerns about child protection services new directors of children's services and new chairs of LSCBs are appointed with little or limited experience of sharp end front-line child protection services.

It has been commented[108] that there are different requirements of being a director of education and seeking to influence what happens in schools led by headteachers compared with the direct accountability and leadership required in having the professional responsibility for directly managed child protection social work. It requires different behaviours. Both are about influence and leadership, but the latter is also about necessary line management authority and accountability for front-line practice and the necessity to be able to know about and judge the adequacy of this practice and of its front-line day-to-day management.

In Mr Balls' media statement there was feedback on the view being taken by Lord Laming who only two weeks before had been asked to review child protection across England. The child protection policies and services now in place in Haringey and elsewhere followed the Victoria Climbié Inquiry undertaken by Lord Laming in 2003. Although, as will be explored later, the changes introduced following the Climbié Inquiry may not have been rooted in the Inquiry's findings and recommendations, Lord Laming was in effect being asked to judge and comment on the changes for which he, at least in part, was seen to have had responsibility.

Mr Balls' media statement noted that Lord Laming was already 'struck by the robustness of the foundation on which current children's services are based'. Bearing in mind that these foundations had been introduced only four years before by a Labour government of which Mr Balls had been and was a member, and apparently based on recommendations from Lord Laming, the view now being taken by Lord Laming must have been reassuring for a government considering whether it held any accountability for the difficulties arising within child protection services. Mr Balls also noted that Lord Laming, despite the media and public clamour, did not support the call for a public inquiry into Peter Connelly's death, arguing that this 'would set back the progress that has been made in many places and divert from the actions needed now to keep children safe in Haringey. I [Mr Balls] agree with this judgement.'

But what was it in the Ofsted quick re-review of Haringey undertaken with the Healthcare Commission and Her Majesty's Inspectorate of Constabulary which justified all the additional inspections and reviews now to be commissioned, the resignation of the Council Leader and the Lead Councillor for children's services, the removal of the Director of Children's Services from her post, and the immediate introduction of new senior managers in Haringey Council? How did the Ofsted view, based on only 13 days (13–26 November) of re-reviewing child protection in Haringey, differ from the former views of Ofsted from lengthier and wider-ranging reviews? After all, Christine Gilbert, Ofsted's Chief Executive, had met with Mr Balls on the morning of his press conference, and he stated that she had told him 'that in her judgement the failings in management, oversight and practice identified by the Inspectors' report in Haringey are "exceptional"'.[109] This might be seen as a contentious statement of confidence in her own judgement by Ofsted's chief inspector about the state of child protection in other areas when it was presumably based on the information from the same inspection procedures and processes which she was now determining had been inadequate and not fit-for-purpose when applied in Haringey. Knowing this, it is also surprising that Mr Balls was readily accepting this judgement.

The November 2008 joint area review (JAR) led by Ofsted was crucial in giving the grounds for the actions that were taken by Mr Balls, actions which centred on Haringey Council and on Sharon Shoesmith. It increasingly came to be seen, however, as a contentious review, with considerable concern about how it was undertaken and how it drew its conclusions. More will become known about this later through the evidence submitted as a part of Sharon Shoesmith's judicial review into her dismissal as Haringey's Director of Children's Services.

In essence, the concerns were about:

- how the rapidly prepared review report went through 17 drafts;
- how it was amended and finalised not by the inspectors who had undertaken the review but by Ofsted senior managers, many of whom had little professional experience in children's social care services and little direct knowledge of Haringey's services;
- how through the drafts the report became more and more damning about child protection services in Haringey with positive comments deleted and negative comments added and strengthened, especially about the leadership and management of child protection in Haringey;
- how it came to focus overwhelmingly on Haringey Council's children's services, with concerning comments about health

services, and especially about the police, apparently removed from the earlier drafts and from the report's recommendations.

This will all be given greater attention in Chapter Three, where there is a focus on the judicial review hearings into Sharon Shoesmith's dismissal. Most of it was publicly unknown in November 2008 when Ofsted, the Healthcare Commission and Her Majesty's Inspectorate of Constabulary produced and published their rushed joint area review report. What was known was the concerns that were stated in the report. The report's section on 'Main findings' is presented in full below:

> The main findings of this inspection, described below, point to significant weakness in safeguarding and child protection arrangements in Haringey. They also show that the arrangements for the leadership and management of safeguarding by the local authority and partner agencies in Haringey are inadequate.
>
> • There is insufficient strategic leadership and management oversight of safeguarding of children and young people from Haringey by elected members, senior officers and others within the strategic partnership.
>
> • There is a managerial failure to ensure full compliance with some requirements of the inquiry into the death of Victoria Climbié, such as lack of written feedback to those making referrals to social care services.
>
> • The local safeguarding children board (LSCB) fails to provide sufficient challenge to its member agencies. This is further compounded by the lack of an independent chairperson.
>
> • Social care, health and police authorities do not communicate and collaborate routinely and

consistently to ensure effective assessment, planning and review of cases of vulnerable children and young people.

- Too often assessments of children and young people, in all agencies, fail to identify those who are at immediate risk of harm and to address their needs.

- The quality of front line practice across all agencies is inconsistent and not effectively monitored by line managers.

- Child protection plans are generally poor.

- Arrangements for scrutinising performance across the council and the partnership are insufficiently developed and fail to provide systematic support and appropriate challenge to both managers and practitioners.

- The standard of record keeping on case files across all agencies is inconsistent and often poor.

- There is too much reliance on quantitative data to measure social care, health, and police performance, without sufficiently robust analysis of the underlying quality of service provision and practice.[110]

This could hardly be more critical. All the main findings were of failure, with no good practice noted within them at all. From the top to the bottom, leadership to front-line practice, it is all inadequate, and not only within the council but also within the health and police services. However, the 14 recommendations that then follow are all targeted at Haringey Council. There are no specific recommendations at all for the NHS or the Metropolitan Police. This contrasts with the first draft of the report that was prepared by those who had actually undertaken the inspection in Haringey. Their report had 33 recommendations, made up of 12 about multi-agency working, 11 for health services, 8 for the council's children's social care services, and 3 specifically for the police.

As discussed in Chapter Three, there is quite a different balance in the final report compared to the initial drafts of the report which were prepared by the seven Ofsted, Healthcare Commission and HM Inspectorate of Constabulary inspectors who actually undertook the inspection in Haringey. They noted and recorded more examples of adequate and good practice in the council, they challenged statements made in later drafts prepared by senior Ofsted managers where the inspectors themselves had found no evidence to validate these statements from their fieldwork in Haringey, and they sought to have specific recommendations for the NHS and the Metropolitan Police included in the report but these were removed by the senior Ofsted managers. Why was this?

One reason might be that on 20 November, in the middle of the inspection, Mr Pullen, a senior manager within Ofsted (but like most of the other senior Ofsted managers, with little experience within children's social care services), attended a meeting with Mr Balls' civil servants at the DCSF. It is reported that:

> It was at this meeting that Mr. Pullen was told that the 'Report must be clear in its judgements and attribution of responsibility'. Those were the words Ofsted managers recorded as being said by David Bell, one of the Permanent Secretaries [and Mrs Gilbert's predecessor as chief executive of Ofsted]. The Permanent Secretary also said that he wanted 'definitive evidence on which the minister can act'. It is also at this meeting that it was said by Mr Bell that the Secretary of State [Mr Balls] considered essential that there be comment on the Baby P case because what was desired was 'closure on the public debate'.[111]

The latter aspiration for the report, that it bring 'closure on the public debate', was not fulfilled even if it may have been the wish of Mr Balls. The aspiration, however, that the report 'be clear in its judgements and attribution of responsibility' was more fully met although Ofsted stopped short of calling for the Director of Children's Services to be removed from her post. However, additions within the later drafts of the review report made a specific issue of leadership in Haringey which was not within the inspectors' initial drafting of the report. The comment was added that 'leadership and management of safeguarding arrangements by the local authority and partner agencies in Haringey are inadequate'.[112] It is an interesting style in the report that largely when critical comments are made the local authority is explicitly named, but the NHS and police are subsumed within a less explicit and recognisable group terminology as 'partner agencies'. The concerns now within the report were apparently enough to determine that Mr Balls would remove Sharon Shoesmith from her post.

Two final comments at this stage about the joint area review report: first, criticisms and recommendations were made of Haringey Council that flew in the face of what was considered at the time to be acceptable and appropriate good practice nationally. It was recommended in the report that Haringey Council 'ensure that all elected members have CRB [Criminal Records Bureau] checks' and that the council 'ensure that all elected members undertake safeguarding training'. Why? These were not seen as necessary or acceptable practice nationally at the time. They are still not universally seen as necessary or acceptable requirements. It is hard to see the rationale for these requirements for councillors who have no access to children or personalised access to information about children. These were not recommendations or requirements Ofsted had been known to be making for other councils. But within the Haringey report it looked as though the council was failing to implement accepted good practice. This was not so.

It was also recommended that Haringey Council 'appoint an independent chairperson to the local safeguarding children board (LSCB)'. Again, this was not what was seen at the time as best practice. It was not then national government policy. It was not the position for other LSCBs. Indeed, the understanding was that by chairing the LSCB the Director of Children's Services was undertaking their role and responsibility to give leadership to the protection of children in their area. Again, within the Haringey report it may look as though Haringey's LSCB was not following accepted best practice. This was not so.

The joint area review report also commented on the first serious case review that had already been undertaken following the death of Peter Connelly. This was the only serious case review completed in Haringey between 2006 and 2008. In November 2008 Ofsted reported its judgement that this serious case review was inadequate. It stated that the individual management reviews by Whittington Hospital NHS Trust, the Metropolitan Police and Haringey Legal Services were good, the review by the FWA was adequate, but that the reviews by Haringey children's social care service, Haringey schools, North Middlesex University Hospital/Great Ormond Street Hospital NHS Trust, Haringey Teaching PCT, Haringey Strategic and Community Housing Prevention and Options Team were all judged to be inadequate. Particular reference was made of the serious case review's failure to 'look at the capacity of front-line services to deliver what was required of them'. Ofsted concluded that 'the serious case review misses opportunities to ensure lessons are learned. Key actions required in order to improve safeguarding are not fully identified.'[113]

It was a surprise to some that Ofsted was now judging Haringey Council's children's social care and safeguarding services to be inadequate, with significant concerns about the leadership and management of the services. However, possibly anticipating the comment that Ofsted had dramatically changed its judgement about children's services in Haringey, Christine Gilbert, within the Ofsted press release on the day of Mr Balls' media conference, noted that 'We also know that performance can go backwards – and what looks promising may not translate into reality'. Ofsted was now proposing that 'Annual inspections will keep a spotlight on services and help to keep children safer'.[114]

The previous judgements, however, were now history. The November judgement of inadequate by Ofsted and the other national inspectors underlay the decisions by Mr Balls that he communicated at the Monday media conference on 1 December. Not surprisingly, coverage of Mr Balls' media conference was extensive. There had been a build-up of attention and anticipation over the days before the

media conference, with much of the media trailing the conference.*
As noted above, it was then the headline story on the 24-hour
television, radio and internet news outlets for the rest of the day.

So, on 1 December, Mr Balls had removed Sharon Shoesmith from
her post as Director of Children's Services in Haringey Council, had
appointed a new interim director and a new interim deputy director,
the leader and lead councillor for children's services had resigned,
and numerous reviews and inspections were under way in Haringey
and nationally. Much, but not all, of what *The Sun* had been seeking
had been achieved. Was this now to be the end of the media frenzy,
as Mr Balls had hoped? Would this story now fade away as happens
quickly with most stories after an initial intensity? Well, not quite!

---

* I had been asked by Sky News, following a live studio interview about the unfolding
'Baby P story', to prepare and present a letter to Mr Balls ahead of his planned media
conference at the start of the following week. 'The letter to Balls' was a five-minute
cameo, shown over and over again in the three days before Mr Balls' media conference,
which was filmed in Kingston University library. I was shown apparently typing the
letter and was saying this was a time which required measured reflection and wisdom
rather than a panic-driven knee-jerk reaction to the media storm, with the danger
of new measures being introduced which would destabilise what was a generally
well-tuned child protection system in England based on decades of development.

Notes

[1] McShane, J. (2009) *It must never happen again: The lessons learned from the short life and terrible death of Baby P*, London: John Blake.

[2] Richards, T. (undated) *Baby P legacy of abuse* [no publisher noted].

[3] Jones, R. (2012) 'Child protection, social work and the media: Doing as well as being done to', *Research, Policy and Practice*, vol 29, no 2, pp 83-94.

[4] Jackson, D. and Cater, B. (2009) 'Fear, failure, outrage and grief: The dissonance between public outrage and individual action?', *Journal of Child Health Care*, vol 13, pp 4-6.

[5] Garrett, P.M. (2009) *'Transforming' children's services? Social work, neoliberalism and the 'modern' world*, Maidenhead: McGraw-Hill, pp 145-52.

[6] Parton, N. (2011) 'Child protection and safeguarding in England: Changing and competing conceptions of risk and their implications for social work', *British Journal of Social Work*, vol 41, pp 854-75.

[7] Barlow, J. and Calam, R. (2011) 'A public health approach to safeguarding in the 21st century', *Child Abuse Review*, vol 20, pp 238-55.

[8] Rogowski, S. (2011) 'Social work with children and families: Challenges and possibilities in the neo-liberal world', *British Journal of Social Work*, vol 4, pp 921-40.

[9] Brandon, M., Bailey, S. and Belderson, P. (2010) *Building on the learning from serious case reviews: A two-year analysis of child protection database notifications 2007–2009*, London: The Stationery Office.

[10] Department for Children, Schools and Families (DCSF) (2010) *Working together to safeguard children: A guide to inter-agency working to safeguard and promote the welfare of children*, Nottingham: DCSF Publications.

[11] Department for Children, Schools and Families (DCSF) (2007a) *Referrals, assessments and children and young people who are the subject of a child protection plan or are on child protection registers, England – year ending March 2007* (http://media.education.gov.uk/assets/files/pdf/sfr282007pdf.pdf).

[12] DCSF (2007a) op cit.

[13] DCSF (2007b) *Children looked after in England (including adoption and care leavers) year ending 31 March 2007* (www.education.gov.uk/researchandstatistics/a00195573).

[14] Pritchard, C. and Williams, R. (2009) 'Comparing possible "child-abuse-related-deaths" in England and Wales with the major developed countries 1974–2006: Signs of progress?', *British Journal of Social Work*, vol 40, no 6, pp 1700-18.

[15] Munro, E.R., Brown, R., Sempik, J., Ward, H. and Owen, C. (2011) *Scoping review to draw together data on child injury and safeguarding and to compare the position of England with that in other countries*, London: Department for Education, p 52.

[16] Pritchard and Williams (2009) op cit, p 1701.

[17] Parsons, T. (2012) 'Don't arm the police, disarm the criminals', *Daily Mirror*, 22 September (www.mirror.co.uk/news/uk-news/dont-arm-the-police-disarm-the-criminals-1337800).

[18] Elsey, S. (2010) *Media coverage of child deaths in the United Kingdom: The impact of Baby P: A case for influence?*, Edinburgh: Centre for Learning in Child Protection.

[19] House of Commons Culture, Media and Sport Select Committee (2012) *News International and phone-hacking*, Eleventh Report, Volume 1, HC-903-1, London: The Stationery Office.

[20] Watson, T. and Hickman, M. (2012) *Dial M for Murdoch*, London: Allen Lane, p 18.

[21] Watson and Hickman (2012) op cit, p 306.

[22] BBC News (2012) 'Profile: Glenn Mulcaire' (www.bbc.co.uk/news/uk-14080775).

[23] Jukes, P. (2012) *The fall of the House of Murdoch: Fourteen days that ended a media dynasty*, London: Unbound, pp 51-2.

[24] Thornton, L. (2008) 'Shannon torment', *Daily Mirror*, 13 November, front page and pp 4, 6-7.

[25] Lawton, J. (2008) 'Shannon drugged and held in noose by mum', *Daily Star*, 13 November, front page and pp 4-5.

[26] Brooke, C. and Greenhill, S. (2008) 'Wicked: Shannon Matthews' mother kidnapped her own daughter', *Daily Mail*, 13 November, front page and pp 4-5.

[27] Taylor, A. (2008) 'Shannon drugged and kept on leash', *The Sun*, 13 November, front page and pp 4-5.

[28] Martin, R. (2009) *Shannon betrayed from birth: The true story of Britain's cruellest mother*, London: John Blake, p 267.

[29] Searches in January 2013 of the Kirklees LSCB, Kirklees Council and the Department for Education failed to find the Shannon Matthews' serious case review executive summary report. Publication of the full report was prevented by a court order following an application by Shannon Matthews' father resisting publication (*Dewsbury Reporter* [2012] 'Judge blocks publication of full Shannon Matthews report', 11 August, www.dewsburyreporter.co.uk/news/local/more-local-news/judge-blocks-publication-of-full-shannon-matthews-report-1-4823646).

[30] Wainwright, M. (2010) 'Social workers cleared, but inquiry warns patterns in Shannon Matthews case not rare', *The Guardian*, 17 June, p 4.

[31] McGuiness, R. (2010) 'Social workers "clear of blame" in Shannon case', *Metro*, 17 June, p 15.

[32] Taylor, A. (2010) 'SHANNON SCANDAL', *The Sun*, 17 June, front page and p 9.

[33] Brooke, C. (2010) 'Not such a bad parent!', *Daily Mail*, 17 June, p 21.

[34] Addley, E. (2008) 'Rapist made daughters pregnant 19 times', *The Guardian*, 26 November, p 9.

[35] March, S. and Pancevski, B. (2009) *The crimes of Josef Fritzl: Uncovering the truth*, London: HarperCollins.

[36] *The Sun* (2010) 'Editorial: Shameless', 11 March, p 6.

[37] Brooke, C., Greenhill, S. and Tozer, J. (2010) '100 care workers ...', *Daily Mail*, 11 March, p 6.

[38] Ferguson, H. (2004) *Protecting children in time: Child abuse, child protection and the consequence of modernity*, Basingstoke: Palgrave Macmillan, pp 206-7.

[39] Chippindale, P. and Horrie, C. (1999) *Stick it up your punter! The uncut story of the Sun newspaper,* London, Simon & Schuster, pp 262-3.

[40] Sky News (2008) 'Pair guilty over toddler's death', 11 November (http://news.sky.com/story/648157/pair-guilty-over-toddlers-death).

[41] Siddique, H. and Jones, S. (2008) 'Two men found guilty of causing Baby P's death', *The Guardian*, 11 November (www.guardian.co.uk/society/2008/nov/11/childprotection-ukcrime).

[42] Metropolitan Police (2008) 'Baby death: Man found guilty', Press release, 11 November (http://content.met.police.uk/News/Baby-death-Man-found-guilty/12602677554559/125).

[43] Siddique and Jones (2008) op cit.

[44] Gray, C. (2008) 'Police speak out on baby killing', *Haringey Independent*, 11 November (www.haringeyindependent.co.uk/news/topstories/3837165.Police_speak_out_on_baby_killing).

[45] BBC News (2008) 'A short life of misery and pain', 11 November (http://news.bbc.co.uk/1/hi/uk/7708398.stm).

[46] Sky News (2008) op cit.

[47] Sky News (2008) op cit.

[48] BBC News (2008) op cit.

[49] Gray, C. (2008) 'Baby death "worse than Victoria Climbié"', *Haringey Independent*, 11 November (www.haringeyindependent.co.uk/news/topstories/3837153.Baby_death_worse).

[50] *The Guardian* (2008) 'Baby P case is worse than Climbié, says child protection group:"Systematic and operational failures" blamed for second child's death while in care of Haringey social services', 11 November (www.guardian.co.uk/society/2008/nov/11/child-protection-climbie-babyp).

[51] www.publications.parliament.uk/pa/cm200708/cmhansard/cm081112-0002/htm#08111228000013

[52] *Daily Star* (2008) 'Spat was shameful', 13 November, p 9.

[53] Treneman, A. (2008) 'Shame, they cried. And they were right', *The Times*, 13 November, p 10.

[54] Cameron, D. (2008) 'Excuses won't do', *The Sun*, 13 November, p 9.

[55] Hope, C. (2012) 'Horsegate: David Cameron knew he was riding a police horse, Downing Street says', *The Daily Telegraph*, 2 March (www. telegraph,co.uk/news/uknews/phone-hacking/9119702).

[56] Leveson Inquiry (2012) 'Rebekah Brooks' evidence', 11 May (www. levesoninquiry.org.uk/wp-content/uploads/2012/05/Transcript-opf-Aftrernoon-Hearing-11-May-2012.pdf), pp 44-58.

[57] Lazzeri, A. and France, A. (2008) 'Baby P: First picture', *The Sun*, 14 November (www.thesun.co.uk/sol/homepage/news/article1931748.ece).

[58] *The Sun* (2008) 'Join our fight', 15 November, p 6.

[59] *The Sun* (2008) 15 November, op cit.

[60] *The Sun* (2011) 'Sylvia Henry: An apology', 10 June (www.thesun.co.uk/ sol/homepage/news/3629756/Sylvia-Henry-An-apology.html).

[61] Greenslade, R. (2012) '*The Sun* changes its stance, yet again, over the Baby P case', *The Guardian*, 2 August (www.theguardian.com/media/ greenslade/2012/aug/02/sun-baby-p).

[62] *The Sun* (2008) 'Baby P petition', 13 November, p 9.

[63] Nasir, N. (2008) 'Baby P: Will you fight for justice?', 17 November (www. thesun.co.uk/sol/homepage/mysun/1927507/Baby-P-Will-you-fight-for-justice.html).

[64] Edemariam, A. (2009) '"When a dead child is known to us, that's the biggest horror. We knew the size of that"', *The Guardian*, 6 February (www.guardian. co.uk/society/2009/feb/06/sharon-shoesmith-haringey-interview).

[65] Wolff, M. (2008) *The man who owns the news: Inside the secret world of Rupert Murdoch*, New York: Broadway Books, p 2.

[66] Chippindale and Horrie (1999) op cit.

[67] Cockerell, M., Hennessy, P. and Walker, D. (1985) *Sources close to the Prime Minister: Inside the hidden world of the news manipulators*, Basingstoke: Macmillan, p 7.

[68] Wall, E. (2008) 'Tortured Baby P: Sack the lot of them', *Daily Star*, 13 November, p 9.

[69] Cheston, P., Lefley, J. and Mendick, R. (2008) 'Boy left to die just like Victoria Climbié', *London Evening Standard*, 11 November (www.standard. co.uk/news/boy-left-to-die-just-like-victoria-climbie-6867336).

[70] Rayner, G. (2008) 'David Cameron says Baby P workers must be sacked, not suspended', *The Daily Telegraph*, 2 December (www.telegraph.co.uk/ news/uknews/baby-p/3542889/David-Cameron-says-Baby-P-workers-must-be-sacked-not-suspended.html).

71 Campbell, D., Jones, S. and Brindle, D. (2008) '50 injuries, 60 visits – failures that led to the death of Baby P', *The Guardian*, 12 November, p 3.

72 Bennett, R. (2008) 'Investigation into brutal death of Baby P increases the pressure on council chiefs', *The Times*, 13 November, p 10.

73 Hughes, M. and Savage, M. (2008) 'Politicians call for action over Baby P case', *The Independent*, 13 November, p 12.

74 Featherstone, L. (2008) 'We need a fresh start in Haringey', 21 November (www.lynnefeatherstone.org/2008/11/we-need-fresh=start-in-haringey).

75 Featherstone (2008) op cit.

76 Twickenham and Richmond Liberal Democrats (2008) 'Laws, Featherstone, Harris and Hemming quiz Balls on "Baby P"', 22 November (http://twickenhamlibdems.co.uk/en/article/2008/025723/laws-featherstone-harris-and-hemming).

77 Dale, I. (2008) 'Baby P: A tale of two MPs', 2 December (http://iaindale.blogspot.co.uk/2008/12/baby-p-tale-of-two-mps).

78 Kavanagh, T. (2012) 'Witch-hunt has put us behind ex-Soviet states on press freedom', *The Sun*, 13 February (www.thesun.co.uk/sol/homepage/news/4124870/The-Suns-Trevor-Kavanagh-Witch-hunt-puts-us-behind-ex-Soviet-states-on-press-freedom).

79 Kavanagh, T. (2008) 'Leftie mafia close ranks over Baby P', 17 November (www.thesun.co.uk/sol/homepage/news/1937117/Leftie-Mafia-close-ranks-over-Baby-P).

80 Pack, M. (2009) 'Baby P's death "could and should" have been stopped', Liberal Democrat Voice, 2 May (www.libdemvoice.org/baby-ps-death-could-and-should-have-been-stopped-14184.html).

81 Lammy, D. (2008) 'Update on the Baby P case', 14 November (www.davidlammy.co.uk/da/90800).

82 Lammy, D. (2009) 'David Lammy responds to the news that the "stepfather" of Baby P has been found guilty of abuse charges against a second child', 2 May (www.davidlammy.co.uk/david_lammy_responds_to_the_news).

83 Leveson Inquiry (2012) 'Transcript of oral evidence given by Rebekah Brooks', 11 May (www.levesoninquiry.org.uk/rebekah+brooks).

84 Leveson Inquiry (2012) op cit, p 47.

85 Hartley, C., France, A. and Lazzeri, A. (2008) 'WHITEWASH', *The Sun*, 25 November (www.thesun.co.uk/sol/homepage/news/article1934185).

86 Leveson Inquiry (2012) op cit, p 46.

87 O'Carrol, L. and Plunkett, J. (2012) 'Judge rounds on Gove as minister resists any curbs on press freedom', *The Guardian*, 30 May, p 14.

88 BBC News (2008) 'Angry leaders clash over Baby P', 12 November (http://news.bbc.co.uk/1/hi/7724541.stm).

[89] BBC News (2008) '"Clear evidence" of Baby P errors', 20 November (http://news.bbc.co.uk/1/hi/uk/7739743.stm).

[90] BBC News (2008) 20 November, op cit.

[91] Groves, J. (2012) 'Leveson Inquiry has created "chilling atmosphere that threatens free speech", says Tory minister Gove', 22 February (www.dailymail.co.uk/news/article-2104406/Michael-Gove-Leveson-Inquiry).

[92] Groves (2012) op cit.

[93] BBC News (2008) 20 November, op cit.

[94] *The Sun* (2010) 'Timeline of mite failed by system', 22 June (www.thesun.co.uk/sol/homepage/news/2443012/Timeline-of-a-tragic-Baby-P-failed-by-system.html).

[95] Mackenzie, K. (2008) 'Idiots who betrayed Baby P must go now', *The Sun*, 16 November (www.thesun.co.uk/sol/homepage/news/1924847/Kelvin-Mackenzie-Idiots-who-betrayed-Baby-P-must-go-now.html).

[96] High Court (2010) Rejoinder on behalf of the claimant to Ofsted's reply dated 26 February 2010 and to the submissions of the Secretary of State and Council dated 22 and 23 February 2010, *R (on the application of Sharon Shoesmith) and (i) Ofsted (ii) the Secretary of State for Children, Schools and Families (iii) Haringey Council*, CO/2241/2009.

[97] *The Sun* (2010) 'Ofsted "changed Baby P report"', 1 April (www.thesun.co.uk/sol/homepage/news/291537/Ofsted-changed-Baby-P-report).

[98] BBC News (2010) 'Ofsted changed Shoesmith report', 1 April (http://news.bbc.co.uk/1/hi/education/8599616.stm).

[99] Balls, E. (2008) 'Baby P: Ed Balls' statement in full', *The Guardian*, 1 December (www.theguardian.com/society/2008/dec/01/baby-p-ed-balls-statement).

[100] Ofsted (2006) *London Borough of Haringey Children's Services Authority Area*, Joint Area Review, p 4.

[101] Ofsted (2006) op cit, p 27.

[102] Ofsted (2007) *Fostering service: London Borough of Haringey Fostering Service*, Inspection report, 29 January.

[103] Ofsted (2008) *London Borough of Haringey fostering service*, Inspection report for LA Fostering Agency, 25 January.

[104] Ofsted (2007) *2007 Annual performance assessment of services for children and young people in the London Borough of Haringey*, 26 November, p 10.

[105] Balls, E. (2008) quoted in *The Queen (on behalf of Sharon Shoesmith) and Ofsted and ORS*, Case number: C1/2010/2635,2635(A),2635(B), Neutral Citation Number [2011] EWCA Civ 642, 27 May 2011.

[106] Balls (2008) op cit.

[107] Rayner (2008) op cit.

[108] Fallon, P. (2009) 'Different strokes', *Society Guardian*, 21 January (www.guardian.co.uk/society/2009/jan/21/letters).

[109] Balls (2008) op cit.

[110] Ofsted, Healthcare Commission and Her Majesty's Inspectorate of Constabulary (2008) *Joint area review: Haringey Children's Services Authority Area*, London: Ofsted.

[111] R *(on the application of Sharon Shoesmith and (i) Ofsted (ii) the Secretary of State for Children's, Schools and Families (iii) Haringey London Borough Council* (2009) Response on behalf of the claimant to Ofsted's post-trial disclosure, CO/2241/2009, p 14.

[112] Ofsted et al (2008) op cit, p 9.

[113] Ofsted et al (2008) op cit, p 6.

[114] Ofsted (2008) 'Haringey requires urgent action to ensure vulnerable children are properly protected', Press release, 1 December (www.ofsted.gov.uk/news/haringey-requires-urgent-action-ensure-vulnerable-children).

THREE

The frenzied media backlash

By the end of 2008, and within the six weeks of the story of 'Baby P' being launched within the media, the story line was already well established, with *The Sun* prominent, although not on its own, in its shaping and telling. The focus was almost exclusively on Sharon Shoesmith, by now already the former Director of Children's Services in Haringey Council, and on a complete organisational line of Haringey Council's children's services managers and social workers. The attention given to the adults convicted of 'causing or allowing' Peter's death had moved from the centre stage of the media's attention. Their media moment would come again in summer 2009. In the meantime, at the end of 2008, they were each in prison awaiting sentence, an event not to take place until six months later.

But for Sharon Shoesmith, the social workers and their managers, the media attention was relentless, with the paediatrician from St Ann's Clinic also receiving media attention, albeit to a lesser extent when she moved away from London.

In Haringey Council the Leader and Councillor who led on children's services resigned from their roles, Haringey Council was required by Mr Balls to appoint a new director of children's services, and three reviews and inspections were under way. One by Ofsted was focused on children's services in Haringey, one was the re-running of the serious case review by Haringey's LSCB with a new chair of the board and a new report author, and the third was a national review by Lord Laming of the state of child protection across England. Further reviews were to be initiated in 2009 and 2010 (the review of social work by the Social Work Reform Board and the Munro review of child protection and social work). All were undertaken within the context of the continuing media attention to the 'Baby P story' and how it had been shaped and how it would be reinforced.

But what was not being given attention within how the 'Baby P story' was being told? First, little attention was given to the police or the NHS, when both services had significant roles and responsibilities in protecting Peter Connelly. In relation to both services there were already known to be concerns about how these services had performed in working with Peter and his family. More will become known later about these serious concerns. But they had not attracted, and never did attract, the same media and therefore public attention as did the overwhelming personalised attention on a small number of social workers and their managers in Haringey Council. So why was there this skewing of media coverage?

Second, Ofsted. Here was the national inspectorate for schools and children's services that had apparently previously failed to properly inspect and grade Haringey children's services. As the same inspection methodology was used everywhere it presumably had failed to properly inspect every other area's children's services as well. There had long been concerns about whether, within its leadership, Ofsted had the wisdom and expertise to understand and inspect children's social care services, including child protection.[1] Ofsted's experience and roots were in schools' inspections. Its board and senior managers primarily had this background, and there was limited social care and social work experience and expertise within Ofsted's senior management and board.

There were subsequently three inescapable questions arising for Ofsted and its Chief Executive, and these questions were asked in Parliament at a hearing of the House of Commons Children's Select Committee. First, as the rushed re-inspection required by Mr Balls produced such conflicting findings with the more timely inspection previously undertaken, why was Ofsted's existing child protection inspection methodology so inadequate? Second, if the judgements previously made about child protection services in Haringey were so flawed, why should there be any confidence in the Ofsted inspections and judgements of other child protection services across England? Third, how did a national inspectorate, where its integrity was in large part based on its assumed independence, come to engage so closely and comprehensively with a government-demanded review which cast aside what was and would be considered as a necessary timescale and process to get a fair and accurate view of an area's child protection services, and how did it come to undertake that fast and rushed review in such close cooperation with the government's civil servants?

Ofsted's Chief Executive was Christine Gilbert, and her role included the 'sole responsibility for inspection judgements'.[2] A former teacher, and then headteacher, she had been a Director of Education in the London Borough of Harrow and then Corporate Director (Education) in Tower Hamlets before becoming the Council's Chief Executive. While at Harrow she married Tony McNulty, who was a local Labour MP and in 2008–09 was a Minister in the Home Office, the government department with responsibility for the police and policing. He himself later became a focus of attention through the media coverage of MPs' expenses claims.[3]

Christine Gilbert replaced David Bell in October 2006 as Ofsted's Chief Executive. David Bell, as noted in the previous chapter, became the Permanent Secretary at the DCSF, and as such was the senior civil servant advising ministers during the media shaping of the 'Baby P story'.

In April 2007 Ofsted was passed responsibility for inspecting children's social care services by the Labour government, following Mr Brown's announcement as Chancellor of the Exchequer in 2005 that for reasons of economy and efficiency the then existing Commission for Social Care Inspection (CSCI) was to be abolished. CSCI had demonstrable expertise and success in inspecting and improving children and adults' social care services, including safeguarding and protection services, but its children's social care inspection responsibilities were to be transferred to Ofsted and its adult social care responsibilities to the Healthcare Commission, which was to be renamed the Care Quality Commission (CQC). Ofsted did not change its acronym, and remained primarily known as the Office for Standards in Education, although children's services and skills were added to its full title. Inspecting schools and teaching within classrooms, however, is quite a different task from inspecting social workers and others working in the community with often very vulnerable children and families.

The serious concerns about the performance of Ofsted were noted in a letter[4] sent in December 2008 to Christine Gilbert by the President of the Association of Directors of Children's Services (ADCS), Maggie Atkinson. Dr Atkinson later became the Children's Commissioner for England. Her letter of 8 December was prompted by an interview article in *The Guardian* on 6 December in which Christine Gilbert claimed Haringey children's services managers had presented data which misled inspectors, and that 'I am concerned that we look at the way this is happening [in other local authorities]'.[5]

The issues that were raised in Dr Atkinson's letter ranged from concerns about Ofsted's inspection processes to the competence of its inspectors. Here is a sample of the issues raised in the five-page letter, and with an indication of the strength of concerns about Ofsted:

> ... why has Ofsted persisted in saying that APA [Annual Performance Assessment] data is sent from LAs [local authorities] to Ofsted, when the reverse is the case [*this is a response to Ofsted claiming that Haringey had sent misleading data to Ofsted*].... This misinterpretation of where data originates and is stored, analysed and used, is both unhelpful and disingenuous.... We formally protest that you have made veiled and unproven accusations about LAs in effect 'lying' over data.... We hereby request the immediate production of Ofsted's formal evidence that backs this claim.
>
> Many of my colleagues in LAs around the country report high levels of concern about the understanding and levels of social care experience amongst your inspectors.
>
> Our concern is that Ofsted seems too focussed on procedural compliance and, indeed, seems possibly to be diagnosing some of the current difficulties as related to lack of compliance rather than striking a balance between procedural compliance, the exercise of professional

judgement and the achievement of outcomes for children
and young people.

This is a damning and devastating critique of a national inspectorate,
with allegations of misrepresentation, inspectors lacking relevant
experience, and concerns about the focus of inspection processes and
judgements. The letter to Christine Gilbert was written in December
2008. Ten months later, in October 2009, Directors of Children's
Services were still expressing their concerns. Kim Bromley-Derry,
who followed Maggie Atkinson as ADCS President, commented that:

> The current inspection regime measures process and
> not practice. There's nothing about improvement in
> the inspection process or how it can be used to ensure
> improvement takes place.[6]

Even more telling in relation to Haringey, John Coughlan, whom
Mr Balls had urgently drafted in to Haringey in November 2008 to
oversee the council's children's services, said at the National Children
and Adults Conference in October 2009:

> We need to ask ourselves, are we auditing or inspecting
> in order to improve? The experience of inspection now
> is an audit of records. We're not doing anything in the
> inspection to improve quality of practice.

Coughlan said the current levels of inspection were turning social
services into a 'spectator sport':

> "It's a very crowded terrace and at the moment there's
> a sense that there are more watchers than players", he
> said to an audience of social workers, who applauded
> and nodded in approval. "The typical chant for spectators
> of course is, 'You don't know what you're doing'", he
> continued. "But then the response would be, 'come and
> have a go if you think you're hard enough'".[7]

It was not only Directors of Children's Services who raised concerns about Ofsted and its inspection and judgement processes. The chair of the Society of Local Authority Chief Executives and Senior Managers, Derek Myers, is also reported as having raised concerns. He said that Christine Gilbert's claim that Haringey Council had previously misled the inspectors by submitting false data to Ofsted 'could in fact have been the product of the pressures of Ofsted's systems'.[8] Derek Myers had himself been a social worker, Director of Social Services and a local council Chief Executive, and provided advice to Haringey's Chief Executive, Ita O'Donovan, as the 'Baby P' media coverage gathered pace.

This criticism by much-respected Directors of Children's Services, and by the Society of Local Authority Chief Executives, of a major high-profile national inspectorate might in itself at other times have been a media bombshell. In the context, however, of how the 'Baby P story' was being shaped and driven by *The Sun* and others, it was given little continuing media or public attention. There were exceptions, as with the report in the *Evening Standard* headlined 'Haringey given a clean bill of health only weeks after the death of Baby P'[9] and, despite all the concerns about Ofsted, 'Balls gives Ofsted vote of confidence'.[10] But overall it was probably seen as an unhelpful complication to the simple story being told about the culpability of Sharon Shoesmith and the social workers and their managers in Haringey for Peter's death. However, the chair of the House of Commons Select Committee on Children, Barry Shearman, was reported 'to have lost confidence in the inspectorate Ofsted over its handling of children's services in Haringey, the north London borough where Baby P died'.[11]

Having confidence in Ofsted would not have been helped by confusion created about Ofsted's varying figures of the number of children dying from abuse. At Mr Shearman's Select Committee Christine Gilbert gave a figure of 210 children dying in England of abuse over a 16-month period from April 2007 (Peter Connelly died in August 2007);[12] an Ofsted report gave a figure of 282 deaths;[13] but Ofsted then reported that between April 2007 and July 2008, 81 serious case reviews were initiated following deaths of children.[14] When the National Society for the Prevention of Cruelty to Children

(NSPCC) was asked for clarification about the number of child homicides in England, it provided figures from 1977 to 2007. The number of child killings over the 30-year period had an average of 76.5 per year, and for the last 10 years to 2007, an average of 72 deaths per year.[15] These latter figures will be much more recognisable to those working in and tracking the performance of child protection services.

Mrs Gilbert remained as Chief Executive of Ofsted until 2011 and was, as will be seen later, a continuing contributor within the 'Baby P story'. However, as will also be seen later, in 2010 and 2011 Ofsted itself became the centre of attention of the House of Commons Select Committee of MPs that reviewed and reflected on Ofsted's performance in inspecting child protection and other children's social care services. It will also be seen later that the concerns about an overwhelming focus on inspectors measuring compliance with procedures rather than having the focus and competence to assess professional practice and judgement was to be taken up in a major review of child protection commissioned by the current Coalition government.

From January 2009 onwards, the telling and shaping of the 'Baby P story' continued relentlessly and with little respite. Opportunities arose to refer to 'Baby P' when other children were killed through neglect or abuse. When further inspections and reviews were reported, whether primarily or more tangentially related to Peter Connelly's death, there was further media coverage. When there was the sentencing of the adults found through the criminal proceedings to have caused or allowed Peter's death there was more coverage, but even then still much of it was targeted at the social workers and their managers. When there were employment tribunals, the related judicial reviews and the hearings before professional bodies related to the social workers, their managers, the paediatrician and the GP, there were further flurries of media attention. This media attention may have had its pinnacles and peaks, but over the next 18 months and beyond there was never a time when the 'Baby P story' went out of view for weeks or months at a time.

Central to the promotion of the story was the continuing personalised attention on the social workers and, especially, on Sharon Shoesmith. She had been removed from her post by Mr Balls on 1 December 2008 and then soon afterwards at a disciplinary hearing within Haringey Council she was dismissed from her employment. Paparazzi photographers continued to stalk her and to besiege her home, and she, along with the other social workers and their managers, were warned by the Metropolitan Police to be fearful for their safety and the safety of members of their family. They had and continued to receive abuse and threats. Maria Ward, the social worker for Peter and the Connelly family in summer 2007, had to move from her home (and has changed address twice since) following threats and harassment.

The serious threats continued, and five years later, when recognised, they still received abuse out on the street and are still tracked by reporters and photographers. When Sharon Shoesmith was photographed going out of her flat in London in January 2009 it became a major photo and story in *The Sun*. Reporters and photographers kept a constant vigil day and night outside her flat for several months. But what was the motivation of *The Sun* and others to continue this personalised threatening intrusion, harassment and vilification of the Haringey children's services social workers and managers?

It was easy to continue to feed the story. Any photograph which showed the suspended and dismissed social workers or their managers with a hostile headline was quick copy for tomorrow's paper. No longer was Peter Connelly the focus of the story. There was little more that could be known or said about his terrible life and death. It was the hunting, harassment and hatred targeted at others that was now the story content. The adults who had a direct responsibility for the abuse of Peter were in prison and only occasionally were there opportunities to bring them back into view. But the social workers and their managers were still available to be taunted, terrorised and traumatised. And this is what happened.

But the continuing telling of the 'Baby P story' required the injection of new information, new comment and new angles to make the continuing coverage newsworthy. For some parts of the

A report from *The Sun* in January 2009

media the new coverage was used to reinforce the story and editorial lines already created and promoted. For other parts of the media the coverage was to challenge the dominant story.

In November and December 2008, even within parts of the broadsheet press that later came to make comment in opposition to the dominant story line targeting Sharon Shoesmith and the social workers, or that came to tell a more complex story about child protection, the focus was initially on the failings of Haringey Council and its children's services:

> Sixty missed chances to save baby 'used as punchbag': Baby P was released from care three times despite terrible injuries caused or allowed by his mother and two men. [*The Guardian*][16]

> Why Baby P was doomed to die: Care agencies have lost their sense of proportion over 'risk' – putting the

most endangered children in even more peril. [*The Daily Telegraph*][17]

Investigation into brutal death of Baby P increases pressure on council chiefs. [*The Times*][18]

Politicians call for action over Baby P case. [*The Independent*][19]

However, and especially as the more specialist social affairs correspondents and coverage came to pick up the 'Baby P story', the comment became more diverse and differentiated. The continuing and escalating targeting of the social workers and their managers was of increasing concern to those who recognised the complexity as contrasted with the simplified black-and-white hero-and-villain story-telling of the tabloids:

This frenzy of hatred is a disaster for children at risk: Britain has one of the best records on child deaths. One case blasted out of all proportion can undo years of good. [*The Guardian*][20]

Attack the professionals, and a tragedy like Baby P will result. [*The Independent*][21]

There was also press coverage of social workers who were willing to speak out against the vilification of the social workers in Haringey, seeking to explain the realities and complexities of child protection social work. 'To protect children we must first protect social workers'[22] was the headline in *The Guardian* for a piece by Harry Ferguson, Professor of Social Work at Nottingham University; a social worker writing under the pseudonym of 'Sally-Anne Jones' described in *The Times* how 'over the past 20 years I have been chased with machetes, threatened with knives and had loads of doors slammed in my face';[23] and in the same pages, a former social worker and Director of Social Services, Bill McKitterick, commented: 'It is a very difficult job to knock on the door of a household that does not want you there....

The social worker is at the sharp end of an inverted pyramid of pressure. It can be an isolating job.'[24] He might also have said that unlike police officers who go out in twos armed with radios and sprays, and doctors who largely see patients in surgeries, clinics and hospitals (which is invariably where Peter Connelly was seen by doctors), social workers routinely and regularly are out on their own visiting homes, often within communities where violence and threat is common. There was also a comment from Anthony Douglas, a former social worker and Director of Social Services and now Chief Executive of the Children and Family Court Advisory and Support Service (Cafcass). His article was entitled 'Baby P's legacy must be better status for children's social workers'.[25]

But for the mass circulation tabloid newspapers, accounts of the reality of social work were not to cloud and confuse the simple story line of blaming the social workers and their managers, and the paediatrician,[26] for Peter Connelly's terrible death. As 2009 unfolded and progressed, so did the victimisation of the social workers, and especially Sharon Shoesmith when she sought to challenge her dismissal by Haringey Council:

FURY AS BABY P BOSS SEEKS £173K PAYOFF.[27]

Sacked Baby P chief launches legal battle for £173,000 payout.[28]

This latter headline and report in the *Evening Standard* was printed beside a picture of Sharon Shoesmith walking along a pavement with the caption 'Sharon Shoesmith shopping the day after her sacking last month'. Not only the reporting but also the intrusion and harassment were still in full flow.*

---

* When in October 2013 there was at last a financial settlement between Haringey Council and Sharon Shoesmith, I was asked to participate in a live BBC *Newsnight* broadcast about the settlement, with the other interviewee being a Conservative MP who was expressing her unhappiness that Sharon Shoesmith should receive any financial settlement. When I arrived at the studios I was asked if I knew the figure for the settlement. I didn't know,

Note continues over

But there was also a backlash, with those who had known and worked with Sharon Shoesmith rallying to her support. A letter signed by 61 headteachers in Haringey was sent to Ita O'Donovan:

> Sharon Shoesmith is a public servant with many years of good work behind her. Since her appointment in Haringey, she has worked unstintingly for young people in the borough. Schools and services, though not perfect, have improved immeasurably during her time here.... The manner in which the Director has been dismissed has greatly disappointed us. We believed that Haringey as a council was more principled than this. We believed that you would adhere to fair employment practice. We believed that you had a duty of care to employees who have dedicated years of their working life to Haringey and its services.... We fear for the recruitment of any quality staff for Haringey for the foreseeable future.[29]

As reported in *The Times*, the headteachers also commented that 'Should the Child P [*with the headteachers correctly acknowledging that Peter Connelly when he died was not a baby*] case result in her loss from the borough, then our children and young people will lose one of their most effective, determined and committed champions'.[30] It is not every departing senior manager who gets such a ringing endorsement from those with whom they have worked and by whom they've been led!

but it was suggested to me that it was a six-figure settlement. On air Jeremy Paxman, who was presenting *Newsnight*, then asked me if it was true that Sharon Shoesmith had received £600,000. The six figures had within less than an hour become £600,000! I subsequently understood that £600,000 was a considerable multiple of the actual amount received by Sharon Shoesmith, although this then became the figure which was picked up in the press and had wide circulation. However, a later BBC online statement noted that 'one government source has told BBC *Newsnight* that the cost to Haringey Council could be as high as £600,000, although that figure reflects the total payment [*which presumably would include legal costs*] and Ms Shoesmith is expected to receive a lower sum' (Morris, J. and Stratton, A. [2013] 'Baby Peter case: Sharon Shoesmith agrees six-figure pay-out', 29 October, www.bbc.co.uk/news/uk-24715666?print=true).

The support for Sharon Shoesmith went wider than Haringey's headteachers, with it reported that 'council staff, local religious leaders, councillors, trade unionists, school governors and more than a dozen fellow children's services directors have stepped up their support for her'.[31] There was even an attempt to get *The Sun* 'to support UK social workers' with a petition set up on the Downing Street website in support of Haringey social workers and their managers.[32] This was an ambitious but doomed-to-failure action by *Community Care*, the weekly 'trade magazine' for social workers. However, what was seen as controversial by some was that Deidre Sanders, *The Sun*'s agony aunt, was to become a member of a government-initiated task force to review, reform and promote social work.

There was, however, not only concern about how Sharon Shoesmith and the social workers in Haringey were being targeted in the media, but also that unrealistic and ill-founded political promises were now being made to prevent such a tragedy as Peter Connelly's death ever happening again in the future.[33]

The attempt to get reality, fairness and balance interjected into the continuing media coverage was challenging. Where this coverage was achieved to counter the blaming and shaming of individual social workers and their managers it was primarily in the broadsheet newspapers, and on radio and television, but not in the tabloids. There were very isolated minor exceptions of more supportive comments about social work in the tabloid press, but they were very rare.[34, 35]

It was not, however, just the mass circulation tabloid print press that continued the coverage with the focus on individual professionals and on social work more generally. For example, the BBC produced and presented three *Panorama* programmes about 'Baby P'. The first[36] was broadcast on 17 November 2008, only six days after Tracey Connelly, Steven Barker and Jason Owen had each been found in the criminal trial to have caused or allowed the death of Peter. It was a special edition of *Panorama* that replaced the edition that was due to be broadcast. This change of a programming schedule was unusual, although not unique, demonstrating the significance and status already attached to the 'Baby P story'. The 30-minute documentary had been prepared over several months, and was ready to be broadcast when it would not have intruded into or had an impact on the criminal trial.

Haringey Council was, therefore, right to anticipate that Peter Connelly's death and the criminal trial would be a focus of media attention. *The Sun* reported,[37] with another opportunity taken by the newspaper to show a photograph of Sharon Shoesmith, that the council had spent £19,000 on buying in from three different sources media, public relations and crisis management expertise. The press strategy that was developed was shared with civil servants in the DCSF, and media training was provided for the council's lead councillor for children's services, the Chief Executive and Sharon Shoesmith as Director of Children's Services. It was decided that Sharon Shoesmith should be the person to front for the council the media conference when the executive summary of the first serious case review was published.[38]

When the public are confronted through the media with the horrors of the terrible torture and death of a toddler, it is not the time to try to paint a picture of pride in improvement. It is not likely to hit the mood of the moment. Sharon Shoesmith was castigated for what was portrayed as her insensitivity. She was accused, incorrectly, of not having expressed distress about Peter's death. It was also claimed by Mark Easton, the BBC's Home Editor, that Sharon Shoesmith had handed out graphs at the media conference about how well Haringey Council's children's services were performing, and that the service had been rated as 'good' by Ofsted. The latter is true. The former, that Sharon Shoesmith handed out graphs at the media conference, was not accurate and led to an impression that in the midst of a media conference about the terrible distressing death of a little boy, Sharon Shoesmith was focused on talking about how well her department was performing.

What, as I now understand it, happened, is that a media briefing pack was given out, not by Sharon Shoesmith, to journalists attending the conference, and that it provided background information for Haringey's LSCB about child protection in Haringey, including the trend data discussed in Chapter Four. This is not unusual. Indeed, being provided with this background contextual data is usually welcomed and asked for by journalists. But the picture created was that of a Director of Children's Services gloating about the performance of the services she led amidst the focus on a child who had died. It may seem a minor issue, and indeed the BBC Trust Editorial Standards Committee decided that 'the script clearly suggested that the Director of Children's Services had personally handed out the graphs' ... but that 'the press packs did not misrepresent the views of the Director, nor give information which was at variance with what she was saying at the briefing or in the interviews. They therefore felt that the effect of the inaccuracy on the viewer's understanding of the story was minimal and not material.'[39]

This should all be of little significance, but amidst the fury and frenzy generated about Sharon Shoesmith, and the hatred and harassment targeted on her, any ammunition that could be fired at her took on a sharp significance. This was picked up in responses to a BBC blog by Mark Easton in February 2009, when the media campaign focused on Sharon Shoesmith was in full flow. In the blog Mark Easton noted that during her interview on Radio 4's 'Woman's Hour' Sharon Shoesmith 'denied "handing out" or "waving" any graphs showing how well her department was doing'. Mark Easton continues: 'I and other journalists were given graphs and information ... whoever did hand them out, the graphs were not a media invention'.[40] Responses to the blog included: 'Does this mean that Mark Easton wants to apologise for misleading viewers/listeners – he seems to be saying that Shoesmith did not hold up or wave any graphs around. Surely this deserves an apology', and 'Mark, are we to understand from your posting that Sharon Shoesmith did not hold and wave them around?... If so, I think this is a disgrace, how is it you are able to make such false claims on national TV?... It seems to me that the reports you made were untrue, in which case, you owe us and, particularly, Sharon Shoesmith an apology.' There was also a comment of: 'A nice slow hand clap for the media. They have managed to turn an individual tragedy into a national disaster. I'm not defending Haringey or anyone involved in this case – but the effect of the media mis-information and witch hunt is social services up and down the country simply cannot fill posts. Many more children will now suffer as a result of this. I am disgusted with the entire media over this whole affair – their manipulation of the public sentiment is a disgrace.'

The Sun made an issue about Haringey Council buying in media expertise when the council already had its own in-house communications team and *The Sun* only five days before had also reported about the membership of this team. *The Sun's* story was that Haringey Council had employed as an Assistant Director for Communication and Strategy someone who had recently worked within the CSCI, an organisation that had received a letter from Nevres Kemal, a former social worker in Haringey, raising concerns about services for children. Lynne Featherstone, the local Liberal Democrat MP, was quoted in the paper as saying 'this is the problem in social services, where people work for the council or inspectors, then swap about. It casts doubt on independent inquiries when everyone seems to know each other.'[41]

Lynne Featherstone was again quoted in *The Sun* a few days later about the money spent by the council on buying in media advice, saying 'it is absolutely outrageous that this money has been wasted on spin doctors. Every penny would have been better spent on improving children's services.'[42]

The 'Baby P' BBC *Panorama* programme in November 2008 was something of a roller coaster of a story. Its focus was very heavily on social work and social workers and 'what went wrong'. Health workers, doctors and police officers and their organisations received only minimal mentions. The programme makers had obtained a 'confidential'[43] police report stating that police officers had wanted Peter removed from his mother after his injuries in June 2007. However, the programme also noted that two police investigations into injuries to Peter had not identified who was living in Peter's home. But despite this being quite an omission and admission, the weight of the discussion and critique within the programme was about social work, and why social workers had failed to identify and act on Peter's abuse.

Contributors to the programme included a social worker who had previously worked in Haringey and who, along with two anonymous social workers, spoke of heavy workloads, and how much time was spent report writing and trapped in the office feeding information into computers. The family friend who had cared for Peter at different times was also filmed and shown in the programme.

Other contributors within the programme included Lord Laming speaking about the Victoria Climbié Inquiry and how it had positively led to a wider children's safeguarding agenda rather than a narrow focus on child protection. This was a point challenged in the programme by Eileen Munro, then Reader in Social Policy at the London School of Economics and Political Science (LSE), but who, as Professor Munro, was later to lead a major national review of child protection. Dr Munro made the comment in the programme that trying to spot children who needed protecting was like 'trying to spot a needle in a haystack, and it gets harder if you make the haystack larger', as happened by broadening the focus from child protection to a children's safeguarding agenda which included, for example, accidents.

Jeremy Vine introduced the programme by noting that the 'social workers and the system have been criticised, some might say crucified' because of the death of 'Baby P', and Alison Holt, the BBC social affairs correspondent, stated towards the end of the programme that there was a national shortage of social workers and 'what social workers don't need is a witch hunt'. Unfortunately a witch hunt was already well under way. The *Panorama* programme inevitably fed into it, with its heavy focus on social work and social workers despite the tale of complexity that it also told.

Less of a roller coaster and more of a directly targeted rocket was a later *Panorama* programme in May 2009 about 'Baby P'. If the first programme bounced around in its coverage of social work, the second programme was largely damning of the social workers in Haringey.

As with the first programme, the second one must have been some time in the making. The broadcasting of the second programme was held back until the end of the criminal trial, when Steven Barker was found guilty of raping a two-year-old girl. He was convicted, quite exceptionally, primarily on the evidence of a little girl aged four about events two years before when she was aged two. The conviction and the process of the conviction, not surprisingly, received comment in the media, including *The Daily Telegraph*:

The 32-year-old targeted his powerless victim in 2007, the same year that he subjected Baby P to months of abuse which ultimately led to the little boy's death. This is the first time the existence of a second case against the part-time handyman can be reported. It is also the first time that the full name of Baby P – Peter – can be disclosed after reporting restrictions were lifted. The two week rape trial was held in secret with the defendant's surname changed in an attempt to hide his true identity from the jury. But the eight man and four woman panel was convinced by the poignant evidence from a little girl who, now aged four, became the youngest victim to give evidence at the Old Bailey.[44]

Steven Barker appealed unsuccessfully against his conviction and then sought to appeal to the Supreme Court, again unsuccessfully, as reported in *The Sun*:

Baby P monster Steven Barker yesterday lost a bid to appeal to the Supreme Court over his conviction for raping a two-year-old girl. Peter's stepdad said his trial was 'unfair' after he was sentenced to life with a minimum of ten years in jail last May. In January the Appeal Court in London upheld his conviction and sentence, with judges calling the rape 'truly appalling'. In the same court yesterday, Lord Chief Justice Lord Judge said Barker could not appeal again.[45]

But back to the May 2009 *Panorama* programme. It was largely based on information provided to the BBC by the Metropolitan Police. As noted in Chapter One, part of the child protection plan for Peter and one of his sisters was to seek to enhance Tracey Connelly's parenting skills and competencies. Tracey Connelly was videoed being interviewed by Sue Gilmore, a manager in Haringey Council's children's services. In the interview Tracey Connelly receives positive comments about her participation and progress. Knowing what came to be known about Tracey Connelly's failure to care for and to protect Peter, the comments from the manager were now seen as inappropriate.

There was concern noted in the *Panorama* programme that the 'solution-focused brief therapy' programme, a programme provided by an organisation called Brief, was not designed for parents where there were concerns about child protection, and that 'the therapy could prove dangerous as the focus shifts from the child at risk to the parent, potentially causing the social workers to lose sight of priorities'.[46] This is a realistic and reasonable concern and one which is also picked up in the second serious case review report, where it was noted that 'not all social workers adopted it ... and some staff [*including Peter's social worker Maria Ward and her manager Gillie Christou*] believed that it did create an ethos which above all emphasised the importance of supporting parents'.[47] This emphasis on supporting parents would have been acceptable, however, if as Sharon Shoesmith said in February 2009 in an interview on BBC Radio 4's 'Woman's Hour', 'social workers believed they were dealing [in the Connelly family] with a chaotic single mother who was honestly worried about a child she kept voluntarily bringing in for medical assessments'.[48]

There is a strong impression of judgements and statements in the *Panorama* programme being made with hindsight, where everyone now knows what was then not known about the abuse of Peter and his imminent death. What was seen as particularly significant by the BBC was that here was clear evidence that Tracey Connelly had a boyfriend, Steven Barker, who had access to Peter:

> Key details that might have saved the life of Baby P were revealed by his own mother on videotape – but never passed to police, the BBC has learned. *Panorama* has found that the baby's mother told a social worker about the new man in her life four months before the child was found dead.... Despite the presence of the new adult in the child's life those details were not handed over to the police investigating suspicious injuries to Peter at that time. They were also not disclosed to police in August 2007 when they began their investigation into the child's death, or the serious case review team sent to examine

> how the child was protected by Haringey. A senior police
> officer tells *Panorama* he is convinced that if the police
> abuse investigation team had been alerted, the boy's life
> could have well have been saved and there would have
> been no need for a murder inquiry.[49]

This was then the story. Someone in Haringey Council children's services knew that Tracey Connelly had a boyfriend, although it has not been alleged that they knew that the boyfriend was living in the Connelly home. But the boyfriend was also known to the school, where a 'man' came with and sometimes without Tracey Connelly to collect Peter's sisters. It is understood it was known at the hospital even back in December 2006, when a 'man', along with Tracey Connelly, came to visit Peter when he was admitted with a whole range of injuries. And it was known to the maternal grandmother and to Peter's father. How, then, did the Metropolitan Police officers, through two criminal investigations, not ascertain that Steven Barker was Tracey Connelly's boyfriend, and then that he, and later Jason Owen, his girlfriend and three children, had moved into the Connelly household? Did they not get this information from the grandmother? Did they not get it from Peter's father? Did they not get it from Tracey Connelly's friend who had been asked to help care for Peter? Did they not find out about Tracey Connelly's male friend from the school or hospital? The people who Tracey Connelly herself was hiding this information from were those key health professionals and social workers who were visiting the family home as part of the child protection plan and who did not know that others had moved into the family home.

The BBC *Panorama* programme had been made with close involvement and cooperation from the police:

> *Panorama* has also seen the police documents that show
> the social work manager who videotaped Baby P's
> mother was directly involved in the decisions about
> his case. The notes show that the officers told her they
> wanted the baby removed from the house until all injuries
> were explained and were baffled when that did not

happen. A senior officer wrote in his log: 'This situation cannot continue.' He goes on: 'I am at a loss as to why our position is at variance to that held by social services. Our concerns for Baby P are valid.'[50]

But how was the video that formed the basis of the *Panorama* programme obtained? The police were told about the video by social workers when the social workers were interviewed, when the rape allegation against Steven Barker was being investigated. A police officer then sought the video from Brief, the organisation that held the video, and took it, as it was potential evidence within a criminal investigation. It was then made available to the BBC.

A *Panorama* programme also included a video of Peter playing in a park with Tracey Connelly and Steven Barker. Surprisingly, what was shown was a little boy smiling, laughing and playing happily with two adults who were responsive towards him, encouraging and praising him as he and they played together with a ball. Anyone seeing these adults and toddler interacting together in the park would have been unlikely to have any concern about his care. Was this what the health visitor, social worker and others saw when they visited the family home? Apparently so, as this is what they wrote in their reports when they observed Peter with his mother.

It is a challenging reminder to those who now see the social workers, and the health workers, as neglectful and naive that maybe not all at the time was black-and-white and clear-cut. The judge in the criminal trial commented how Tracey Connelly had set out to mislead and misinform visitors to her house about what was happening to Peter and his sisters, including the account that she put chocolate on Peter's face to hide bruising.[51] The picture of how Peter was being cared for may not have been so clear and consistent as is now assumed by those with the benefit of unclouded hindsight providing 20:20 vision. But the overall impression and impact of the *Panorama* programme was of naive and gullible social workers easily fooled by a mother who they were too ready to encourage and believe, and with the police complaining that information was being withheld from them.

But what explanation was given for the police not being given or told about the video earlier? The BBC reported that:

> Haringey Council has told Panorama that its former head of children's services, Sharon Shoesmith, and her deputy, Cecilia Hitchen – both since dismissed – were responsible for handing over any relevant documents and information to investigators. Mrs Shoesmith has told the BBC that she cannot comment on the videotape. On the disclosure of documents she said: 'This is always done in line with the advice of lawyers and in this case with a barrister. Everything was disclosed with only those documents that our barrister advised were subject to Public Interest Immunity withheld and the Crown Prosecution Service would know what they are.'[52]

It should be noted, however, that the videotape was not in the possession of the council, but was held by and was the property of another organisation.

Possibly part of the explanation for the confusion about who knew what and when lies within the comments to the BBC from Tracey Connelly's mother, and the BBC report about what had been said by Haringey social workers. Peter's grandmother claimed that she had told social workers in December 2006 about Tracey's new boyfriend, Steven Barker, but also went on to say that her daughter was 'manipulative', and the BBC stated that 'Haringey social workers maintained that Baby P's mother had appeared to be cooperative with them and deliberately hid her violent boyfriend from them'.[53]

The BBC were, however, along with other television and radio media, often contributors of complexity within the otherwise often simplistic telling of the 'Baby P story', including, as will be seen later, raising concerns about Great Ormond Street Hospital NHS Trust and the paediatric services it provided at St Ann's Clinic. Television and radio interviews at significant points in the story's development allowed a range of voices and opinions to be heard. And in February

2009 within 'Woman's Hour' on BBC Radio 4 one of those voices was Sharon Shoesmith in an interview with Jenni Murray.

In the interview Sharon Shoesmith reflected on her dismissal, and the actions being taken against the social workers and managers. Haringey Council had dismissed Sharon Shoesmith at a disciplinary hearing on 8 December, only four working days after Mr Balls had announced to everyone, including to Sharon Shoesmith, that she was to be immediately removed from her post. Sharon Shoesmith was dismissed with no notice period, no compensation and no immediate payment of her pension.

On 1 December, minutes before Mr Balls' press conference, Haringey Council's Assistant Chief Executive telephoned Sharon Shoesmith and told her she was immediately suspended pending an investigation, but Sharon Shoesmith noted that no investigation then took place. Instead, on 3 December, she was instructed to attend a disciplinary hearing on 8 December. This was only two working days notice from Haringey Council of the hearing. It was all very rushed and moving at a pace. The day after the hearing she received a letter stating that she had been summarily dismissed. The letter was included in evidence to the High Court judicial review of Sharon Shoesmith's dismissal. It stated that:

> The effect of the Direction of the Secretary of State made on 1 December 2008 in relation to the position you hold and the allegation that the relationship of trust and confidence in you has been fundamentally breached following receipt of the report of the Joint Area Review which sets out failures in the effectiveness of the management of child protection services at the most senior level within the Council.... The Panel found that the effect of the Direction of the Secretary of State on 1 December 2008, which it had no reason to suppose was not valid and lawful, was to remove the responsibility for all duties and functions of your post as Director of Children and Young People's Services. The Panel further found that no significant elements of that post could be exercised outside of the effect of

that direction.... The Panel found that the relationship of trust and confidence in you had been fundamentally breached as a consequence of the summary judgement and main findings of the Joint Area Review which identified a catalogue of shortcomings across the service. In particular the Panel had regard to the lack of effective supervision and management within the service e.g. child protection planning and assessment.... The Panel noted that the Joint Area Review recognised substantial failings within other agencies but were not able to comment as they were not within its remit.... Therefore the decision of the Panel is that sufficient evidence was presented ... to justify summary dismissal with immediate effect.[54]

In essence, the only reasons and evidence given by Haringey Council for Sharon Shoesmith's dismissal were the action taken by the Secretary of State and the recent rapid joint area review led by Ofsted. In the statement above, the council presented no evidence or argument based on information it held within itself about Sharon Shoesmith's performance.

This may not be surprising when it is also known, as reported in the later judicial review High Court proceedings, that after the November serious case review case conference, Haringey Council's Chief Executive had taken Sharon Shoesmith out for dinner to thank her for handling the press conference, and on the same evening she was telephoned by the lead children's services councillor who complimented her on handling the press conference interviews so well. Mr Young, the council's Assistant Chief Executive, and who only a few weeks later was to send Sharon Shoesmith the disciplinary hearing letter, also emailed on the night after the press conference, 'Hope all is OK ... think you did very well on the news tonight'. She also received an email from Paul Ennals, Chief Executive of the National Children's Bureau, commenting: 'Well done, Sharon, on how you have been handling the media attention over this case. Seriously tricky stuff, but you have been getting the tone just right.'[55] Here was someone, Sharon Shoesmith, who was being widely thanked and appreciated. But this did not last for long.

Sharon Shoesmith appealed within the council's procedures against her dismissal, and a panel of councillors heard her appeal over three days in January 2009. They upheld the decision that she should be dismissed, largely restating the reasons for dismissal given after the initial disciplinary hearing. The letter recording the findings and decision of the appeal panel also noted that:

> The Panel reached its own independent conclusions without any outside influence. In particular, the Panel had not taken account of any press reporting and had expressed its displeasure about material reported in the press at the time of this hearing....The Panel appreciated that you had submitted information that questioned the validity of the JAR's [joint area review] conclusions. The Panel also noted that the JAR records substantial failings in services other than Haringey [*presumably meaning health services and the police*]. However, this Panel had no opportunity to verify your information through questioning the authors of the JAR.[56]

As noted above, the media coverage at the time of Sharon Shoesmith's appeal hearing within Haringey Council focused on how much she might get paid as compensation if her appeal was successful. The *Evening Standard* report included quotes from the leader of the Liberal Democrat group within Labour-controlled Haringey Council and from Lynne Featherstone, the local Liberal Democrat MP, reflecting the continuing Party political dimension to the 'Baby P story':

> Robert Gurrie, leader of the Liberal Democrats on Haringey Council, said today: 'Residents will be rightly outraged if Sharon Shoesmith gets a large payout as a result of her failures. She has to be seen to be paying for all the gross failures made under her watch – dismissal without compensation'. Lynne Featherstone, the local MP and leading critic of Haringey's handling of the case, said: 'Sharon Shoesmith should not receive a penny. I hope she does not succeed with this appeal'.[57]

With her dismissal from Haringey Council now confirmed, Sharon Shoesmith lodged an appeal to the Employment Tribunal, but it was never heard as she also lodged a judicial review application with the High Court about the process of her dismissal. This was heard first and was subsequently followed by a Court of Appeal judgment that she had been wrongfully dismissed (more of this later).

But it was not only Sharon Shoesmith who was to be dismissed. Gillie Christou and Maria Ward had previously been the subject of disciplinary investigations within Haringey Council a year before in April and May 2008 following the death of Peter Connelly. They had each been given written warnings after it was found that there were omissions in recording, and during one time of three weeks the contact frequency with Peter was not as planned, but that there was no gross misconduct. This process and the outcomes had been agreed with the Council's Leader, Chief Executive, Head of Legal Services and Head of Human Relations.[58] It might be assumed, therefore, that that was the conclusion to these disciplinary processes. But with the media clamour for further sackings continuing, Ita O'Donovan, the council's Chief Executive, re-opened the disciplinary proceedings with a former Director of Social Services from elsewhere in London brought in to review and advise. The outcome was that they were subjected again to disciplinary hearings, and this time they were each dismissed, as were the council's Deputy Director for Children and Families (Cecilia Hitchen) and the Head for Children's Safeguarding (Clive Preece). The net capturing anyone in Haringey Council's children's services had been thrown wider so that anyone who could be seen as having had any management or professional role that might be seen to have related to Peter Connelly was subsequently dismissed.

As Sharon Shoesmith noted in 2012, when Maria Ward and Gillie Christou had their Employment Tribunal case fail:

> The new disciplinary processes led to both Gillie and Maria being dismissed in a blaze of publicity along with others *The Sun* had campaigned to sack. The crucial legal act is that Gillie and Maria were tried twice on the same evidence and subjected to 'double jeopardy'.[59]

Gillie Christou had 26 years' experience as a social worker and team manager. Maria Ward had five years' experience of front-line social work. These were people who had assisted and protected hundreds and thousands of children in their careers as social workers. They were also much respected by their colleagues in children's services. Andrew Anthony, in an extensive feature in *The Observer* in August 2009, noted that 'one child protection police officer told me that Ward was one of the best she had worked with'.[60] But their careers were now prematurely, punitively and primitively ended.

The line management chart below shows how, right through the organisation of Haringey Council's children's services, a complete tranche of managers and practitioners were punished and penalised. Although Peter Connelly had died in August 2007, it was only 16 months later, when the media fury started, in November 2008, with *The Sun* campaigning for sackings, that suspensions and then dismissals took place within Haringey Council.

Line management list showing who was dismissed

Resigned

Leader of the Council (George Mehan)

Lead Councillor for Children's Services (Liz Santry)

All dismissed

Director of Children's Services (Sharon Shoesmith)

Deputy Director, Children and Families (Cecilia Hitchen)

Head of Safeguarding (Clive Preece)

Team manager (Gillie Christou)

Social worker (Maria Ward)

Although it was Sharon Shoesmith and the social workers and their managers who were ultimately dismissed, a solicitor within Haringey Council had also been given a written warning but continued to be employed. Although not a hidden part of the story, the part played by Haringey's legal services has received relatively little press, political or public attention.

On two occasions following injuries to Peter, social workers and their managers sought, as would have been required from within the council, legal advice about whether there were grounds to make an application to the court through care proceedings to have Peter removed from the care of his mother. Although the media often claim that social workers can remove – 'snatch' – children from families, this is not so, despite the headlines:

> State child snatchers: As social workers hand back a child they falsely claim was abused, an investigation exposes one of the great scandals of our age. *Daily Mail* readers will have been horrified to read the story of the South Gloucestershire couple whose two young children were removed from them because social workers thought their son's bone fractures must have been caused by physical abuse.[61]

Just a moment's informed reflection would undermine the either uninformed or mischievous and deliberately misleading argument in Christopher Booker's piece above in the *Daily Mail*. First, it would not have been social workers but specialist doctors who would have carried out the examinations and tests about the injuries to the children and who would have then submitted their diagnosis and assessment to the court. And second, social workers do not have the power to 'snatch' children from families (although if it is urgent, police officers can take this action). Social workers have to apply to and make an argument in the family courts that on the balance of probabilities to protect a child, the court should order that the child be removed from the care of the parents. This is a dramatic and drastic action and one that courts do not readily or easily agree to take. It is almost always contentious and contested by parents.

It is why councils require that social workers seek legal advice and guidance before the council will make an application for care proceedings in the court. If the proceedings were likely to be unsuccessful, they would not be initiated. The same happens, for example, with criminal proceedings, where the police present their evidence to the Crown Prosecution Service, and where a decision is then taken about whether the evidence is likely to lead to a successful prosecution. For example, the police, with the Crown Prosecution Service, decided they did not have the evidence to prosecute Tracey Connelly or anyone else following Peter's injuries in December 2006 and in June 2007.

The view taken by the solicitors in Haringey Council's legal services department in summer 2007 was that, despite the concerns of the social workers who knew Peter and his family, there was insufficient evidence for successful care proceedings. But legal services within Haringey Council were in some disarray and difficulty, with an inexperienced locum solicitor with limited supervision and little experienced management oversight.[62] It was stated that:

> 16 Nov 2008: *The Sunday Telegraph*: ...The senior lawyer at Haringey council is facing questions over his role in the Baby P tragedy after it emerged that just nine days before the toddler's death his department advised that the child should not be taken into care. At a meeting of council officials on July 25 last year [2007], a lawyer advised social workers that the evidence that Baby P was being abused was not strong enough to warrant removing the child from his mother. On August 3, Baby P was found dead. One lawyer has been given a written warning, as have two social workers. John Suddaby, the head of legal services at Haringey, north London, admitted last night to *The Sunday Telegraph* that it was 'of concern' that such advice had been given....The executive summary [of the first serious case review], which was disclosed last week, suggests that:
>
> - One of the factors in Baby P's death was a delay in holding legal meetings and in providing legal advice

on whether social workers could justify steps to have the toddler removed from his mother.

- Legal advice was given by recently recruited lawyers whose work was not checked by a senior member of staff.
- The council was short of experienced specialist child protection lawyers and did not have the systems in place to obtain advice from outside firms.[63]

In the first serious case review report there were seven recommendations for legal services in Haringey Council, including that 'pending a strategic review, Legal Services should ensure that sufficient numbers of lawyers with strong experience of acting for a local authority in child care proceedings are recruited or alternative methods of service provision are explored'.[64] Strangely and surprisingly, the re-commissioned second serious case review, required by Mr Balls and completed and reported only four months later in March 2009, had no recommendations at all for Haringey Council's legal services department. However, in the text of the second serious case review report it is stated that 'Legal services accept completely that the service in this case was inefficient and did not meet the standard and they have made improvements to prevent a recurrence'.[65]

But no recommendations at all for legal services? As will be seen later, it was not only the council's legal services that received no recommendations in the second serious case review as, unlike in the first serious case review report, there were also no specific recommendations for NHS organisations or for the Metropolitan Police. All the recommendations instead were for the LSCB and, in particular, for Haringey Council's children and young people's services. The focus and attention in the second serious case review, as with the media and political focus and attention, had now fallen overwhelmingly and almost exclusively on social workers and the council's children's services.

Sharon Shoesmith made a judicial review application to challenge the process of her dismissal, and she, Maria Ward, Gillie Christou and Cecilia Hitchen each made applications to the Employment Tribunal to challenge their dismissals. These provided a further opportunity for

The Sun to attack the social workers, feeding off the arguments put by Haringey Council in support of its change of mind when, after previously giving the social workers formal warnings, it then later decided they should be dismissed. *The Sun's* coverage in September 2010 at the time of the Employment Tribunal hearing, over a line of photographs of 'tortured ... little Peter', 'liar ... Tracey Connelly', 'fired ... Gillian Christou' and 'failures ... Maria Ward', was 'EVIL BABY P MUM'S LIES "JUST ACCEPTED": Social worker's bruise blunder'.[66]

The Guardian report at the same time noted that Gillie Christou was critical of the 'family support model to aid Peter's mother', and that, 'in hindsight this was a wholly inappropriate way to deal with child protection cases', and 'she also said working in Haringey was "never easy", with social workers overstretched and the number of children on the child protection register in the borough soaring 39% in the first half of 2007'. She continued, 'Peter Connelly was one of many children from deprived backgrounds we were dealing with.... Unfortunately his case did not present as being exceptional prior to his death.'[67]

A BBC report summarised the Employment Tribunal hearing and findings:

> Mrs Christou and Ms Ward were sacked after an investigation revealed there was a period in mid-2007 when they did not know where Peter was. The hearing was told Peter's mother said she had taken her son to visit her sick uncle in Cricklewood, north-west London, despite being told to return home. Ms Ward was found to have failed to meet a requirement to see Peter at least once a fortnight. Mrs Christou had argued both she and Ms Ward had been sacked to appease the press and politicians. She said: 'Haringey were wrong to make us scapegoats and to add our names to the list of Tracey Connelly's victims'. The pair admitted failing to ensure Peter was visited regularly enough, failing to keep adequate records and losing contact with the family at one stage. The employment tribunal conceded that there 'may have been media pressure and those involved

had in mind the tragic death'. But it found that 'poor professional judgement' was responsible for both sackings. The panel was ruling on whether Haringey Council was right to dismiss the pair's initial internal appeal against losing their jobs. The inquiry criticised Haringey Council for its 'inadequate' disciplinary proceedings. But it concluded: 'It is not our view that those involved in the appeal panels bowed to the pressure to which we have referred.'[68]

After their Employment Tribunal applications challenging their dismissals failed in October 2010, Gillie Christou and Maria Ward appealed, with their appeal against the Tribunal findings not heard until February 2012 and with the outcome announced in May 2012. The outcome of the Employment Tribunal appeal hearings was an upholding of the earlier Employment Tribunal judgment that they had been fairly dismissed. They then made unsuccessful applications to the Court of Appeal in relation to the Employment Tribunal decisions.

The General Social Care Council (GSCC) also considered Gillie Christou and Maria Ward's registration as social workers. Without being registered with the GSCC they could not be employed again as social workers. In 2012 Sharon Shoesmith reflected on the GSCC's conduct review of Gillie Christou and Maria Ward's registration:

> Maria and Gillie were subject to a disciplinary process in April and May 2008. This was conducted properly by their managers and overseen by the chief executive using a 'simplified' version of the disciplinary process. The 'simplified process' is a part of Haringey's human resources policy and procedures and is used if there is no evidence of gross misconduct. Having studied Maria's involvement in the case, it was the view of the chief executive, the leader of the council, human resources officers and me that there was no gross misconduct.... In Gillie's case there was never any question that she had committed gross misconduct. As a team manager she had

a 26 year exemplary career behind her in one of the most challenging settings the country can offer. However, it was thought she should go through the simplified process such was Haringey's desire to do things properly. The GSCC was informed that there was no gross misconduct involved and having looked at the case it took no action either, that is not until after the public reaction.[69]

Following the GSCC Conduct Committee hearings in May 2010, which considered the professional conduct of Maria Ward and Gillie Christou, the outcome was that, each having already been suspended for 16 months following their dismissals by Haringey Council and the council's referring them to the GSCC, Maria Ward was suspended for a further two months and Gillie Christou for a further four months.

The GSCC found that for Maria Ward she had a backlog of entering recordings on 'Framework-I', the council's children's social care database, had not followed the child protection plan frequency of visits between 1 June and 11 July 2007, and had not ensured there was an adequate replacement for the childminder following her withdrawal on 23 July 2007, and that Maria Ward was not aware of the precise location of Peter Connelly for a period of time (it was, in fact, only days) in July 2007. Similar issues were identified for Gillie Christou.

At some length, however, the GSCC Conduct Committee noted mitigating factors in relation to Gillie Christou and Maria Ward, including that:

- Tracey Connelly was a skilled and manipulative liar intent on deceiving any agency and anyone responsible for assessing her parenting skills....
- ... the Registrant did bring some of her concerns regarding Peter's case, her workload and her recording to the attention of management, and took advice accordingly....
- ... the Framework-I system was not an easy one to use and caused problems for many people [and] the Registrant did maintain handwritten notes....

- ... the Registrant's actions and/or inactions must be viewed in the context of the working environment at Haringey as a whole – it was, to say the least, a challenging environment; there were shortages of staff, excessive workloads and a lack of managerial support and supervision; the family support model in relation to child protection was perhaps adopted too generically within Haringey....
- ... not only were there systemic failings within Haringey but failures of other outside agencies....
- ... the Registrant has an unblemished record as regards her professional conduct both before and after this series of events.[70]

Much of what happened at the GSCC hearing will send a chill down the spine of many social workers and others who work to protect children. Explanation and reason can be played down as mitigation. When a child dies, actions are intensely scrutinised, but they are scrutinised in isolation. It is not overall workload, performance and context that are examined. It is actions with regard to this one child, this one case. Judgement is made based on measuring performance judged against the perfect meeting of the myriad procedures and processes to be followed, even if time and resources meant that it was impossible to do everything that now, in retrospect, is being judged. And Haringey was a pressurised place in which to seek to protect children, as graphically told in Andrew Anthony's piece in *The Observer* in August 2009 with quotes such as, "'I think [the social worker] was in a fog", says [another] social worker, "because it was like that sometimes. We used to call it 'Nam' – 'Tott Nam'. Because it was just constant. You'd come out sometimes and you'd be absolutely exhausted. You'd think, 'Oh, I've lived another day'"'.[71]

The GSCC hearing, however, gave *The Sun* the opportunity for further comment and with yet another opportunity to print a photograph of Maria Ward:

Baby P bunglers can apply for new jobs. Two social workers whose blunders led to Baby P's death could be back at work within weeks.... Ward and Christou admitted misconduct. They were sacked in April 2009 after a *Sun* petition but plan to sue for unfair dismissal. They could start hunting for news jobs in weeks and have vulnerable children placed in their care.... [Baby P's] gran fumed: 'Allowing these two to practice again makes my blood boil'. Michelle Elliot of charity Kidscape accused the GSCC of 'defending their own'.[72]

The GSCC Conduct Committee were clearly aware, as inevitably they were bound to be, of the media-generated public vindictiveness aimed at the social workers, and it commented that:

The Committee considered whether the Registrant's conduct was sufficient as to merit removal. Not only did the Committee consider that such a course was disproportionate to the facts admitted at this hearing, but if it did remove it felt that it would only be doing so to satisfy a perceived public blame and punishment for a Registrant who does not present a continuing risk – that would be wrong. Her conduct was not so serious that removal was required.[73]

The stance, judgement and opinion of the GSCC, therefore, was considerably at variance with the actions taken by Haringey Council to dismiss Maria Ward and Gillie Christou. The GSCC Conduct Committee recognised the pressure it was under, as exemplified by *The Sun* reference above, but made an explicit statement that it was not having its decision determined by this pressure, albeit it should still be remembered that it *had* suspended Maria Ward for 18 months and Gillie Christou for 20 months.

But, as noted by the GSCC's Conduct Committee, there were failings by other agencies. What actions were taken by those agencies and the professional conduct committees of the workers involved with Peter Connelly? As far as is known, no disciplinary action was taken against any of the police officers who had any part or responsibility for the two criminal investigations into Peter's injuries before he died, despite the criminal investigations apparently not ascertaining who was living in the Connelly household. With regard to the first criminal investigation, it was lost sight of mid-stream. In the second investigation, according to the first serious case review report, 'unfortunately there was a week's delay before photographs were taken, the elder siblings were not interviewed, and [Tracey Connelly] was not asked specifically about the household composition'.[74]

With regard to the NHS organisations and professionals involved with Peter, no disciplinary or professional conduct action was taken against any manager (despite, as will be seen later, Dr Al-Zayyat being appointed to a post when she did not meet the requirements for the job), but Peter's GP and the paediatrician, Dr Al-Zayyat, who saw him at St Ann's Clinic, both of whom saw Peter days before he died, were each reported to their professional body, the GMC.

Dr Ikwueke, the GP, was suspended and his professional conduct was considered at a GMC hearing in July 2010. It was concluded that he had 'failed to consider the possibility of child abuse, failed to refer the baby for urgent paediatric assessment and failed to share information with other professionals'.[75] In July 2011, one year on, the *Evening Standard* reported 'GP who bungled Baby P case to be reinstated', with a report that 'former patient Justin Hinchcliffe, chairman of Tottenham Conservatives said, "The authorities were desperate to pin the blame on someone. But he was the first to raise the alarm about Baby Peter. He has been scapegoated. If he had done anything then he would have been struck off – he wasn't".'[76] Dr Ikwueke's suspension was ended at the GMC case review hearing in July 2011 and he was able to resume his practice as a GP.

Dr Al-Zayyat, the paediatrician, was suspended but later withdrew herself from the GMC register, which meant she was never formally removed from the register by the GMC. This is discussed in more detail later.

In 2012, referring back to 'Baby P', the GMC published guidance after doctors had been complaining that there was a 'climate of fear' about child protection. They were concerned that, following Peter Connelly's death, doctors were being penalised for not acting on and reporting child abuse, but also, as happened with Dr Southall, a paediatrician who was publicly hounded and then disciplined by the

GMC for identifying possible child abuse,[77] penalised if they did act on suspicions of abuse.* Heather Payne, a consultant paediatrician and a member of Professionals Against Child Abuse, noted that 'people do not want to do child protection as they know it might end up in court'.[78] There was to be difficulty in the future in recruiting community paediatricians as well as social workers to work in child protection services. Niall Dickson, Chief Executive of the GMC, and who had previously been the BBC's social affairs correspondent (when he left he was replaced by Alison Holt), commented that child protection was a 'complex and emotionally challenging area of work for doctors'.[79]

It was also a complex and challenging area of work for social workers and their managers, and in addition to being complex and challenging, it was controversial and professionally catastrophic. For Sharon Shoesmith there were further proceedings ahead. She initiated a High Court judicial review alleging that proper process had not been followed in determining her dismissal from Haringey Council with Haringey Council, Ofsted and the Secretary of State for Children, Schools and Families each named as defendants in the judicial review application.

The judicial review proceedings ran and ran, starting in October 2009 but with judgment not given until April 2010, a Friday when the BBC had arranged that I be at the High Court of Justice on The Strand in London to give my instant comments on television and radio to the judgment. I, along with many others, was wrong-footed. The judgment that she had not succeeded in her judicial review was not as many anticipated.

---

* Dr Southall was a paediatrician and Professor of Paediatric Medicine who was in the spotlight through much of the time the 'Baby P story' was at its peak. He was not associated with the 'Baby P story'. Indeed, he was at the other end of the spectrum of media and public concerns about child protection. The doctors and others who knew Peter Connelly were castigated for not identifying child abuse. Dr Southall was campaigned against because it was argued he too readily and incorrectly identified child abuse. There was little media comment, however, and certainly not in the tabloid newspapers, bringing into focus the challenges, conflicts and controversy of the 'too little ["Baby P"] – too much [Dr Southall]' debate on the identification of child abuse.

This real-life courtroom drama was seen by some as a game of two halves, with the result not reflecting the flow of the match. It was also a match that went into extra time because of repeated failings within Ofsted to identify and declare relevant materials to the court. Indeed Ofsted and its behaviour and performance increasingly became 'the story' within the judicial review proceedings.

But at the start in October 2009, Sharon Shoesmith was on the back foot, with BBC headlines such as 'Minister defends Baby P sacking'[80] and 'Baby P boss ran "worst ever" unit',[81] and with *The Sun* contributing the headline of '**1.6M "WRONG"**' and that:

> The barrister acting for Sharon Shoesmith yesterday poured scorn on petitions by an incredible 1.6m *Sun* readers. They demanded the sacking of Shoesmith and others responsible for failing to protect tragic baby Peter. A team of *Sun* reporters led by Political Editor George Pascoe-Watson delivered *The Sun's* petition to Downing Street last November. But James Maurici told the High Court: 'Petitions from a national newspaper are not properly evidence of public concern. They are evidence of the expression of uninformed feeling on a very emotional issue.'[82]

The judicial review was scheduled to last for three days between 7 and 9 October 2009, but on 12 October the BBC carried a news report that 'Shoesmith demands Ofsted reports ... the request comes after allegations the assessment of Haringey's children services was secretly downgraded from "good" to "inadequate".... Her lawyers argue she was unfairly and unjustly dismissed after Mr Balls allowed himself to be influenced by a "media storm and witch-hunt" over the Baby P case.... In a statement [Ofsted said] "Ofsted completely refutes the allegations that it manipulated any results".'[83]

It was stated that:

> *The Guardian* revealed ... that a whistleblower had claimed an official report on Haringey children's services was secretly downgraded from "good" to "inadequate".[84]

The Ofsted chief, Christine Gilbert, will be ordered to attend an emergency parliamentary committee to answer questions that inspectors were forced to downgrade an official review of Haringey's children's services after the death of Baby P was made public. Barry Shearman, chair of the children, schools and families committee, was today urgently seeking approval to set up the meeting after receiving leaked documents suggesting that Ofsted had at least twice marked Haringey down following the outcry over Baby P's death.[85]

But it was now to get worse for Ofsted. Ofsted was increasingly in trouble within the judicial review processes for failing to declare documents, claiming documentation did not exist which it then very belatedly found, and also it had been claimed that an instruction had been given within Ofsted to delete emails related to the Haringey inspection and to 'Baby P'.[86] It was stated by the Ofsted senior manager who had given this instruction that this was because of concern that the emails might become known to the media that were heavily engaged in reporting about 'Baby P'.[87]

Here was an inspectorate that, even if not undertaking deliberate deception, was apparently disorganised and in some disarray, and was casual and careless in providing information to the court. Whatever the reasons, it did not reflect well on a national inspectorate and its leadership, as was noted in November 2009 by the *London Evening Standard* in a report which it headed 'Shoesmith edges to victory':

> An unhappy Christmas is brewing in the household of Christine Gilbert and Tony McNulty [*who had been the minister at the Home Office responsible for the police, and Minister for London*] ... Ms Gilbert is Ofsted's chief inspector and was closely involved in the watchdog's critical report into Haringey council's social services department last December in the wake of the Baby P scandal. This report was relied on by the Children's Secretary Ed Balls to order the dismissal of the council's director of children's services, Sharon Shoesmith, which she is currently

contesting in the High Court. Before ordering Haringey to sack Ms Shoesmith, he received a verbal briefing from Ms Gilbert herself.[88]

The *London Evening Standard* then reported the concerns about Ofsted:

> Ofsted was forced to make a grovelling apology to the High Court after admitting it had failed to produce hand-written notes written by one of the inspectors who carried out an emergency inspection of Haringey at Mr Balls' request. It also admitted that another inspector held a draft of the Haringey report on his computer – a report that had been sought by Ms Shoesmith's legal team since August. Ofsted first claimed the report was of no consequence and then said it did not exist. And then it told the truth. There is a whiff of the Ofsted report having been spiced-up, possibly to meet Mr Balls' apparent wish to remove Ms Shoesmith. This has not been said explicitly in court but Mr Justice Foskett did say yesterday: 'Suggestions have been made that these drafts have been altered in some way'.[89]

So what did the judge think of it all? According to the *London Evening Standard*:

> Mr Justice Foskett appears a mild-tempered man but his face was noticeably reddening with anger when events unfolded before him in court 76. The existence of the extra documents – which could have a major bearing on Ms Shoesmith's claim for judicial review – only came to light when Ofsted was in the process of responding to a freedom of information request....The judge demanded that Ofsted spend the next 14 days ensuring it does not hold any other documents pertinent to the Shoesmith case, and expects a signed letter from an Ofsted boss guaranteeing this to be the case.

It concluded:

> Yesterday's developments will have added to the sense
> of injustice that Ms Shoesmith claims to have suffered
> at the hands of Mr Balls and Ofsted. If the judgement
> eventually goes in her favour, Ms Gilbert could well join
> Mr Balls in the hall of fame.

The *Daily Mail* picked up on the same story in November 2009,
but with a story line that presented Sharon Shoesmith as primarily
interested in getting a big financial settlement following her dismissal.
Getting a financial settlement would have been important to her.
As had been reported, 'despite stories about multi-million pound
pensions, she now has nothing – no savings, no income, and no
pension. She is being supported by family and friends before she
can get back on her feet.'[90] Getting back on her feet was difficult,
however, when she was finding that she was unemployable and had
become apparently professionally untouchable.[91]

This was no Bob Diamond, Chief Executive of Barclays Bank,
who, in 2012, resigned when it was found he was heading up an
organisation that had deliberately and inappropriately manipulated
the financial markets. He was already very rich, but was still stated
to have been given a further £2 million when he left the bank and
the bank the previous year paid £5.7 million to cover his tax bills.[92]
This was no Rebekah Brooks, resigning from News International in
2011 when it was found that she had been heading up an organisation
where there had been deliberate and intentional illegal acts including
phone hacking and with herself charged with perverting the course
of justice. But she was still rich and able to retreat and retire to her
Cotswold estate with a pay-off reported to be £10.8 million.[93]
Sharon Shoesmith and the social workers were never alleged to
have deliberately committed any intentional criminal or other
wrongful act. The allegations against them were essentially of errors
of judgement, good people who (may have) got it wrong. But they
were left destitute and unemployable.

It was the seeking of a financial payment, however, which was the
tabloid story line in the *Daily Mail*:

Disgraced Baby P council chief could pocket huge payout after Ofsted 'destroyed draft report': Sharon Shoesmith hopes to use a secret report into Haringey's performance over the Baby P scandal to win a six-figure compensation deal. The sacked boss of Haringey children's services is demanding to see a draft report by Ofsted, which insiders claim was binned in the wake of Baby P's death as it was too favourable to the council. According to a whistleblower at the children's inspectorate, the initial review into the council's performance rated it 'good', but in later editions it was downgraded to 'inadequate' due to the furore over the death of Baby P.... But the 2008 assessment was then hurriedly deleted and rewritten to condemn Haringey as inadequate with just one star in the key category, insiders say....The documents are the second set of draft reports Ofsted has tried to keep secret. It was criticised earlier this month by Mr Justice Foskett for withholding drafts of the emergency inspection report ordered by Mr Balls.[94]

So, in November 2009 it may have looked as though Sharon Shoesmith's judicial review would be successful and Ofsted was in trouble. The materials belatedly submitted to the court by Ofsted did indeed indicate that its report on Haringey's children's services was substantially strengthened in its criticisms between the first draft, prepared by the inspectors who had actually undertaken the Haringey inspection, and, apparently after 17 iterations, the final version, which was shaped by Ofsted senior managers before being submitted to Mr Balls. The Ofsted documentation also showed there had been engagement between Mr Balls' DCSF senior civil servants and Ofsted senior managers as the Ofsted report was amended and amended. The numerous draft versions of the report also showed how more and more the focus was heavily on Haringey Council, its children's services and with comments added about the leadership of these services, and how less and less attention was given to the concerns about NHS organisations and the Metropolitan Police. This was despite this joint area review of child protection in Haringey being a joint inspection of all the services and agencies conducted together between Ofsted, the Healthcare Commission and Her Majesty's Inspectorate of Constabulary.

The scene was set for Mr Justice Foskett's judgment that came on a Friday afternoon in April 2010. To many, including possibly the reporters at the *Evening Standard* and *Daily Mail* quoted above, it was a surprise. The BBC News website immediately ran the story with the headline 'Baby Peter sacking was lawful, the High Court rules' and went on:

> The former head of children's services at the north London council had claimed she was made a scapegoat and unlawfully sacked after a media outcry. But at the High Court, Mr Justice Foskett said the decision to remove Ms Shoesmith 'could not be impugned on the grounds of unfairness'. He said, 'I have rejected as "too simplistic" the suggestion that the Secretary of State's decision to commission the Ofsted inspection was driven by "party politics", as indeed I have also rejected the suggestion that he was improperly influenced in making the decision he did on 1 December 2008 by a petition presented to him a few days previously by a national newspaper.'[95]

But the judge also noted that he dismissed Sharon Shoesmith's application 'with a lurking sense of unease' and 'I cannot think that any party will truly look back at how matters were handled in this case with complete satisfaction'. Mr Justice Foskett expressed his concern that Mr Balls was 'persuaded to offer his opinion' that Ms Shoesmith should be dismissed. But he said he could find 'no sustainable basis' for the suggestion that there was 'political or other improper interference in the Ofsted inspection, or the report-writing process by, or on behalf of, the Secretary of State'.

However, as the report continues, the reasons for the judge's 'lurking sense of unease' become clear:

There were 'strong grounds' for thinking that Ms Shoesmith and others subjected to the Ofsted inspection did not have a fair opportunity to explain their position – but that 'did not invalidate what Ofsted did'.... The judge expressed concern over Haringey's decision to dismiss her, but said it was for an employment tribunal to decide whether she had been treated unfairly by the council. He said: 'In a nutshell, I have not been satisfied the procedures at Haringey gave the appearance of fairness'.[96]

It was reported that 'the judgement has been welcomed by Ofsted and the Children's Secretary, Ed Balls, but Ms Shoesmith may appeal'. Mr Balls was quoted as saying: 'It is clear from the judgement that my motivations were the right ones and I have acted in a proper and right way', and Christine Gilbert was quoted as saying: 'I am pleased that the judge's conclusion is clear: Ofsted inspection process has been vindicated.... We carried out a robust inspection, came to a sound conclusion based on the evidence and acted fairly'.[97]

The headlines the next day which followed the judgment were not unpredictable even if they were not always accurate (the judge noted that it was for an Employment Tribunal to determine whether Sharon Shoesmith had been treated unfairly by Haringey), with *The Sun* celebrating the judgment, and also applauding itself for its part in the outcome, and having a full page with the headline '**SHOESMITH LOSES CASE: Baby P bungler fairly sacked, says judge ... but she demands STILL demands £1m**'. It went on:

> Baby Peter's death in August 2007 horrified the nation. *The Sun*'s petition for the sacking of Shoesmith and other bunglers who betrayed him became the biggest in newspaper history. Last night Haringey MP Lynne Featherstone renewed her demand for a full-blown public inquiry into what went wrong in Shoesmith's department. The Lib Dem said of the High Court judge ruling against Shoesmith, who still plans an industrial tribunal case: "I'm very pleased. She was the accountable person".[98]

The Sun, 24 April 2010, p 10 (and where *The Sun* shows several of its previous front pages)

The *Daily Mail* seemed to realise more than *The Sun*'s headline writers that the judgment did not mean, as *The Sun* claimed, that Sharon Shoesmith was 'fairly sacked'. Rather it noted that:

> Disgraced Baby P official Sharon Shoesmith was yesterday handed fresh ammunition in her £1.5m compensation battle. A High Court judge criticised Haringey Council for rushing to sack its controversial director of children's services after Children's Secretary Ed Balls ordered her removal.[99]

The *Daily Mail* also noted that Haringey Council was facing unfair dismissal claims from Cecilia Hitchen, Colin Preece, Maria Ward

---

and Gillie Christou, all of whom the council had dismissed in April 2009, and that Dr Al-Zayyat was claiming unfair dismissal from Great Ormond Street Hospital NHS Trust.

In September 2010 it was reported[100] that Sharon Shoesmith had been given leave to appeal against the High Court judicial review judgment. The judge who heard the judicial review was clearly not totally happy with what he had heard about Ofsted, the Secretary of State or Haringey Council. He rejected their claims that Sharon Shoesmith should meet their legal costs of £350,000 and said in relation to the substantive judgments he had made, that 'it is by no means fanciful that the Court of Appeal may differ from my view'.

Sharon Shoesmith did appeal. The appeal was heard in March 2011 and the Court of Appeal gave judgment on 27 May 2011. It was a damning judgment for Mr Balls, the by now former Secretary of State for Children, and for Haringey Council, both having been found to have acted inappropriately through procedural unfairness. With regard to Ofsted, the Court of Appeal upheld the earlier judicial review decision that Ofsted had fulfilled its duty of fairness.[101]

In his final observations, Lord Justice Kay noted 'I cannot leave this case without commenting on the way in which Ms Shoesmith was treated'. He quoted Lord Justice Sedley from another case:

> It seems that the making of a public sacrifice to deflect press and public obloquy, which is what happened to the appellant, remains an unaccepted expedient of public administration in this country. (*Gibb v Maidstone and Tunbridge Wells NHS Trust* [2010] EWCA Civ 678, at para 42)

Lord Justice Kay then commented specifically in relation to Sharon Shoesmith:

> In my view this is what happened in the present case. Those involved in areas such as social work and healthcare are particularly vulnerable to such treatment. This is not to say that I consider Ms Shoesmith to be blameless or that I have a view as to the extent of her or

anyone else's blameworthiness. This is not the business of this Court. However, it is our task to adjudicate upon the application and fairness of procedures adopted by public authorities when legitimate causes for concern arise, as they plainly did in this case. Whatever her shortcomings may have been (and, I repeat, I cannot say), she was entitled to be treated lawfully and fairly and not simply and summarily scapegoated.[102]

So there it is. Official. Sharon Shoesmith was scapegoated.

And how did the press react? Here are some of the tabloid headlines and coverage at the time:

> SHE'S OVER THE MOON: HE'S UNDER THE EARTH. Shoesmith to get £2.5m; Baby P's family still mourn. [*The Sun*][103]

> No shame: The idea that anyone can be 'absolutely thrilled' over any aspect of the tragic Baby P case speaks volumes about Sharon Shoesmith.... She has pursued her claim for a payout with a zeal that was woefully lacking from her department's approach to child protection.... Ed Balls acted decisively when he fired her and he was right to do so. The buck stopped with her. **Shoesmith should have done the decent thing in the first place – and resigned BEFORE she was sacked**. [*The Sun*][104]

> THE £1M SMIRK: Shoesmith set for huge payout – but still won't say sorry for Baby P. [*Daily Mail*][105]

> £1m for shameless Shoesmith. If only she'd fought as hard for children as she did for herself. [*Daily Mail*][106]

> Baby P: SHAME OF CARE BOSS: I'VE NO GUILT: Shoesmith says "I don't do blame": Now her payout may double to £4m. [*News of the World*][107]

Kid's hell can't be dismissed.... A reminder: Baby P died pitifully and painfully at the hands of his warped 'guardians' despite being under the watch of Ms Shoesmith's social workers. Outraged as many will be at this week's legal ruling, we must concentrate on what really matters. The best possible care for children everywhere. Ms Shoesmith believes her victory will give social workers a confidence boost. Others feel it is a sad defeat for public accountability.... Meanwhile, Ms Shoesmith's compensation could make her a multi-millionaire. But as she points out, she was 'never in it for the money'. *So we can surely expect a big donation to children's charities very soon. [News of the World]*[108]

Blame is not just a game, Ms Shoesmith ... where life and death are concerned, especially the lives and deaths of helpless children, there must always be blame and there must always be people who are prepared, in the end, to accept it. [Editorial, *Mail on Sunday*][109]

Of all the press comments on the appeal court judgment, this Editorial comment from the *Mail on Sunday* is possibly the most frightening. It would certainly serve as a rationale and justification for the hostile coverage that every week social workers and other professionals working in the public sector receive in the *Daily Mail* and the *Mail on Sunday*.

What it is saying is that no matter how well you work, no matter how competent and conscientious, and no matter how great your care and commitment, if a child dies, someone should be blamed. The blame is not attached to the person who committed the killing. It is to be allocated to the professionals who had contact with the child. 'There must always be blame and there must always be people willing to accept it.' A patient dies – a doctor or nurse must be to blame. Someone commits a criminal offence – a police officer must be to blame. A child does not pass an exam – it must be the fault of the teacher. A child is killed – it must be a social worker who is to be held accountable. This is the mentality that not only feeds a blame culture but the pages every day of so much of the tabloid press.

But what of Sharon Shoesmith? *The Times* included an interview with her:

> Sharon Shoesmith is not a woman who cries easily. But when she heard that she had won her appeal court case, the tears flowed. "I cried my heart out. I felt at last somebody sees it, somebody understands what I went through, that I was made a scapegoat. I really hope never again will a social worker be vilified like this."[110]

She went on to comment that "Ed Balls had over a year to prepare for it [the response to Peter Connelly's death]. He knew it was coming. We needed someone to steady the ship, not just in Haringey but across the country.... But he was reckless, irresponsible. Instead of a serious response about the nature of children's services, he went the other way. 'She's the one. Everything else is fine. Get rid of her and all be well' was his reaction".[111]

The Guardian front-page headline was 'Shoesmith turns on Balls after court win: Baby P "scapegoat" in line for £500,000 payout as judges criticise former minister'.[112] The £500,000 noted in *The Guardian* is somewhat short of the £4 million now being stated in the tabloids, and *The Guardian* report on its inside pages is also rather more measured, with a headline of 'Euphoria but regrets for child care director who was sacked over death of Baby Peter':

> Shoesmith, who was director of children's services when [Peter Connelly] died in August 2007 said: "I'm very relieved to read the judgment but this started with a death of child so there's no great joy in that sense. I'm relieved to see that [what I experienced] has been recognised, but always with that sadness at the death of a child at the heart of the story".[113]

The Guardian's Editorial on the same day notes that:

The court of appeal was extremely clear where the blame lay for the way Ms Shoesmith was dismissed. It lay with Mr Balls for rushing his fences too eagerly and Haringey for following him over them too blindly.[114]

But it is hardly sympathetic to Sharon Shoesmith:

> Very few people who have studied the Baby P case in detail will be in much doubt that Ms Shoesmith bears a very serious share of the responsibility for the Baby P case failings and for the unacceptable state of child services in her borough at the time. If proper procedures had been followed it is unlikely she would have remained long in her post or have had any case against her dismissal.

This is a surprising, if not staggering, statement, and from *The Guardian*. It was absolutely 'on message' with the tabloid story line. Sharon Shoesmith carried a special responsibility for what happened to Peter Connelly and she should be sacked, albeit sacked through the proper process.

I was telephoned several times by the media on the morning the Court of Appeal judgment was announced. Standing in a shopping centre car park I gave a live interview to BBC Radio 5. I welcomed the judgment, recalling and remarking on all the bullying and bigotry of the tabloid press. I also said it would never be known whether Sharon Shoesmith should have been dismissed from her post in Haringey as no proper disciplinary process or hearings had taken place and what had happened in dismissing her was now known to have been wrong. I also said that whether or not there was error by Sharon Shoesmith, it did not warrant or justify the terror that *The Sun* unleashed on her and on the social workers. It was a surprise, then, the following day to read the cavalier and dogmatic Editorial in *The Guardian*.

Only four days later, however, *The Guardian* included another comment piece, this time from Patrick Butler, its Society Editor. It was something of a volte-face compared to the previous Editorial:

A powerful warning rang out loud and clear from the appeal court ruling on the dismissal of Sharon Shoesmith, one that politicians would do well to reflect upon before they puff out their chests and promise swift and decisive action in the wake of the next public scandal: 'Accountability is not synonymous with "heads must roll"'.... Shoesmith was brutally removed from her job, without warning and on live TV by children's secretary Ed Balls at the height of Baby Peter hysteria in December 2008, then hastily sacked without compensation by her employers, Haringey council. The appeal judges ruled last week she had been unlawfully dismissed and 'summarily scapegoated'.[115]

Butler went on to comment:

The ruling was not about a legalistic technicality trumping the moral righteousness of Balls' decision, but about the proper exercise of accountability. Social workers and health professionals are particularly vulnerable to the vicious blame games played by the media and politicians, [the Appeal Court judges] noted. Without legal safeguards, who would do these jobs?

And commenting on the parts played by Mr Cameron and Mr Balls, Butler wrote:

Politicians last week showed no sign of having learned from the fiasco. Balls blustered about 'constitutional' issues.... Yet the judges did not question whether Balls had the legal power to remove Shoesmith, but simply pointed out that he used his powers unfairly. Balls, predictably, told reporters: "I would make exactly the same decision today" ... Cameron was whipper-up-in-chief when the Baby Peter hysteria took hold, demanding sackings at the now infamous question time appearance. Balls, too, spotted an opportunity and was happy to collude. For both, the political gains were immediate, the longer-term consequences of their opportunism disastrous.

The consequences of Mr Cameron and Mr Balls tying themselves into *The Sun's* call for vengeance targeted on Sharon Shoesmith and the social workers will be explored in Chapter Five, but one not surprising immediate consequence was that Haringey Council was unable to recruit and retain social workers. It had to send out a plea to other councils asking for help from their social workers to undertake child protection work in Haringey.[116] But other councils were also struggling to recruit and retain social workers within the climate of fear and professional vulnerability that had been created. None of this would have helped keep children safer in Haringey or elsewhere.

It was a danger previously noted in an Editorial in *The Times* in 2010 at the time of Sharon Shoesmith's earlier judicial review hearing:

> [The judge] warned that employment processes could be subverted by political or media pressure unless those involved took extra care to act with "scrupulous fairness". He wondered who might take on the important job of Director of Social Services if they faced being fired.... [*and the Editorial goes on to note*] The system has failed not only Peter Connelly but also people responsible for his care.[117]

Coverage following Court of Appeal judgement

Mr Gove, who by 2011 with a change of government had replaced Mr Balls as Secretary of State for Children, gave a commitment that he would launch a challenge to the Court of Appeal judgment. He failed when the Supreme Court rejected the appeal application in August 2011, and Sharon Shoesmith's successful judicial review stands.[118] *The Sun* called it an 'insult', and reported that 'Mr Balls declared he was "surprised and concerned" [and that] Haringey Council said: "We stand by everything we have done".'[119]

As for Maria Ward and Gillie Christou, who were dismissed in April 2009, in May 2012 their appeals were unsuccessful against an earlier Employment Tribunal judgment in October 2010 that found they were fairly dismissed (the Employment Tribunal application by Cecilia Hitchen in December 2012 was also unsuccessful). The 2010 Employment Tribunal had noted 'there may have been media pressure' but that 'it is not in our view the case that those involved in the appeal panels bowed to the pressure to which we have referred'. There was criticism of Haringey's 'inadequate' disciplinary proceedings, but it was concluded that 'poor professional judgement' was responsible for both the dismissals.[120]

So the story of 'Baby P' continued well beyond November 2008 when it was first shaped and captured by *The Sun*. In 2013, and no doubt beyond, it was still being told. As noted at the beginning of this chapter, the continuation of the story was fed by news about the Employment Tribunal, judicial review and Court of Appeal hearings and judgments and by the hearings before professional conduct committees. It was also fed, as will be noted in the next chapter, by the reports of all the official reviews and inquiries Mr Balls launched in December 2008, and which reported over the subsequent year and beyond.

The 'Baby P story' was also brought into view when other children's social care or child protection concerns arose, with reference made to 'Baby P' as a means of setting the scene for the new story. One example from *The Sun* in September 2009 mentions 'Baby P' and also manages to target Haringey Council with a full front-page headline of: '**ANOTHER HARINGEY SCANDAL**: Baby P council let foster kid live with terrorist' and a 'Sun Says' editorial comment about Sharon Shoesmith headlined 'Good riddance':

> A foster child was sent to live with the leader of the liquid
> bomb airliner pilot – by the SAME council that betrayed

Baby P. Shamed Sharon Shoesmith was children's services boss in Haringey, North London, as evil Abdullah Ahmed Ai, 28, made plans to take kids on doomed flights. An MP raged: "It beggars belief".[121]

The Sun, 12 September 2009, front page

There was also an apparent eagerness by *The Sun* to wind and whip up a continuing hostility towards the Haringey social workers it had specifically decided to target back in November 2008. A headline in *The Sun* in March 2011 read 'Baby P staff are quizzed on own kids'.[122] Who were the 'Baby P staff' who had 'been quizzed over allegations involving their own children'? Anyone reading this headline might reasonably understand that it is apparently about the Haringey social workers and their managers who had involvement with Peter Connelly and who *The Sun* had been naming and shaming and hunting and haunting for the past four years. Wrong, although this may be exactly the impression and message *The Sun* was seeking to give.

The information was provided to *The Sun* by Haringey Council following a freedom of information request from *The Sun*. Maybe *The Sun* was looking to find a new angle to promote its continuation of its 'Baby P' story line. What it was told by the council was that, as in every other council, it had investigated any complaints about care of children made about its own staff. But these complaints were not about the social workers and managers involved with Peter Connelly. Indeed, how could they have been, as, following the demands of *The Sun*, they were all dismissed three years previously in 2009? Still, it gave *The Sun* the opportunity to approach again members of Peter Connelly's family, one of whom it quotes as saying, 'Nothing really surprises us any more but we had all hoped Haringey had learned some lessons from Peter's death. We can only hope these investigations were carried out far more thoroughly than in his case.'[123]

However, not only did *The Sun* major on the 'Baby P story', with its relentless focus on Sharon Shoesmith and Haringey's social workers, but it also, with other tabloid papers, shaped the words used in how the story was told. For example, *The Sun* repeatedly wrote about '*shame*' as in 'SHAMEFUL, disgusting, cowardly and disgraceful' (13 November 2008), '5 WHO HAVE NO SHAME' (15 November 2008), 'Shoesmith shamed in damning Baby P report' (2 December 2008), 'Shameless Shoesmith spotted as new row starts' (12 January 2009), 'Baby P: Shame of care boss' (29 May 2011), and with the first serious case review described as 'a shameful whitewash' (27 October 2010).

The Sun also, as noted above, repeatedly called Sharon Shoesmith and the social workers '*bunglers*'* as in 'Baby P's bungler's grovelling text' (9 October 2009), 'Baby P bunglers can apply for new jobs' (27 May 2010), and '*The Sun*'s petition for the sacking of Shoesmith and the other bunglers ...' (28 May 2011), and this was also a description

---

* 'Bungling' has not, however, been a term reserved by *The Sun* only for social workers. On 11 August 2012, and possibly reflecting the then less warm and close relationship between *The Sun* and the Metropolitan Police following the phone hacking and related inquiries, 'The Sun Says' Editorial noted that 'when the case is over, the Met must answer for those humiliating bungles'. What were these 'bungles'? In 2012, over a period of a week, there was a big police operation with the public and press trying to find a missing schoolgirl, Tia Sharp. She was last seen at her grandmother's house. The police searched the house twice. It was only on a third search that her dead body, which had been there all the time, was found within the house (France, A. [2012] 'UNFORGIVEABLE', *The Sun*, 11 August, pp 1, 6-7 and 12).

picked up and used elsewhere as in 'Bunglers who let a tot "cook to death"'.[124] So who were these 'bunglers' who left a 13-month-old boy in his buggy in front of a fire? It was the 'social workers [who] missed 17 chances to save a baby left by his drunken mum to roast in front of a roaring gas fire', although there was the comment two paragraphs later that 'a serious case review published yesterday found Alex was also the victim of many failures by several agencies which were meant to protect him'.

Indeed, this determination to target social workers when other professionals and agencies were the primary decision-makers is a repeated theme within the tabloid press, as illustrated by the quotes below in a *Daily Mail* story[125] which was headlined 'Mother whose children were taken away for eight months … because of nappy burns':

> A mother whose daughter suffered nappy burns had her children taken into care because social services wrongly thought she had scalded her deliberately.

This is the first paragraph of the report, a point at which many people may stop reading. But several paragraphs later it is noted that it was not social services and social workers who believed the mother had abused her daughter, but doctors and police officers (and that social workers and the courts would have been acting on the views of the doctors and the police):

> [The mother] took her [daughter] to hospital, but when doctors examined her, they called the police and [the mother] was arrested on suspicion of abusing the little girl by scalding her with hot water.

Social services placed the children with their paternal grandmother while the court considered the concerns of doctors and the police, and 'a specialist in burns and plastic surgery at Alder Hey Hospital [in Liverpool], said [at the court hearing] that she believed the injury was "most probably a scald"'.

And, albeit this report was in the *Daily Mail* in July 2012 five years after Peter Connelly died and almost four years after *The Sun* and other media majored on the 'Baby P story', the actions taken by the doctors and police in Liverpool (although wrongly reported to have been primarily because of the view taken by social services) were related to 'Baby P' with the mother quoted as saying 'They said they were trying to protect Adele [her three-year-old daughter] and did not want another Baby P case'.

So, in this one report social services were blamed for suspicions and concerns held by doctors and the police which led to the court (not social workers) determining that children should not remain with their mother. The social workers actually arranged for the two children to remain within their extended family with contact with the mother, not dissimilar to the actions taken for Peter Connelly at Christmas 2006 when arrangements were made for him to stay with a family friend. And in this report there is a further example five years on of referencing back to the death of 'Baby P', illustrating how the 'Baby P story' had become a resource within the media to blame social workers when children were killed and also to blame them when action was taken to protect children. A further report from the *Daily Mail* of social workers being blamed – 'let down by social services' – is in a case where a mother with severe post-natal depression killed her two sons when it was health services and professionals who 'missed key warning signs' and there was no contact with social workers or social services.[126]

The Sun, therefore, may have championed and sought to capture the 'Baby P story' as its own, with vilification and vengeance targeted at Sharon Shoesmith and social workers, but it was not alone. Nor was the terrible death of Peter Connelly the only opportunity to promote and pursue, however inaccurately, the targeting of social workers.

But what of all those reviews and inquiries that were launched when the story of 'Baby P' was first being told? What did they conclude and how did the media report them? This is the focus of the next chapter.

Notes

[1] Jones, R. (2009) 'No substitute for experience', *The Guardian*, 14 January (www.guardian.co.uk/society/joepublic/2009/jan/14/child-protection).

[2] Ofsted News (2009) 'Christine Gilbert' (www.ofstednews.ofsted.gov.uk/article/98).

[3] *The Daily Telegraph* (2009) 'Tony McNulty resigns following expenses shame', 5 June (www.telegraph.co.uk/news/politics/5454342/Tony-McNulty-resigns-following-expenses-shame.html).

[4] Atkinson, M. (2008) Letter to Christine Gilbert, 8 December, Manchester: Association of Directors of Children's Services.

[5] Curtis, P. (2008) '"We have to take responsibility"', *The Guardian*, 6 December (www.guardian.co.uk/education/2008/dec/06/ofsted-baby-p-inspector-chief).

[6] Bromley-Derry, K. (2009) quoted in Cooper, J. (2009) 'ADCS and Ofsted lock horns on inspections', *Community Care*, 2 November (www.communitycare.co.uk/Artices/Article.aspx?liArticleID=113037).

[7] Coughlan, J. (2009) quoted in Cooper, J. (2009) 'ADCS and Ofsted lock horns on inspections', *Community Care*, 2 November (www.communitycare.co.uk/Artices/Article.aspx?liArticleID=113037).

[8] Curtis, P. (2008) 'Balls "was irresponsible" to promise Baby P case will not happen again', *The Guardian*, 12 December (www.guardian.co.uk/society/2008/dec/12/ed-balls-child-protection).

[9] Ross, T. (2008) 'Haringey given a clean bill of health only weeks after death of Baby P', *Evening Standard*, 14 November, p 4.

[10] Press Association (2008) 'Balls gives Ofsted vote of confidence', *The Guardian*, 11 December (www.guardian.co.uk/society/2008/dec/11/ed-balls-child-protection-ofsted).

[11] Curtis, P. (2008) 'Ofsted accused of complacency on child protection', *The Guardian* (www.guardian.co.uk/education/2008/dec/11/ofsted-christine-gilbert-baby-p).

[12] Merchant, S. (2008) 'Baby P: Shock child abuse figures', Sky News, 10 December (www.sky.com/skynews/Home/Politics/Baby-P-Shock-Abuse-Figures-Revealed).

[13] McVeigh, T. and Doward, J. (2008) 'Ofsted's child abuse report was misleading', *The Observer*, 23 November (www.guardian.co.uk/society/2008/nov/213/ofsted-child-abuse).

[14] McVeigh and Doward (2008) op cit.

[15] NSPCC (2008) Personal correspondence, 17 December.

[16] Jones, S. (2008) 'Sixty missed chances to save baby "used as punchbag"', *The Guardian*, 12 November, pp 4-5.

[17] Riddell, M. (2008) 'Why Baby P was doomed to die', *The Daily Telegraph*, 13 November, p 23.

[18] Bennett, R. (2008) 'Investigation into brutal death of Baby P increases pressure on council chiefs', *The Times*, 13 November, p 10.

[19] Hughes, M. and Savage, M. (2008) 'Politicians call for action over Baby P case', *The Independent*, 13 November, p 12.

[20] Toynbee, P. (2008) 'This frenzy is a disaster for children at risk', *The Guardian*, 18 November (www.theguardian.com/commentisfree/2008/nov/18/comment-social-services-child-protection).

[21] Campbell, B. (2008) 'Attack the professionals, and a tragedy like Baby P will result', *The Independent*, 13 November, p 11.

[22] Ferguson, H. (2008) 'To protect children we must first protect social workers', *The Guardian*, 13 November, p 32.

[23] Jones, S. (2008) '"He blocked the door and pulled a knife"', *Times 2*, 13 November, p 2.

[24] McKitterick, B. (2008) 'Being constantly suspicious is part of the territory', *Times 2*, 13 November, p 3.

[25] Douglas, A. (2008) 'Baby's P legacy must be better status for children's social workers', *The Guardian*, 23 November (www.theguardian.com/society/2008/nov/23/baby-p-child-protection).

[26] Erwin, M. (2008) 'Doctor's despair at Baby P death', *Metro*, 20 November, p 11.

[27] Moriarty, R. (2009) 'Shamed children's boss fights dismissal', *The London Paper*, 6 January, p 1.

[28] Mendick, R. (2009) 'Sacked Baby P chief launches legal battle for £173,000 payout', *Evening Standard*, 6 January, p 5.

[29] Haringey Headteachers (2008) Letter to Dr Ita O'Donovan, 16 December.

[30] Timesonline (2008) 'Headteachers back Sharon Shoesmith', 15 November (www.thetimes.co.uk/tto/news/uk/crime/article1875257.ece).

[31] Butler, P. and Lightfoot, L. (2009) 'Protests at "Baby P" sacking', *The Observer*, 18 January (www.guardian.co.uk/society/2009/jan/18/baby-p-protest-campaign).

[32] Lombard, D. (2009) '*Community Care* calls on *Sun* to support UK social workers', 29 January (www.communitycare.co.uk/blogs/social-work-blog/2009/01/community-care-calls-on-sun-to).

[33] Curtis (2008) op cit.

[34] Jones, R. (2009) 'Why we got it so wrong', *News of the World*, 8 March, p 2.

[35] Jones, R. (2010) Letter, *The Sun*, 25 January, p 41.

[36] BBC (2008) 'What happened to Baby P', *Panorama*, 17 November.

[37] France, A. (2009) 'Council paid £19k for Baby P "spin"', *The Sun*, 8 December (www.thesun.co.uk/sol/homepage/news/2014141/Haringey-Council-paid-19000).

[38] High Court of Justice (2009) *R (on the application of Sharon Shoesmith and (i) Ofsted, (ii) The Secretary of State for Children, Schools and Families, (iii) Haringey London Borough Council*, Skeleton Argument on Behalf of the Claimant, C0/2241/2009.

[39] BBC Trust (2009) *Editorial Standards Findings: Appeals and other editorial issues to the Trust considered by the Editorial Standards Committee, November 2009*, issued December 2009, pp 61-2.

[40] Easton, M. (2009) 'Graphs in a crisis', 9 February, BBC (http:/bbc.co.uk/blogs/thereporters/markeaston/2009/02).

[41] France, A. and Quick, A. (2009) 'Baby P: Fury at £70k Haringey inspector', *The Sun*, 5 December (www.thesun.co.uk/sol/homepage/news/article2006171.ece).

[42] France (2009) op cit.

[43] *Metro* (2009) 'Council responds to "Baby P" claims', 11 May (www.metro.co.uk/news/405283-council-responds-to-baby-p-claims).

[44] Gammell, C. (2009) 'Paedophile step-father of Baby P faces life in jail for raping two-year-old girl', *The Telegraph*, 2 May (www.telegraph.co.uk/news/uknews/baby-p/5258941/Paedophile-step-father-of-Baby-P-faces-life-in-jail-for-raping-two-year-old-girl.html).

[45] *The Sun* (2010) 'Baby P's stepdad loses appeal bid', 21 April (www.thesun.co.uk/sol/homepage/news/2941153).

[46] BBC News (2009) 'Baby P: The whole truth?', 3 May (http://news.bbc.co.uk/1/hi/uk/8029832.stm).

[47] Haringey Local Safeguarding Children Board (LSCB) (2009) *Serious case review 'Child A'*, March, published by the Department for Education, 26 October 2010, p 51.

[48] Edemariam (2009) op cit.

[49] BBC News (2009) op cit.

[50] BBC News (2009) op cit.

[51] Jones, S. (2008) 'Baby P death: "They rubbed chocolate on his face to hide bruises"', *The Guardian*, 11 November (www.guardian.co.uk/society/2008/nov/11/childprotection-ukcrime2).

[52] BBC News (2009) op cit.

[53] BBC News (2009) op cit.

[54] High Court of Justice (2009) *R (on the application of Sharon Shoesmith and (i) Ofsted, (ii) The Secretary of State for Children, Schools and Families, (iii) Haringey London Borough Council*, Skeleton Argument on Behalf of the Claimant, C0/2241/2009, p 36, para 109.

[55] High Court of Justice (2009) *R (on the application of Sharon Shoesmith and (i) Ofsted, (ii) The Secretary of State for Children, Schools and Families, (iii) Haringey London Borough Council*, Skeleton Argument on Behalf of the Claimant, C0/2241/2009, p 14, para 47.

[56] High Court of Justice (2009) *R (on the application of Sharon Shoesmith and (i) Ofsted, (ii) The Secretary of State for Children, Schools and Families, (iii) Haringey London Borough Council*, Skeleton Argument on Behalf of the Claimant, C0/2241/2009, p 41, para 124.

[57] Mendick (2009) op cit.

[58] Shoesmith, S. (2012) 'Case of Baby P social workers crucial for future of profession', *Community Care*, 19 June (www.communitycare.co.uk/blogs/childrens-services-blog/2012/06/shoesmith-case-of-baby-p-social-workers-crucial-for-future-of-profession/#.UqnO4o2d5_k).

[59] Shoesmith (2012) op cit.

[60] Anthony, A. (2009) 'Baby P: Born into a nightmare of abuse, violence and despair, he never stood a chance', *The Observer*, 16 August (www.guardian.co.uk/society/2009/aug/16/baby-p-family).

[61] Booker, C. (2011) 'State child snatchers', *Daily Mail*, 29 August (www.dailymail.co.uk/news/article-2027272/South-Gloucestershire-social-work).

[62] *The Daily Telegraph* (2009) 'Baby P: Haringey Council's lawyers admit he "should have been in care before he died"', 22 May (www.telegraph.co.uk/news/uknews/baby-p/5365020/Baby-P-Haringey-Councils-lawyers-admit-he-should-have-been-in-care-before-he-died.html).

[63] Barrett, D., Harrison, D. and Sawer, P. (2008) 'Baby P: Now spotlight falls on lawyer who sided with mother. Haringey's legal department decided evidence was too flimsy', *The Daily Telegraph*, 16 November (www.telegraph.co.uk/news/uknews/law-and-order/3464202).

[64] Haringey Local Safeguarding Children Board (LSCB) (2008) *Serious case review 'Child A'*, Executive Summary, November, London: Department for Education, p 15.

[65] Haringey LSCB (2009) op cit, p 63.

[66] Lazzeri, A. (2010) 'Evil Baby P mum's lies "just accepted"', *The Sun*, 22 September, p 6.

[67] Press Association (2010) 'Baby P social workers thought his mum was "caring"', *The Guardian*, 24 September (www.guardian.co.uk/society/2010/sep/24/baby-p-social-workers-employment-tribunal).

[68] BBC News (2010) 'Baby P social workers lose case', 22 October (www.bbc.co.uk/news/uk-england-london-11605453).

[69] Shoesmith (2012) op cit.

[70] General Social Care Council (GSCC) (2010) *Notice of Decision of the Conduct Committee*, Case reference: 1042389, p 10.

[71] Anthony (2009) op cit.

[72] Haywood, L. (2010) 'Baby P bunglers can apply for new jobs', *The Sun*, 27 May, p 15.

[73] GSCC (2010) op cit.

[74] Haringey LSCB (2008) op cit, p 116.

[75] *The Guardian* (2010) 'Baby P's doctor failed him, tribunal finds', 8 July (www.guardian.co.uk/society/2010/jul/08/baby-p-doctor-gmc-ruling).

[76] Goodchild, S. (2011) 'GP who bungled Baby P case set to be reinstated', *Evening Standard*, 15 July, p 12.

[77] BBC News (2010) 'Paediatrician David Southall "may do child work again"', 5 May (http://news.bbc.co.uk/1/hi/health/8661639.stm).

[78] Boseley, S. (2010) 'The campaign against David Southall', *The Guardian*, 6 May, pp 12-13.

[79] BBC News (2012) 'Doctors "should not fear raising child abuse alarm"', 10 July (www.bbc.co.uk/news/health-18773101).

[80] BBC News (2009) 'Minister defends Baby P sacking', 7 October (http://news.bbc.co.uk/1/hi/england/london/8295840.stm).

[81] BBC News (2009) 'Baby P boss ran "worst ever" unit', 7 October (http://news.bbc.co.uk/1/hi/8293971.stm).

[82] *The Sun* (2009) '1.6M "wrong"', 9 October, p 9.

[83] BBC News (2009) 'Shoesmith demands Ofsted reports', 12 October (http://news.bbc.co.uk/1/hi/england/london/8302842.stm).

[84] Butler, P. (2009) 'Sharon Shoesmith lawyers demand Ofsted documents', *The Guardian*, 12 October (www.theguardian.com/society/2009/oct/12/shoesmith-demands-ofsted-documents).

[85] Curtis, P. (2009) 'Ofsted chief will be told to attend emergency meeting over Haringey review', *The Guardian*, 13 October (www.theguardian.com/society/2009/oct/13/ofsted-chief-haringey-review).

[86] Williams, R. (2009) 'Judge demands explanation from Ofsted on Baby P emails', *The Guardian*, 2 December, p 8.

[87] High Court of Justice Queen's Bench Division Administrative Court (2010) *The Queen on the Application of Sharon Shoesmith and (1) Ofsted (2) Secretary of State for Children Schools and Families (3) London Borough of Haringey*, Case Number CO/2241/2009, Neutral Citation Number: [2010] EWHC 852 (Admin).

[88] *London Evening Standard* (2009) 'Baby P: Ofsted joins Balls in the dock as Shoesmith edges to victory', 11 November (http://lydall.standard.co.uk/2009/11/baby-p=ofsted-joins-balls-in-the-dock).

[89] *London Evening Standard* (2009) op cit.

[90] Edemariam, A. (2009) op cit.

[91] *The Guardian* (2009) 'Sharon Shoesmith sacking "a breach of natural justice"', 7 October (www.theguardian.com/society/2009/oct/07/baby-peter-shoesmith-sacking).

[92] Treanor, J. (2012) 'Ex-Barclays boss Bob Diamond under pressure to hand £2m payoff to charity', *The Guardian*, 10 July (www.guardian.co.uk/business/2012/jul/10/barclays-bob-diamond-payoff-charity).

[93] BBC News (2012) 'Rebekah Brooks receives £10.8m News International payoff', 12 December (www.bbc.co.uk/news/business-20705535).

[94] Camber, R. (2009) 'Disgraced Baby P council chief could pocket huge payout after Ofsted "destroyed draft report"', *Daily Mail*, 29 November (www.dailymail.co.uk/news/article-1231853/Disgraced-Baby-P-council-chief).

[95] Harrison, A. (2010) 'Baby P sacking was lawful, the High Court rules', 23 April (http://news.bbc.co.uk/1/hi/education/8639496.stm).

[96] Harrison (2010) op cit.

[97] Harrison (2010) op cit.

[98] Wells, T. and Wheeler, V. (2010) 'Shoesmith loses case', *The Sun*, 24 April, p 11.

[99] Allen, V. (2010) 'Now Shoesmith is in line for £1.5m payout', *Daily Mail*, 24 April, p 5.

[100] Butler, P. (2010) 'Sharon Shoesmith given leave to appeal against court ruling on dismissal', *The Guardian*, 12 September (www.guardian.co.uk/society/2010/sep/01/sharon-shoesmith-appeal-ed-balls).

[101] Court of Appeal (2011) Judgment approved by the Court, Neutral Citation Number: [2011] EWCA Civ 642, paras 37-38.

[102] Court of Appeal (2011) Judgment approved by the Court, Neutral Citation Number: [2011] EWCA Civ 642, paras 134-135.

[103] Syson, N. and Peake, A. (2011) 'She's over the moon: He's under the earth', *The Sun*, 28 May, p 9.

[104] *The Sun Says* (2011) 'No shame', *The Sun*, 28 May, p 8.

[105] *Daily Mail* (2012) 'The £1M smirk', 28 May, p 1.

[106] Pendlebury, R. (2011) 'If only she'd fought as hard for children as she did for herself', *Daily Mail*, 28 May, pp 6-7.

[107] Wooding, D. (2012) 'Baby P: Shame of care boss', *News of the World*, 29 May, p 11.

[108] *News of the World* Editorial (2012) 'Kid's hell can't be dismissed', 29 May, p 6.

[109] *Mail on Sunday* Editorial (2011) 'Blame is not just a game, Ms Shoesmith', 29 May, p 27.

[110] Bennett, R. (2011) 'Balls put more children at risk', *The Times*, 28 May, p 3.

[111] Sharon Shoesmith, quoted in Bennett (2011) op cit.

[112] Butler, P. and Watt, N. (2011) 'Shoesmith turns on Balls after court win', *The Guardian*, 28 May, p 1.

[113] Butler, P. (2011) 'Euphoria but regrets for child care director who was sacked over death of Baby Peter', *The Guardian*, 28 May, p 10.

[114] *The Guardian* Editorial (2011) 'Sharon Shoesmith ruling: Welcome but few cheers', 28 May, p 40.

[115] Butler, P. (2011) 'Shoesmith decision sends out warning', *The Guardian Society*, 1 June, p 4.

[116] Curtis, P. (2009) 'Baby P council issues urgent appeal for staff', *The Guardian*, 26 January (www.guardian.co.uk/society/2009/jan/26/haringey-social-workers-baby-p).

[117] *The Times* Editorial (2010) 24 April (www.timesonline.co.uk/tol/comment/leading_article/article7106704).

[118] Ramesh, R. (2011) 'Supreme court rejects bid to challenge ruling on Sharon Shoesmith sacking', *The Guardian*, 2 August (www.guardian.co.uk/society/2011/aug/02/baby-p-ruling-backs-sharon-shoesmith).

[119] Schofield, K. (2011) 'Baby P killer is free on Friday', *The Sun*, 2 August (www.thesun.co.uk/sol/homepage/news/3729798/One-of-the-evil-trio-jailed-over-Baby-Ps-death-will-walk-free-on-Friday.html).

[120] BBC News (2010) 'Baby P social workers lose case', 22 October (www.bbc.co.uk/news/uk-england-london-11605453).

[121] Parker, N. (2009) 'Another Haringey scandal', *The Sun*, 12 September, p 1.

[122] Wells, T. (2011) 'Baby P staff are quizzed on own kids', *The Sun*, 1 March (www.thesun.co.uk/sol/home[page/news/3438581).

[123] Wells, T. (2011) op cit.

[124] Lawton, J. (2011) 'Bunglers who let tot "cook" to death', *Daily Star*, 3 February, p 25.

[125] Narain, J. (2012) 'Mother whose children were taken away for eight months ... because of nappy burns', *Daily Mail*, 18 July, p 9.

[126] Pemberton, C. (2011) 'Social workers blamed for health visitors' mistakes', *Community Care*, 2 August (www.communitycare.co.uk/blogs/childrens-services-blog/2011/08).

FOUR

The influence of reviews and reports

In November and December 2008, when *The Sun* in particular, but with other media as well, started to frame the 'Baby P story', and when Mr Brown was cornered by Mr Cameron about 'Baby P' at Prime Minister's Question Time, Mr Balls announced a whole tranche of inspections and reviews. Some, as with the hasty November joint area review led by Ofsted and the second serious case review into Peter Connelly's life and death, were focused on Haringey. Some, as with the Laming review and the CQC's national review of the NHS, were broader and looked at child protection practice throughout England. And one, undertaken by the Social Work Task Force, was to look at the state of social work more generally.

What is missing from this list of the reviews is any specific mention of the police. The child protection performance and practice of the police in Haringey or nationally had little focused public attention beyond coverage within the more general joint area review and serious case review, which in themselves concentrated very heavily on Haringey Council's children's services.

But the review that had partly triggered the media attention in November 2008 had not been commissioned by Mr Balls. This was the first serious case review following Peter Connelly's death. When it had been decided at the criminal trial of Tracey Connelly, Steven Barker and Jason Owen that they had 'caused or allowed' Peter's death, it became permissible to publish the executive summary of the serious case review. At the time, in 2008, only executive summaries could be published to protect personal confidential information about

———

family members that would be contained within the full report. The executive summary could not, however, be published before the determination of guilt at the criminal trial, as it might otherwise have interfered with the trial process and the evidence to be submitted at the trial. However, the preparation of the report would not have been stalled waiting for the conclusion of the criminal trial; it would have been started soon after it was known that Peter had died as a consequence of abuse.

The process would have been that an independent expert, who was not employed by any of the agencies that had had any involvement with Peter and his family, and who had no prior involvement with the case, would be appointed to write the serious case review report. Each agency would prepare an individual management review on the involvement of their agency with the case and these would then be used in preparing the serious case review overview report. Immediately after it was known that Peter had died, the case records and files in each agency should have been secured so that they could not be altered or amended, and these records would be used in preparing the individual management reviews. These should have been prepared in each agency by a manager or other senior person with no involvement or responsibility for the agency's work with Peter and his family. All of this process is within the government's statutory child protection guidance,[1] which includes the requirements about when and how serious case reviews should be undertaken.

In December 2008, just as the 'Baby P' media story was gaining momentum, Ofsted published a report on its evaluation of 50 serious case reviews it had received between April 2007 and March 2008. (It had the role of evaluating the appropriateness and adequacy of each serious case review.[2]) In Ofsted's judgement, 20 of the reports were 'inadequate' (and would have to be revised or done again), 18 were 'adequate', 12 were 'good' and none were 'outstanding'. The first Peter Connelly serious case review report was not in this Ofsted sample, but it was later determined by Ofsted to be 'inadequate', a not unusual Ofsted judgement at the time.

As noted in DCSF guidance on serious case reviews, 'the prime purpose of a serious case review is for agencies and individuals to learn lessons to improve the way in which they work both individually and collectively to safeguard and promote the welfare of children'.[3] However, as illustrated by the response to Sharon Shoesmith, Director of Children's Services, and social workers in Haringey, serious case reviews, along with joint area reviews undertaken by Ofsted with other national inspectorates, may be used for the allocation of responsibility and blame. It may not be the stated intention, of course, but it is the reality.

Every two years the government commissions an overview of the lessons from serious case reviews, and these overviews have been prepared by Marian Brandon and colleagues at the University of East Anglia. Three overview reports were prepared for the previous two-year periods up to March 2009. The overview for 2007–09[4] would have included the first serious case report concerning Peter Connelly.

Within the Brandon report it is noted that there were 268 serious case reviews between April 2007 and March 2009, and that 152 (57 per cent) related to a child death. This gives an annual rate of 76 child deaths, but these would have included suicides by children and young people, or accidental death as a consequence of alcohol or drug misuse, so were not all related to death as a consequence of abuse or neglect. The 268 serious case reviews also included cases where children and young people were, for example, sexually abused outside the family home by non-family members.

In a summary it is noted that:

> Throughout the three annual reviews we have emphasised the complexity of each child's circumstances and the consequent difficulties professionals face in making sound professional judgements. It is the individual *differences* in each child's case that pose the most challenges for understanding and hence for practice and decision making. The demands and the complexity of the task of protecting children and the importance of supporting professionals, especially social workers, to make sound professional judgements has been accepted by policy makers and, increasingly, by the public.[5]

This analysis is well informed and clear, but the conclusion that the complexity of child protection work is increasingly accepted by the public is more contentious, as shown by the continuing vilification of Sharon Shoesmith and the social workers, and by the media coverage of new instances of child abuse as they emerged.

But what were the findings of the first Haringey serious case review undertaken following the death of Peter Connelly? The executive summary[6] notes that Ofsted was informed on 6 August 2007 that a serious case review was being undertaken, three days after Peter died; that a sub-committee of Haringey's LSCB was convened on 8 August, agreed the scope of the review and met seven times between September 2007 and July 2008; and that an independent consultancy, CAE Ltd, had been commissioned to prepare the overview report drawing on the individual management reviews from each agency. It was noted that Peter Connelly's father declined an opportunity to contribute to the review, and Peter's mother did not respond to an invitation to contribute.

There was a particular mention in the section on 'the conduct of the review' about the involvement of health services with Peter and with the review. It was noted that those involved in the serious case review process 'recognised a need for, commissioned and received expert medical opinions about particular aspects of child A's receipt of health services and those judgements are reflected in the recommendations for action'. This, as will be seen later, became an uncertain and contentious issue. An independent expert medical opinion from two experienced and much respected paediatricians was sought and received about the paediatric care received by Peter, especially from St Ann's Clinic and from Dr Al-Zayyat. But there is confusion and conflict about how, to what extent and when these opinions were made available in the serious case review process. This was of some significance as the independent expert medical opinion raised serious concerns about the services, and the management of the services, of Great Ormond Street Hospital NHS Trust, concerns that were not noted in full depth or range in the serious case review reports.

The first serious case review report was completed in July 2008, but with further amendment in October 2008 to make more specific the recommendation to Haringey NHS PCT about the need to 'ensure that the Primary Care Trust has in place robust arrangements for each child subject to a child protection plan to have active oversight and monitoring of her/his medical treatment'.

So what were the conclusions of the first serious case review? The 'lessons learned' covered 16 paragraphs over three pages and related to issues and concerns about communication, delays in the paediatric development assessment and in the legal planning meeting and the advice given at that meeting, that only limited efforts were made to involve Mr Connelly in the early period of intervention, and about the inability to identify and prosecute a perpetrator for Peter's injuries. The report noted:

> The main finding of this serious case review is that, despite a great deal of professional input, the conclusions of the various assessment processes had not reached an adequate understanding of the:
>
> - cause of [Peter Connelly's] injuries and bruising;
> - nature of [Tracey Connelly's] relationship with [Steven Barker] and the extent of his involvement with the family;
> - value of the input by the family friend who provided care alternative care in December 2006 and oversight of [Peter] after the June 2007 incident.[7]

The report also noted:

> There were many factors that contributed to the inability of the agencies to understand what was happening to [Peter]. With the possible exception of the paediatric assessment on 01.08.07 [*when Peter was seen at St Ann's Clinic two days before he died*], none on their own were likely to have enabled further responses that might have prevented the tragic outcome. The factors in combination contributed to the lack of understanding of

the family's functioning and consequently compounded the risk to [Peter].

But what were these factors? They included:

- 'There were no concerns about the welfare of any of the children in the family prior to mid December 2006....'
- 'From the time of [Peter's] first presentation at hospital, observations and assessments of the relationship between [Tracey Connelly] and her children remained largely positive and she was considered to be cooperating with the child protection plan....'
- 'Various professionals noted that [Peter] was an active child who was observed to throw his body around and head-butt family members and physical objects ... an element of the child protection plan was to obtain a developmental paediatric assessment to ascertain if there was an organic reason for such behaviour....'[*]
- 'With one exception [*when Tracey Connelly was seen outside the school to slap the face of one of Peter's sisters*], the two elder siblings both under eight years old did not give cause for significant concern. They attended school regularly and there was no evidence from schools of any concerns about their home life or any indication of changed circumstances....'[8]

One of the most significant conclusions of the first serious case review was that:

- 'All the professionals working with the family understood the household composition to be [Tracey Connelly] with her four children. Although it was known that [Steven Barker] was a friend, neither his intimate relationship with [Tracey Connelly] nor his presence within the household had been discerned by any professionals. With the benefit of hindsight, the indication that [Steven Barker] may have been present in the household from

---

[*] Knowing what is known now, Peter Connelly's unusual behaviour of headbutting and throwing his body around might be understood as a sign of distress, not an organic disorder.

February (current finding of the police investigation following [Peter's] death) offers a new perspective'.[9]

So, the first serious case review noted that after receipt of the separate agency individual management reviews, including from the Metropolitan Police after their two criminal investigations between December 2006 and August 2007, none of the agencies or professionals knew that Steven Barker or later Jason Owen had moved into Peter's home. The police investigation following Peter's death concluded that Steven Barker had moved into the Connelly family home in February 2007 at about the time the family moved from their overcrowded flat to their larger housing association house:

> The reality was that the local professionals were wholly unaware that [Steven Barker] had been living with [Tracey Connelly] for some months [and] that five other individuals had been staying at the home for approximately a fortnight before [Peter] died.[10]

As the serious case review concluded:

> The absence of previous concerns about [Tracey Connelly]'s four children and the positive observations of her parenting led to a high level of trust of [her]. This was further reinforced by her predominant behaviours and presentation (the current criminal proceedings may reveal whether the positive picture was more apparent and real) ie her:
>
> • co-operation with most professional visits and appointments.
> • positive responses to offers of help.
> • frequent initiation of communication with professionals, often relaying information between them, openness of manner.

> As a consequence of the professional perceptions of [Tracey Connelly], coupled with the lack of an identified perpetrator, [Peter's] injuries were perceived to be largely a consequence of insufficient supervision and of his own observed behaviours.[11]

The first serious case review had 45 paragraphs of recommendations, within many of which there was more than one recommended action. There were five recommendations for the LSCB itself, four for the FWA, nine for Great Ormond Street Hospital NHS Trust, one for local NHS services more generally, one for the NHS PCT, 13 for Haringey Council's children and young people's services and seven for its legal services, two for schools and three for the Metropolitan Police. All the agencies were, therefore, given recommendations for actions to drive improvement. What a contrast with the second serious case review ordered by Mr Balls after the media storm erupted in November 2008 and with the second serious case review undertaken at the height of the storm and completed in March 2009. It had only 15 recommendations, all of which were for Haringey's LSCB and children's services. There were *no* specific recommendations at all for any NHS organisation or for the Metropolitan Police. As with the media coverage, the focus was no longer spread across the agencies but was largely fixed on Haringey Council and its children's services. The previous significant concerns exposed and expressed about the health services and the police had apparently evaporated and become extinct. Why?

In November 2008, when the first serious case review executive summary was published, Haringey LSCB also published two briefing notes. The first was titled 'Support offered to family of child A', noting that:

> [The family] were seen 60 times in eight months – on average twice a week:
>
> • The family were seen 18 times by Children and Young People Service staff, including announced and unannounced visits to their home.

- They were seen 37 times by health staff, including three visits to their home.
- They were seen 5 times at their home by the Family Welfare Association [now called Family Action].
- In the past month of his life, the mother took her son to health professionals 8 times.[12]

A second briefing note[13] was also issued at the same time by the LSCB. It detailed the number of child protection investigations, and the number of children with child protection plans, in Haringey:

	Child protection investigations within the year	Child protection plans on 31 March year end	Child protection plans per 10,000 under-18s on 31 March year end	
			Haringey	Similar councils
2004–05	563	238	47.6	36.3
2005–06	494	200	40.3	33.6
2006–07	455	156	31.5	34.0
2007–08	594	232	47.4	–

Note: Figures were also given for March 2007 (455) and March 2008 (427) for the number of children in the care of the council.

What were the trends within these figures published by Haringey's LSCB? In the three years up to the time when Peter Connelly died, there was a year-on-year reduction in both the number of child protection investigations and the number of children with child protection plans. There was also a reduction over the two years for which information was given in the number of children in the care of the council. Indeed, figures were actually given from 2001 to 2008, but only for child protection plans, and these showed that the 156 plans in 2007 was the lowest by a margin of any year between 2001 and 2008, with 2006 having the next lowest number of plans at 200 (2004 had the highest number of plans at 238).

Why this reduction in child protection activity and numbers of children in care in Haringey? One explanation could be Haringey children's services' focus on working in partnership with parents on parenting competencies and confidence. It was an approach that was noted in Chapter Three to be controversial when applied to families where there were children with child protection plans, and this had been the subject of a critical *Panorama* programme. Or maybe it was due to the concerns noted in Chapter Two, expressed by Lynne Featherstone, one of the two local MPs, that Haringey Council had budget pressures and was seeking to cut back on expenditure. Or it could be that Haringey Council had had a particularly high level of child protection activity following the Victoria Climbié inquiry on its patch, and was now getting back to a level of activity more comparable with elsewhere.

It is always difficult to give any meaningful comment on figures and trends without having comparable information from other areas, and especially in this instance, areas that were within Haringey's comparable 'family' of similar authorities. So, were the reductions of child protection investigations, child protection plans and children in care in Haringey in line with the trends elsewhere? The information above, taken from the Haringey LSCB 'Background Information' note, helps to answer this question as it gives comparable information for similar areas for the proportions of children and young people aged under 18 with child protection plans.

What the figures show is that Haringey *did* have a comparatively high proportion of its child population with child protection plans in 2004–05, and this may well have been the Victoria Climbié Inquiry effect, with more defensive decision-making within the local agencies which were bruised and battered by the Inquiry and its media coverage. However, by 2006–07, the year in which Peter Connelly and one of his sisters had child protection plans, the proportion of children with child protection plans in Haringey was lower than comparable areas. This suggests that there may indeed have been an impact on decision-making from either or both the model of working in partnership with parents on parenting competencies and on needing to cut back on expenditure (although this would be more related to reducing the number of children in council care than the number of child protection plans). There was a bounce back in the number of child protection plans in Haringey in 2007–08, the year in which Peter Connelly's serious case review was undertaken (but before the media coverage started in November 2008), but no comparative figures with other areas are given for this year (no comparative figures are available from government until later in the autumn after the 1 April–31 March year has ended).

But how was the *second* serious case review undertaken from December 2008 to February 2009, and what were its findings? It was commissioned after the media furore and frenzy had started in November 2008. The second serious case review report was prepared by an ex-Assistant Chief Inspector in the Department of Health's Social Services Inspectorate, and he was preparing the report for Haringey's LSCB. The Board now had Graham Badman, a former teacher, headteacher and recently retired Director of Children's Services in Kent, as its chair, and Mr Badman also chaired the panel that oversaw the second serious case review process.[14]

The serious case review overview report was, as was the national process and the process with the first Haringey report, based on individual management reviews from each of the agencies that had had contact with Peter and his family. However, for the second serious case review these were prepared very quickly to hit a tight timetable for the completion of the overview report. This tight timetable was set in the midst of the considerable continuing media interest and pressure, and the consequent political interest and pressure.

The pace at which the second serious case review was undertaken was indicated within the report itself. The serious case review LSCB panel met seven times between 11 December 2008 and 25 February 2009.[15] Taking out the Christmas and New Year holiday period, this is almost once a week. It was an exceptional timescale in which to have gathered, collated, considered and drafted all the individual agency management reviews and then prepared the overview report. It would certainly have been a rushed task for everyone involved.

The rush to undertake and complete the report is explicitly noted in the individual management review that was prepared on behalf of NHS London. A copy of this was provided to the BBC. The BBC asked me to comment on it when concerns arose about the health service involvement with Peter Connelly and his family, and whether issues about NHS provision and practice were properly reflected in the first and second serious case reviews. This subsequently became the subject of a BBC London television documentary, focused on Great Ormond Street Hospital NHS Trust, in May 2012.[16]

In the individual management review prepared for NHS London by Verita, an independent consultancy company, it is noted that:

> Verita was commissioned on 12 December 2008 by Haringey Teaching NHS Trust (HTPCT) and Great Ormond Street Hospital (GOSH) [*who at the relevant time provided paediatric medical cover at the North Middlesex Hospital (NMH)*] to undertake the revised individual management review (IMR) following the joint area review published on 3 December 2008.... The repeat serious case review (SCR) had to be completed by the end of March 2009. Each IMR therefore had to be delivered in draft by 10pm on 29 January 2009. After discussion with the commissioners and given the amount of work involved in the health IMR and shortness of time, on 22 January the chair of Haringey Local Safeguarding Board (LSCB) agreed an 18-hour extension.[17]

The individual management review authors then noted that it was not until 19 December 2008 that they were informed of the LSCB's terms of reference for this second serious case review, and that 'the tight timescale for delivering this report obliged us to decide who to interview before we could consider all the documents and information'.[18]

In essence, the tight timescale was skewing the process of undertaking the review. It meant for these authors that they only had between 12 December and 29 January (a period which included Christmas and the New Year) to identify, collect and read all the relevant NHS records, procedure statements and so on across several NHS organisations. They then had to interview the NHS practitioners and managers whom they saw as particularly relevant in understanding the NHS involvement with Peter Connelly and his family and the application of the child protection policies, procedures and practices of each NHS organisation. Finally, they had to capture and collate all that was relevant within the individual management review they were to prepare. And all in a period of not much more than 20–25 working days. The concern of the authors is represented in their statements that, 'It would have been helpful to meet some individuals again but time was too short' and 'we have conducted our work to a tight timescale and made our findings to the best of our ability and with the information available to us'.[19]

Why such a rush? Was it not more important, especially for the re-run of the serious case review process into the life and death of Peter Connelly, to ensure that it was thorough and well considered? After all, Mr Balls had already appointed a new Director of Children's Services for Haringey and a new chair of the LSCB, so what could be seen as emergency action had been taken to ensure any possible major shortcomings and concerns were identified and addressed. In addition, the first serious case review had recently been rated by Ofsted as 'inadequate', so presumably, it was very important that the second serious case review was at least 'adequate' and preferably 'good'. But the press and political interest may have been what required a review that was quick and rushed.

What, then, were the findings of this rapid and rushed second serious case review? Early in the report it is noted that:

> In order to fully understand and do justice to professional actions in safeguarding and protecting children we need to see them in the fullest social, economic and knowledge contexts in which they take place.[20]

This comment about context is important. It widens the view so that as well as drilling down into the case and actions that are the major focus of the serious case review, it also looks at the broader experience of the workers at the time: their overall workload; the resources they could draw on to help children and families; organisational stability or change; working relationships across agencies; national and local policy and procedural requirements. All of these factors and more make it easier or harder for workers to work well.

So what was it like in Haringey in 2007, at the time that Peter Connelly died? First, the second serious case review noted that there was anticipated and actual organisational disruption within local children's health services:

> Haringey Teaching Primary Care Trust was responsible for GP and Children's Community Services at the time of [Peter Connelly's] death. Since April [*2007, four months before Peter died*], Great Ormond Street Hospital provided community paediatric services, commissioned by the PCT, now known as NHS Haringey.[21]

Second, there were changes within and an historic and continuing shortage of health visitors:

> Following a Health Equality Audit a number of health visitor posts were moved from the west part of Haringey, and a system of coloured folders for targeted children was set up. The health visiting service was under pressure in 2006/2007 because, although most posts were filled, there was 8% sickness absence. The system was changed to team caseloads with individual allocations of blue and red folders, and individual caseloads averaged 607 families in 2007.[22]

What this would have meant for health visitors, and for children and families, were changes and lack of continuity in the contact of health visitors with families, losing the opportunity to build relationships and knowledge over time. For the health visitors, each with 607 families, there would be the considerable task of juggling contact with a large number of children and families, especially in an area such as Tottenham, with high levels of deprivation and diversity, as noted in Chapter One.

And the high workload and workload pressure was not just the experience of health visitors:

> The caseload of the social worker [Maria Ward] responsible for leading on the child protection plan for [Peter Connelly] had almost doubled from January

2007 to July 2007 and was 50% above the caseload recommended by Lord Laming in the Report of the Inquiry into the death of Victoria Climbié. The social worker described her caseload as made up of various 'types of case and categories of [child protection] registration' and that 'it was a lot of work' and that 'she never had time to do everything'.[23]

No comments were given about resource or context issues for the Metropolitan Police and whether these had an impact on the unsuccessful two criminal investigations into Peter's injuries. This reflects and repeats the apparent lack of attention given to police practice and performance right through all the inquiries, accounts and comments following the death of Peter Connelly.

What is also missing in the context and resources section of the second serious case review report is any comment about the significant and long-standing concerns regarding the medical staffing and organisational arrangements of St Ann's Clinic. This was the responsibility of Great Ormond Street Hospital NHS Trust, and is explored more fully below. It was of considerable importance in relation to Peter Connelly as it related to both the delay in getting the appointment for the paediatric assessment required within Peter's child protection plan, and it also had an impact on the failure for Peter to be assessed when he belatedly did get an appointment at the clinic. It is a significant omission in the second serious case review that these major concerns about Great Ormond Street Hospital's resourcing and management of the paediatric services at St Ann's Clinic were not detailed and discussed.

There is also no reference in the context section to the capacity and competence concerns regarding Haringey Council's legal services. However, as with the paediatric services at St Ann's Clinic, issues around capacity, competence and consultation, and about wider organisational and management grip and oversight, were significant for Peter Connelly. There was a delay in implementing the child protection plan requirement to get legal advice about whether the grounds for care proceedings were met, and when belatedly this advice was provided, there were concerns about its quality.

In concluding the section on resources in the second serious case review report, it was noted that 'There has been some examination of the resources available to the service at the time and consideration of both budget available and budget pressures informs a recommendation'. So far so good. This serious case review was looking at context as well as the case (albeit without taking into its view any context issues in particular for the police or St Ann's Clinic), and with its consideration of the resource context presumably to inform the second serious case review's conclusions and recommendations.

But now there is a disjunction between the context and resource issues described in the report and noted above, and what then appears in the conclusions and recommendations. First, there is no reference in the conclusions and recommendations about NHS resource issues, despite the information about the considerable difficulty and pressure for the health visiting service, a service which had a significant part to play in Peter Connelly's child protection plan. Second, as is consistent throughout the 'Baby P story', the attention is overwhelmingly turned on Haringey's children's services and its social workers.

In the report's conclusion there was an inconclusive comment about 'budgetary movements' and the 'overall quantum of resource' within Haringey's children's social care services, but this was then followed by a much more assertive comment that 'further resources in themselves [*eg more social worker time*] would not have impacted on the outcome of this case':

> Implicit within this report has been the consideration of the resourcing of children's social care in Haringey. It is clear that there were budgetary movements in the period 2005/06, 2006/2007 and 2007/08, but these did not reduce the overall quantum of resource. Within the scope of this review it is difficult to determine whether or not that quantum of resource should have been deployed differently. However, what is clear from the detailed consideration of workload and deployment

of front-line staff is that further resources in themselves
would not have impacted on the outcome in this case.[24]

This is a brave and bullish statement. It is not one, however, that fits
easily with the GSCC's findings quoted in Chapter Three that '[Maria
Ward's] actions and/or inactions must be viewed in the context of the
working environment at Haringey as a whole – it was, to say the least,
a challenging environment; there were shortages of staff, excessive
workloads and a lack of managerial support and supervision'.[25]

So why this statement in the second serious case review report
that 'further resources in themselves would not have impacted on the
outcome in this case'? The report was prepared early in 2009 at the
height of the media and political storm, and the press, political and
public vilification of Haringey children's services, its managers and
social workers. It was also, as noted earlier, prepared rapidly and in
a considerable rush. The GSCC's comments were from 2010, when
the 'Baby P story' was still continuing but with a little less intensity,
and with the GSCC having more time to receive evidence and to
reflect and consider their comments and conclusions. The difference
in the second serious case review report and the GSCC's report
may, however, have nothing to do with when and how quickly the
two reports were prepared, but may reflect a significant difference
of view about how resource and time issues had an impact on social
work practice.

But how did all of this get reflected in the recommendations of the
second serious case review? The only recommendation that related
to resource issues was that:

> The Local Authority should secure an external audit
> of resources made available to children's services
> between 2005 and 2008, to satisfy themselves that their
> expenditure was sufficient to meet the needs of those
> services and with a view to establishing the appropriate
> level of resource to meet the requirements of the [joint
> area review] action plan.[26]

The first serious case review was prepared over nine months in 2007–08, and graded by Ofsted as 'inadequate' in November 2008 as the 'Baby P story' was breaking and building. The second serious case review was prepared in 11 weeks (including Christmas and the New Year) at the height of the shaping and telling of the 'Baby P story' between December 2008 and February 2009. It was graded by Ofsted as 'good' and has retained that grade. But, as noted earlier, the first serious case review is much more extensive and comprehensive in its account of actions, analysis and recommendations. It also has recommendations for all the agencies. The second serious case review is much more limited in its recommendations and only has specific recommendations for Haringey's LSCB and children and young people's services. Why this very marked and significant difference? And why did Ofsted conclude that the more limited second serious case review was so much better than the more comprehensive first review?

The absence of any recommendations at all in the second serious case review for the NHS, Metropolitan Police and Haringey Council's legal services is all the more surprising when considered alongside the media statement[27] issued in May 2009 by Graham Badman, as chair of Haringey's LSCB, following the finalisation of the second serious case review. In his statement he noted that 'doctors, lawyers, police and social workers [should have] adopted a more urgent, thorough and challenging approach' and if this had happened 'the case would have been stopped in its tracks at the first serious incident'. If this was the view of the LSCB chair who oversaw the preparation of the second serious case review, why were there no specific recommendations from this review for this wider range of professionals or their agencies?

When the full first and second serious case review reports were both published by the Department for Education in October 2010, it provided an opportunity and the ammunition for a further flurry of 'Baby P' media coverage, but with a difference in the commentary. *The Guardian*, for example, had the headline:

> Official report reveals serious inadequacies in 'every agency involved' in Baby P's death: social workers, lawyers, doctors and police blamed: abuse of Peter 'could have been stopped in its tracks'.[28]

In contrast, *The Sun*'s front page, shared with a picture of bikini-clad Coleen Rooney, wife of the footballer Wayne Rooney, was 'NEW ABUSE PROBE; BABY P cover-up finally blown: FIRST REPORT HID BUNGLES'.[29]

The Sun's front page, 27 October 2010

The Sun had coverage of the story over four pages. Its headline message was 'THE TRUE HORROR: Shoesmith whitewash condemned'.[30] It then had a full page describing 'How new inquiry exposed bungling', which included criticisms of the police, doctors and lawyers as well as social workers, but the photographs shown alongside that of Peter Connelly were of Sharon Shoesmith, social workers Gillie Christou and Maria Ward, and the GP, Dr Ikwueke. *The Guardian* only showed photos of Peter, Tracey Connelly and Steven Barker. There were no photographs in *The Sun* of police officers or of NHS or Metropolitan Police managers or senior officers. This relentless focus and fixation in *The Sun* on Sharon Shoesmith, the social workers and Haringey Council was reflected in *The Sun*'s Editorial. This made no mention at all of reported failings within the NHS or the Metropolitan Police but attacked the council and the

The Sun's inside pages, 27 October 2010

social workers and praised Mr Cameron, now, in 2010, the Prime Minister:

> Time and again Peter could have been saved while he was being tortured to death. But nobody could be bothered. Danger signs were ignored. Nothing was followed through. Why? Partly because Haringey council had already given up, mentally writing off Peter's squalid home circumstances as a typical sink estate mess from which nothing could be expected. The attitude led to children across the borough being neglected by social workers. David Cameron, who was 'shocked' by yesterday's revelations, has the chance to bring good out of tragedy. There is a clear link between what happened in Haringey and the Coalition's historic mission to end welfare addiction and the violent, degenerate behaviour it can foster. But nothing can excuse the shame of individuals whose failures to help Peter have been exposed.[31]

So, as before, *The Sun* and Mr Cameron continued to make politics a central thread in the 'Baby P story', with selective political and professional targeting a theme throughout how the 'Baby P story' was shaped and told.

When the first and second full serious case review reports were published in October 2010, Mr Loughton, Minister of State for Children, was quoted as saying that he hoped the reports would bring 'some form of closure' so that everyone in the case could move on. This was a forlorn hope. Sharon Shoesmith and the social workers continued to be pursued by *The Sun* and other papers, and Peter's family continued to be contacted by papers when they could add a quote within new stories that would build links back to the story of 'Baby P'. There was no rest, remission or respite.

The Department for Education statement concerning the publication of the two serious case reviews noted that:

> The first SCR was commissioned in August 2007 by Haringey Local Safeguarding Children Board (LSCB), under the chairmanship of Sharon Shoesmith, and the executive summary was published by the LSCB in November 2008. This SCR was evaluated as 'inadequate' by Ofsted.
>
> In December 2008, the then Secretary of State for Children, Schools and Families directed the appointment of a new LSCB Chair, Graham Badman, and asked the Haringey LSCB to begin a new SCR on the case of Peter Connelly. This second SCR was evaluated as 'good' by Ofsted and the executive summary was published in May 2009.[32]

But look at what is found when the two reports are compared:

- Both were written by independent authors.
- Both serious case review processes were overseen by a panel of managers from each statutory agency involved with the family (including the council, NHS organisations and the police).
- The first was started soon after Peter Connelly's death; the second was started one year five months after Peter died.

- The first was substantially completed over a period of 14 months before the 'Baby P' media and political story exploded; the second was completed in a very short timescale of 11 weeks immediately after the 'Baby P story' exploded.
- The first was much more extensive and comprehensive, at 129 pages; the second was considerably shorter and less comprehensive in its account and analysis of what happened and was almost half the length, at 73 pages.
- The first had 64 paragraphs of 'conclusions and lessons learned'; the second had eight paragraphs of 'conclusions'.
- The first had 46 paragraphs of recommendations; the second had 15.
- The second serious case review had *no* recommendations for the FWA, Haringey Council's legal services, NHS organisations or the Metropolitan Police. In comparison, the first serious case review had four recommendations for the FWA, one general recommendation for the NHS, nine recommendations for Great Ormond Street Hospital NHS Trust, 13 for Haringey Council's children and young people's services, two for schools, seven for Haringey Council's legal services and three for the Metropolitan Police.
- Ofsted rated the first much more extensive and comprehensive report as 'inadequate'; the much more limited, quickly undertaken second report, with its focus heavily and more narrowly on Haringey Council's children's services, was rated as 'good'.

Both reports were available to access on the Department for Education website by searching 'Peter Connelly' and were available for anyone to make their own judgement about the comparative standard and adequacy of the two reports.

One of the contentious issues for both serious case reviews, but especially for the second review, was how concerns about the NHS paediatric service at St Ann's Clinic were noted and addressed. This in itself became a focus of a BBC London television programme in 2012.[33] The paediatric service was managed by Great Ormond Street Hospital through a contract with Haringey NHS PCT. There had already been concerns expressed by clinicians about the amount and quality of service they could provide, including by Dr Kim Holt, a community paediatrician, who was then suspended and only returned to work in October 2011. She is quoted as saying: 'I believe if our concerns had been treated seriously at the time we raised them, then we could have prevented the death of Baby Peter'.[34]

It was Great Ormond Street Hospital that, prior to April 2008, had the responsibility for the doctors at St Ann's Clinic. From April 2008 Great Ormond Street Hospital had full responsibility for the clinic. At the time, therefore, when Peter Connelly was referred to and seen at the clinic in the summer of 2007, Great Ormond Street Hospital employed the doctors at the clinic and was responsible for their management and the quality of their service.

In 2007 there was a delay of four months in Peter being seen at the clinic. A referral was first made to the clinic by a health visitor, as part of Peter's child protection plan, in April 2007. The intention was to get Peter assessed by a paediatrician to see if it could be understood why he was headbanging. It took a further referral by Peter's social worker and a further continuing delay before Peter was seen at the clinic at the beginning of August. He was then not examined as the paediatrician decided he was too unwell, she thought probably with an infection, to be examined and assessed.

The first NHS individual management review was completed in autumn 2007, but in January 2008 Jane Collins, Chief Executive of Great Ormond Street Hospital, commissioned a 'review of child protection practice of Dr Al-Zayyat'. Why this delay? What triggered the action in January 2008, five months after Peter had died, and after the first NHS independent management review had been completed? Possibly it was in response to the authors of the first serious case review report requesting an expert paediatric opinion to consider the implications of the results of Peter Connelly's post-mortem,[35] or possibly it may have been a response to Jane Collins herself becoming more aware of the range and seriousness of Peter Connelly's injuries.

The review was to be undertaken by two eminent doctors, Professor Sibert, a recently retired Professor of Child Health at Cardiff University and a consultant paediatrician, and Dr Hodes, a consultant paediatrician within Camden NHS PCT. Their initial terms of reference set by Dr Collins were to concentrate on the competence of Dr Al-Zayyat, the consultant paediatrician at St Ann's Clinic who had seen Peter at the beginning of August 2007, just before he died. However, the two doctors undertaking the review had it agreed that in addition they should also 'review the settings and systems where child protection cases are seen at St Ann's Hospital'.[36] This was significant and led to findings and conclusions that supported the concerns previously raised by doctors at St Ann's Clinic.

So what did the Sibert and Hodes review find?

- First, there were concerns about Dr Al-Zayyat's experience and expertise. It was found that she had been appointed to the post of consultant paediatrician although she did not meet the person specification and the requirements for the post. She was not on the specialist register for paediatrics and child health, and had not undertaken a specialist training programme which was a requirement before being appointed to the consultant's post. She had little experience or training related to child protection. Her background was primarily focused on child development and children with complex disabilities.
- Second, Dr Al-Zayyat, when at St Ann's Clinic, was working within a service where there was no named doctor (a national requirement) for child protection. She would not, therefore, have had – as was required – a specific colleague with expertise in child protection with whom she could consult.
- Third, the review noted that there should have been four consultant paediatricians at St Ann's Clinic, but there were only two, and the majority of child protection referrals were seen by more junior doctors.
- Fourth, there were difficulties in linking with North Middlesex Hospital which provided the acute hospital paediatric and in-patient services. In particular, there were no special arrangements for doctors at St Ann's Clinic to have skeletal surveys, bone scans, photographs or blood tests undertaken at the hospital, and communication and contact between the hospital and clinic was limited. This was reflected in the notes about Peter Connelly and

his injuries when seen at North Middlesex Hospital not being available to doctors working at St Ann's Clinic (there were no notes available at the clinic from any of Peter's 37 contacts with health professionals).

• Fifth, doctors working at St Ann's Clinic had no nurses at the clinic to assist them in their work, with the consequence that they had to undertake tasks that might more appropriately be undertaken by a nurse.

In the Sibert and Hodes review report there is a statement quoted from another doctor at St Ann's Clinic:

> She says that it is a 'clinically risky situation' ... and feels that she is fire-fighting all of the time. There are a number of shortfalls:
>
> • Too few staff.
> • There is no nurse to help in the clinic and the doctors have to weigh and height the patients.
> • It is very difficult to link with the North Middlesex Hospital.[37]

Professor Sibert and Dr Hodes concluded:

> The concerns [described above] we believe need urgent consideration by the Trust. We appreciate that the bringing together of the North Middlesex and St Ann's should help considerably. Having a combined child health service should also help in the management of young children and those with significant abuse.
>
> In particular, we recommend that there is nursing support in the clinic to help with child protection (and indeed other) cases. This would help considerably in what is an isolated clinical situation.
>
> We also believe that the arrangements for children under two with bruising should be reviewed. They need a skeletal survey and bone scan ... and we do not believe

it is adequate to just give a form to the social worker. We noted that skeletal surveys and bone scans were not done on [Peter Connelly, when he was a patient] at the North Middlesex Hospital.[38]

This is all a quite damning catalogue of concerns, and goes some way to understanding why, for Peter Connelly, there was a delay in his referral to St Ann's Clinic being accepted, why the clinic did not have Peter's medical or hospital history, and why, when belatedly he was seen at the clinic, he was not examined and assessed.

The concerns above relate to systems, procedures and working practices, and not only at the clinic but at North Middlesex Hospital. But at St Ann's Clinic the concerns also relate to clinical capacity and, for Dr Al-Zayyat, competence. Indeed it seems that she should never have been appointed to the consultant clinician post. In addition, in that post she was very exposed and without the specialist oversight and support she should have had from the missing 'named doctor' for child protection.

Professor Sibert and Dr Hodes concluded with regard to Dr Al-Zayyat that:

> From our examination of the child protection cases [Dr Al-Zayyat] has seen at St Ann's, this [*the concerns about her response to Peter Connelly*] does not appear to be an isolated event. In other cases she saw, there were significant concerns.... We do not believe that Dr Al-Zayyat has actually had much training in child protection in her career and has been on only one course. Whatever her future, we believe she needs further significant training and experience in child protection. We do not believe she has reached an appropriate standard for a Consultant Community Paediatrician.[39]

It is hard to avoid the conclusion that Dr Al-Zayyat was bound to fail. She did not have the experience and expertise for the post to which she was appointed, and was known not to meet all the requirements for the post. She was then working in a clinical context which was isolated, could not readily access hospital diagnostic services, with information about patients not available, which was 50 per cent below its senior medical capacity, with no named doctor for consultation and oversight of child protection work, and where there were no nurses on site so that doctors' roles were skewed to undertake tasks that should have been within the role of nurses.

Professor Sibert and Dr Hodes made 14 recommendations to Great Ormond Street Hospital NHS Trust about community child health services in Haringey. Some were about medical staffing, some were about the relationships and practices between the clinic and the hospital, and some were about the joint working with social workers. All in all, their report raised serious and significant concerns about the paediatric service at St Ann's Clinic that was the responsibility of Great Ormond Street Hospital NHS Trust.

How was this reflected in the two serious case reviews that followed Peter Connelly's death? And how was it later covered and reported by the media? This all became an issue of considerable contention with four players, in particular, key in the debates and disputes that ensued.

First, there was Dr Jane Collins, Chief Executive of Great Ormond Street Hospital NHS Trust since 2001, and previously a consultant paediatric neurologist at the hospital. Second, Dr Kim Holt, a consultant paediatrician at St Ann's Clinic from 2003, and who, with colleagues, had raised concerns about the capacity and organisation of St Ann's Clinic that led to her being on 'special leave' until 2011. Third, Lynne Featherstone, the local Liberal Democrat MP, who, as noted in Chapter Two, was raising concerns about St Ann's Clinic in 2008. Fourth, there was Graham Badman, whom Mr Balls appointed in December 2008 to be the new chair of Haringey's LSCB.

The Sibert review was a thorough inquiry into Peter Connelly's contact with St Ann's Clinic and into the service provided by the clinic. The full Sibert review report was not, however, made available to inform the first serious case review. Only an edited and incomplete version was made available. So why was the full report not made available, and why were critical comments and concerns taken out of the edited report that was made available? Great Ormond Street Hospital stated in a later press release that the Sibert report was only available towards the end of the process of completing the first serious case review, and that 'it did not send the full report [to the serious case review report authors] following legal advice from the police. The Trust wanted to make sure that it did not prejudice the forthcoming criminal trial'.[40]

But it is difficult to understand how criticisms and concerns about St Ann's Clinic, for example, that a doctor was appointed who did not meet the criteria for the consultant paediatrician's post, would have prejudiced the criminal trial. It has also been reported that the police denied giving Great Ormond Street Hospital advice that information in the Sibert review should be withheld from the serious case review.[41] One of the authors of the first serious case review, Edi Carmi, is reported to have been 'shocked by the information withheld, saying much of it concerned resources, training and recruitment, and management issues fundamental to her inquiry'. Ms Carmi is also quoted as saying: 'I've never been aware of any agency withholding this sort of information from a SCR. I find it unbelievable this level of information was not provided.'[42]

So there is apparently no dispute that information was withheld by Great Ormond Street Hospital NHS Trust from the first serious case review about significant issues and difficulties at St Ann's Clinic that were prevalent at the time Peter Connelly was taken to the clinic in August 2007. Even so, and based in part on the incomplete and less than comprehensive edited version of the Sibert report that was made available by the hospital for the first serious case review, the first serious case review report had five specific recommendations for action for Great Ormond Street Hospital. However, the first serious case review could not address many of the most significant concerns about the management, resourcing and isolation of St Ann's Clinic as the identification of these concerns had been deleted from the edited version of the Sibert report.

But if these concerns were held back from the first serious case review, were they made known by Great Ormond Street Hospital to those undertaking the later hasty joint area review ordered by Mr Balls in November 2008 and the almost as hasty second serious case review that he also ordered? Both reviews were undertaken in weeks and would have been heavily dependent on open and full access to relevant information and reports. They were also undertaken after the findings of guilt at the criminal trial. The Sibert review would have been of particular relevance and importance within both the joint area review and the second serious case review.

It is stated that the Sibert report was made available to the Healthcare Commission that led on NHS and healthcare issues for the November 2008 joint area review. Astoundingly the Sibert report was apparently not seen as relevant by the Healthcare Commission inspectors who, although they had received it, ignored it when undertaking the joint area review. The Healthcare Commission is reported to have stated 'The GOSH [Great Ormond Street Hospital – Sibert] report related to a single individual and activities around a specific incident in the past rather than current safeguarding systems and was not therefore considered relevant to include within the JAR [joint area review]'.[43]

But this is not correct. The Sibert report, because Professor Sibert and Dr Hodes asked that their terms of reference be extended, went beyond one doctor (Dr Al-Zayyat) and one patient (Peter Connelly) to consider the wider context of community paediatric services in Haringey. How this could not have been seen as relevant for the 2008 joint area review, completed in a rush only six months later, is incomprehensible. The consequence was to minimise any focus on Great Ormond Street Hospital and not to distract from all the media and political attention on Haringey Council, its Director of Children's Services and its social workers.

But surely the second serious case review undertaken between December 2008 and February 2009 would fully take into account and report on the serious concerns identified in the Sibert report? Again, no. Why not? There has been a continuing dispute and uncertainty about whether the second serious case review report writers and panel received the full unedited Sibert report. Great Ormond Street Hospital has stated[44] that the full Sibert report was given to Graham Badman, who oversaw the second serious case review. Graham Badman is reported to have said that he had never seen it.[45] The second serious case review report, however, not only fails to address the serious concerns in the full Sibert report, but also fails to effectively address the concerns within the edited and abridged Sibert report. There are no recommendations for action or improvement specifically for Great Ormond Street Hospital in the second serious case review report.

So how should this all be understood? A report prepared by two acknowledged experts identifies significant management and service failings in the community paediatric service provided by Great Ormond Street NHS Trust at St Ann's Clinic in Haringey at the time Peter Connelly was taken to the clinic. These concerns were not fully declared by Great Ormond Street Hospital at the time of the first serious case review in summer 2008. They were apparently all made known to the NHS national inspectorate, the Healthcare Commission, at the time of the joint area review in November 2008 but not seen as relevant and were ignored and not taken into account. They may or may not have been fully declared at the time of the second serious case review completed in February 2009, but there were no recommendations in the second serious case review report to remedy the concerns or confirmation that all the concerns had been remedied.

However, they were subsequently given attention and exposure by Tim Donovan, the London political editor for the BBC,[46, 47, 48] by Andrew Gilligan at *The Daily Telegraph*,[49] in *The Lancet*[50] and in *Private Eye*,[51] with Lynne Featherstone[52, 53] consistently demanding the dismissal of Jane Collins for withholding the information in the Sibert report and, along with consultant doctors at Great Ormond Street Hospital,[54] calling for an investigation.[55] It has also been claimed that what has been called 'the audit trail of suppression … has protected one of Britain's most cherished hospitals and deflected the blame for Baby P's death disproportionately'[56] on to Dr Al-Zayyat and Haringey's children's services.

But what about the emerging information in 2008 and 2009 related to the issues concerning the Metropolitan Police? There was media coverage and comment, but it was fleeting and soon ended. When even within the limited reports about the Metropolitan Police's involvement with the Connelly family came to be known, the story was still structured to heavily focus on the social workers. This was illustrated by a *Daily Mail* report in November 2008 with the headline 'At least two doctors believed Baby P had been abused and police WERE told about his injuries ... but still no one would save him'.[57] But in the following report there was no information about the two unsuccessful criminal investigations and about how the first investigation stalled and was delayed, about how photographs of Peter's injuries were not taken at the earliest opportunity, and how it was not determined who was living in the Connelly household and who had access to Peter,[58] all culminating in insufficient evidence to press charges against any of the adults who were living with Peter. Instead, it is stated that:

> The evidence was deemed insufficient to bring a prosecution, because it was impossible to prove precisely how and when the injuries had been caused and exactly who had inflicted them. The news will raise new questions about why Baby P was not taken into care by Haringey council in response to medical backing for suspicions that he had been abused. In particular, it [the second serious case review] will focus attention on why, even if was impossible to bring a criminal case, the fact that such a young child had suffered deliberate injuries while in the care of his mother did not result in a decision to remove him.

But within the *Daily Mail* report itself there is an explanation as to why a decision was not taken to remove Peter. The assertion that Peter 'had suffered deliberate injuries' was rather stronger than the comment quoted in the report from doctors at Whittington Hospital that Peter's injuries were 'suggestive of non-accidental harm'. It was this suggestion and suspicion that the Metropolitan Police were following up and investigating and where the social workers and their managers were waiting for the findings of the investigation. None of this, however, stopped the rest of the *Daily Mail* article concentrating again on the social workers, with a picture of Peter Connelly and a body map of his injuries, and with pictures also of Steven Barker, Sharon Shoesmith and Maria Ward with the caption 'Accused: Social worker Maria Ward and her boss Sharon Shoesmith'.

There is no naming or identification of the police officers, and no further comment on the limited criminal investigations and why the investigations were unsuccessful in finding out what had happened to Peter and who was living with him. The police briefly came into view, but almost instantly were taken out of the story.

There was a further flurry of comment about the Metropolitan Police in April 2009 when Tim Donovan, political editor for BBC London, received a copy of the first full serious case review report. The media reporting was now explicit about the errors within the police investigations and that 'police mistakes meant a chance to charge Baby's P mother with assaulting him was missed several weeks before his death, an unpublished report says'.[59] The BBC report notes concerns about 'several police errors' that included:

- Police did not photograph [Peter's] bruises for a week and failed to photograph his home, a potential crime scene [in December 2006]....
- Furthermore, the review found that officers did not visit the home with the social worker and kept no detailed notes of conversations with the mother....
- The Crown Prosecution Service asked police to get an independent medical review of the toddler's injuries. A specialist was identified to carry it out. But in March 2007 the detective in charge transferred to a different part of the Metropolitan Police without formally handing the case over to another officer in breach of standard operating procedures....
- With no officer allocated for two months the case drifted [and] the review said: '[If it had not drifted] this might have made it more likely that all the subsequent incidents were reported to the police and that arguably the child might have been more effectively safeguarded'....
- In June 2007, when Baby P was taken into hospital yet again with extensive bruises and scratches, his social worker did contact the police. Baby P's mother was arrested but again it was a week before photos were taken

of the boy's injuries and police did not talk to his older siblings....

• And the review questions why the mother was not asked – at interview – who else was living in the family home. It might have shed light on the presence of her boyfriend, the man now convicted of having caused or allowed the death of Baby P....

It is hard not to conclude from this liturgy of errors and failings that of all the agencies and workers who had contact with Peter Connelly and his family, the most significant subsequent span of concerns following Peter's death might have been focused on the Metropolitan Police. Evidence was not collected or sought. Records were not adequately kept. Actions were not followed through. Basic information was not sought and basic questions not asked. And possibly most concerning of all, an investigation which was already delayed and drifting was lost track of altogether when a police officer changed job and did not hand the case on. The consequence was that 'delays securing an independent medical opinion meant that the six-month legal deadline passed within which to charge the mother with common assault'.

As far as is publicly known, no police officer has been formally disciplined for any of these failings, and no publicly reported inquiry has been undertaken focused on the Metropolitan Police's role and response concerning Peter Connelly and his life and death. Mr Cameron and Mr Balls have not called for the sackings of any police officer or senior officer, and the Home Office and its ministers with responsibility for policing have been unheard and unseen. Quite unlike what has been experienced by Sharon Shoesmith, the social workers, and the paediatrician and GP. Why?

These concerns about the Metropolitan Police were known to the government in November 2008 when the 'Baby P story' started to be told and before Mr Balls' December press conference, as they were included in the first serious case review report. They did not, however, receive the same attention in the second serious case review or the joint area review commissioned by Mr Balls in November 2008. Why not?

But there *were* expressions of concern about the errors and failings of the Metropolitan Police. The Metropolitan Police stated to the BBC in April 2009 that they could not comment on the concerns for 'legal reasons'. Lynne Featherstone, the local MP, felt no restriction and is quoted as saying that there had been a 'monumental failing' by the police; the BBC report noted that:

> Valerie Brasse, a member of the Metropolitan Police Authority and an adviser to the Victoria Climbié Inquiry, said the findings were "appalling" and "not acceptable". "There is no accounting for poor, sloppy police investigation and if that is what is emerging then that is poor investigation. The issue remains though that if an investigation is poor and of that quality, what then the role of the supervisor and why wasn't that picked up?"[60]

There was a further report in the *Daily Mail*, again using the favoured tabloid term 'bungling'. It was headed 'Bungling police missed chance to charge Baby P's mother before his death, says report'.[61] It also quotes Ms Featherstone as saying 'What on earth was going on that nobody was doing their job properly', and this time it is stated that 'Scotland Yard yesterday said it would be "inappropriate" of them to comment on a leaked document'.

And what about *The Sun*? How would it handle this information emerging into the public arena and being reported by the BBC and now other newspapers about the failings of the Metropolitan Police, a service where it became known in 2012 through the Leveson Inquiry that it had close personal and professional relationships? Its report was short. It was 24 lines long and, although headed 'Cops "let Baby P's mum go": Blundering cops squandered a chance to charge Baby P's mum with child abuse before his death, a leaked report claims',[62] it managed to turn the story away from the Metropolitan Police with the comment that 'social workers and doctors missed terrible injuries inflicted on Baby P, who was 17 months old when he died in his cot in August 2007'.

What discussions were going in *The Sun*'s offices on 10 April 2009? On Thursday 9 April the BBC first carried the story about the police and 'Baby P'. On Friday 10 April, the following day, it was picked up and covered by other newspapers including the *Daily Mail*. But this was about 'Baby P', the story *The Sun* had largely made its own, and here was a significant new story line that *The Sun* seemed reluctant and remiss in not covering. Could or should *The Sun* leave it uncovered? With only one more day, Saturday 11 April, before the weekend break in *The Sun*'s publishing, there was only one more contemporary opportunity to refer to the new story line of which the public-at-large were already aware but which *The Sun* had so far not reported. What happened? It was covered, kept brief, and with another opportunity to leave the blame solely with the social workers and doctors.

The Sun and the other tabloids' contrasting coverage of the police compared to the social workers did not go unnoticed, albeit it was noticed and commented on within the professional social work press. Under the headline 'Baby P: One rule for police: one rule for social workers' it was noted that:

> Blundering, bungling....You guessed it. I'm reading the adjectives used in several tabloid news articles about the latest leaked information from the Baby P serious case review. What do these words tell us (other than that someone didn't make it past the letter B in their pocket thesaurus)? A great deal, actually. For once, these words were not used to describe social workers. The target in this case is police officers.
>
> So far, so familiar – this is exactly the type of language that we are used to seeing in reports about social workers. So does this mean that social workers are treated no worse by the press than other professions? Not exactly.
>
> *The Sun*'s article is uncharacteristically short – its pieces about child protection of late have been long and detailed. And while the articles about social workers in the case have routinely named the practitioners involved, no mention is made here of the individual police officers involved.

Neither is there an overt call for the police involved to be disciplined or sacked – a common component of the paper's articles about social workers. So, as far as *The Sun* is concerned there is obviously one rule for social workers and another for police officers.

The *Daily Mail* dedicated more space to the story but also avoids pointing the finger at specific officers or making outlandish judgements. It can't, however, resist the opportunity to have a dig at social workers, despite the facts implying that social workers do not bear the burden alone – in the story a pull-out quote links readers to a separate article about a mother 'forced to give up her son' after hitting her son with a hairbrush in a 'moment of madness'. The association clearly reinforces the dichotomous baby snatchers vs leaving-the-child-with-unfit-parents stereotype of social work that the paper favours.[63]

In the next chapter there are reflections on the more wide-ranging and general national reviews of child protection and social work initiated by the government during the telling of the 'Baby P story', and their impact on child protection policies and practice, but there were two further specific reviews focused on Haringey. One was the *Review of the involvement and action taken by health bodies in relation to the case of Baby P.*[64] It was commissioned by Alan Johnson, the then Secretary of State for Health, in December 2008 after the publication of the joint area review ordered by Mr Balls.

The review report was published in May 2009 by the CQC, the successor body to the Healthcare Commission from April 2009. It looked at the responses to Peter Connelly during his lifetime from NHS services provided by Haringey Teaching PCT, North Middlesex University Hospital NHS Trust, Whittington Hospital NHS Trust and Great Ormond Street Hospital for Children NHS Trust. It noted that Great Ormond Street Hospital had been contracted by the PCT and North Middlesex Trust to provide paediatric services in Haringey.

In a press release at the time of the publication of the CQC report, Cynthia Bower, the CQC Chief Executive, is quoted as saying:

This is a story about the failure of basic systems. There were clear reasons to have concerns for this child but the response was simply not fast enough or smart enough. The NHS must accept its share of the responsibility. The process was too slow. Professionals were not armed with information that might have set alarm bells ringing. Staffing levels were not adequate and the right training was not universally in place. Social care and healthcare were not working together as they should. Concerns were not properly identified, heard or acted upon.[65]

In the full CQC review report it is stated that:

We have identified systemic failures [within health services] in a number of areas leading up to the death of Baby P, in particular:

- Poor communication between health professionals and between agencies, leading to a lack of urgent action with regard to child protection arrangements and no effective escalation of concerns.
- Lack of awareness among some staff about child protection procedures, and lack of adherence, by some staff, to these procedures.
- Poor recruitment practices combined with lack of specific training in child protection, leading to the risk of some staff being inexperienced in the arrangements to protect children.
- Shortages of staff at St Ann's [Clinic], leading to delays in seeing children. This included shortages in consultants, nurses and administrative staff.
- Failings in governance in the trusts concerned, excluding the Whittington NHS Trust.[66]

Earlier in the CQC report particular mention was made of 'chronic recruitment' and staffing problems:

The children's services at Haringey Teaching PCT have
been subject to chronic recruitment problems for many
years and are still noticeably understaffed. Great Ormond
Street Hospital has been unable to recruit and retain a
sufficient number of paediatricians, and the post of named
doctor for child protection was vacant for a long time,
despite this role being a part of the statutory guidelines.
The named doctor post was recruited to on 29 January
2009. Before this, the role was being covered by the
designated doctor, which we see as unsatisfactory, given
the demanding and serious nature of both of these roles.[67]

The CQC, however, found not only a shortage and absence of
paediatricians and specialist child protection doctors, but also:

Due to the recruitment problems, there is also an
insufficient number of health visitors, school nurses
and support staff, which is resulting in current staff
having to take on excessive workloads in what is already
a demanding and challenging environment. These
recruitment difficulties have been further exacerbated
by the media attention since the case of Baby P was
highlighted, resulting in even higher staff turnover in
some areas due to the pressure of working for a trust
that is so much in the public eye.[68]

So there is specific reference here to the media coverage that had
started six months before having hindered rather than helped the
protection of children in Haringey. But what is also of note is that
this catalogue of concerns about NHS services in Haringey, and
especially services to protect children, was not reflected in the
conclusions and recommendations of the second serious case review
which was undertaken at the same time as this CQC review, nor
in the November 2008 joint area review, which was undertaken
by Ofsted with the Healthcare Commission. What is all the more
surprising was that the CQC reported in its May 2009 press release
that there were still, almost two years after Peter Connelly's death,

and six months after the start of all the press and political attention, continuing significant 'shortfalls' in NHS provision in Haringey:

- Some staff at North Middlesex Hospital NHS Trust were still not clear about who is responsible for following up child protection services to social services.
- The attendance of healthcare professionals from North Middlesex Hospital and Haringey PCT at child protection case conferences was not good enough.
- The A and E service for children at North Middlesex Hospital NHS Trust was perceived by some staff to be potentially vulnerable as there was no paediatric department after 7pm.
- The report recommended Haringey PCT and North Middlesex Hospital must work with Great Ormond Street Hospital (GOSH) to ensure they have a sufficient number of appropriately qualified paediatric staff.
- Haringey PCT is still under-staffed in terms of health visitors, school nurses and support staff. In addition, the report recommended that [GOSH] must review the consultant cover at St Ann's [Clinic] to make sure it is adequate.[69]

In its full report specific mention was made of the difficulties and shortfalls at St Ann's Clinic and with particular reference to the impact for Peter Connelly:

> St Ann's [Clinic], where the assessment [of Peter in August 2007] was carried out, is notably isolated from a paediatric health professional community [*the clinic itself is a stand-alone building located and with the appearance of being somewhat lost within a large, rambling old hospital site*]. The hospital's consultant did not have any joint meetings or regular interaction with their consultant colleagues from Great Ormond Street Hospital and North Middlesex University Hospital, at which it may have been possible to share concerns, discuss cases and therefore provide

a better overview of concerns. The consultant who examined Baby P on 1 August 2007 did not have any direct contact with the social worker assigned to Baby P's care – either prior to or following the assessment – which would have provided an opportunity to discuss the concerns and could have provided the consultant with appropriate background information. At the assessment, the consultant was the only health professional present. Having nurse support on this occasion may have proved beneficial, as nurses often provide a further opinion and additional information.[70]

How all these considerable concerns, some still continuing in summer 2009, about NHS provision in Haringey were not reflected in the conclusions and recommendations of the November 2008 joint area review and in the March 2009 second serious case review is a mystery. It is a significant omission in both reviews. How this went without much media comment and political action is also possibly surprising, but maybe not when it is recalled how the 'Baby P story' had already been shaped and was being sustained to focus on Haringey Council and then primarily on Sharon Shoesmith and the social workers.

There was short-term coverage of the findings of the May 2009 CQC report, with headlines such as 'Baby P "failed by NHS staff who saw him 35 times"'.[71] But the 'Baby P story' quickly returned to a focus on Sharon Shoesmith and the social workers. There were no calls for sackings of NHS managers, who remained unnamed and unidentified, and no continuing outcry about the NHS issues, despite the CQC reporting that there were outstanding concerns that still needed to be addressed. The 'systemic failures' and 'shortfalls' within the NHS in Haringey were not to confuse or complicate the main story line focused on naming, blaming and shaming Sharon Shoesmith and the social workers. As will be seen in the next chapter, this was not without its consequences, not only for individuals but also for child protection more generally.

There is one other review specific to Haringey that reported in 2009. This was the further joint area review ordered by Mr Balls in

December 2008. As with the November 2008 joint area review it was led by Ofsted along with the Care Standards Commission and Her Majesty's Inspectorate of Constabulary. The report of this new joint area review was published in July 2009. It noted progress in tackling a backlog of assessments, attendance of workers across agencies at case conferences, and with some developments in workload and performance management. But not surprisingly, it told a sorry tale of child protection services in difficulty, and difficulties that had been compounded by the lack of stability and capacity (presumably not helped by experienced managers and practitioners being suspended and sacked) which had increased since December 2008:

> Operational management of the referral and assessment service within children's social care has been very unstable. This is linked to the suspensions of staff involved with the case of Baby P and also to staff sickness and special leave. More recently further disruption has been caused by the restructuring of the referral and assessment service and additional suspensions and dismissals from post as the current senior management team began to tackle poor practice and capability concerns about individual managers and social workers. Key vacancies remain and a considerable proportion of posts, including some in the senior management team, are filled by interim and agency managers.[72]

The 'overall judgement' of the July 2009 joint area review was that:

> It is only six months since the last inspection and although progress can be seen in some areas, the council and its partners have made limited progress overall in addressing the areas of weakness identified in the November 2008 joint area review....These are concerns exacerbated by the serious capacity issues of the council and some of its partners.[73]

The picture from the 2009 joint area review is that it had become more difficult to protect children in Haringey, with significant issues of vacancies and disruption in the workforce and in management. This is hardly a surprising outcome from the media and political targeting of child protection workers in Haringey, targeting that created fear and threat among those who should be supported in the task of protecting children experiencing threat and trauma.

Notes

1. Department for Education and Skills (DfES) (2006) *Working together to safeguard children: A guide to inter-agency working to safeguard and promote the welfare of children* (http://webarchive.nationalarchives.gov.uk/20130401151715/https://www.education.gov.uk/publications/eOrderingDownload/WT2006%20Working_together.pdf).

2. Children Act 2004, section 20 (www.opsi.gov.uk/Acts/acts2004/ukpga-20040031-en-3#pt2-pb4-1g20).

3. Department for Children, Schools and Families (DCSF) (2010) *Working together to safeguard children: A guide to inter-agency working to safeguard and promote the welfare of children*, Nottingham: DCSF Publications, Chapter 8, p 233.

4. Brandon, M., Bailey, S. and Belerson, P. (2011) *Building on the lessons from serious case reviews: A two-year analysis of child protection database notifications 2007-2009*, London: Department for Education.

5. Brandon, Bailey and Belerson (2011) op cit, p v.

6. Haringey Local Safeguarding Children Board (LSCB) (2008) *Serious case review 'Child A'*, Executive summary, November.

7. Haringey LSCB (2008) op cit, p 6.

8. Haringey LSCB (2008) op cit, p 3.

9. Haringey LSCB (2008) op cit, p 5.

10. Haringey LSCB (2008) op cit, p 7.

11. Haringey LSCB (2008) op cit, p 5.

12. Haringey Local Safeguarding Children Board (LSCB) (2008a) *Support offered to family of child A*.

13. Haringey Local Safeguarding Children Board (LSCB) (2008b) *Background information*.

14. Haringey Local Safeguarding Children Board (LSCB) (2009) *Serious case review 'Child A'*, March 2009; full report published 26 October 2010, London: Department for Education p 9.

15. Haringey LSCB (2009) op cit, p 4.

[16] Donovan, T. (2012) 'Great Ormond Street Hospital "victimising concerned staff"', BBC News, 18 April (www.bbc.co.uk/news/uk-england-london-17733798).

[17] Lowton, A. and Bos, S. (2009) *An individual management review into the care of PC on behalf of NHS London*, February, London: Verita.

[18] Lowton and Bos (2009) op cit, p 6.

[19] Lowton and Bos (2009) op cit, p 7.

[20] Haringey LSCB (2009) op cit, p 9.

[21] Haringey LSCB (2009) op cit, p 15.

[22] Haringey LSCB (2009) op cit, p 15.

[23] Haringey LSCB (2009) op cit, p 15.

[24] Haringey LSCB (2009) op cit, p 68.

[25] General Social Care Council (GSCC) (2010) *Notice of Decision of the Conduct Committee*, Case reference: 1042389, p 10.

[26] Haringey LSCB (2009) op cit, p 70.

[27] Haringey LSCB (2009a) Statement on new Baby P serious case review, 1 May.

[28] Williams, R. (2010) 'Official report reveals serious inadequacies in "every agency involved" in Baby Peter's death', *The Guardian*, 27 October, p 6.

[29] West, A. (2010) 'Baby P cover up finally blown', *The Sun*, 27 October, pp 1, 4–5 and 8.

[30] West, A. and France, A. (2010) 'The true horror', *The Sun*, 27 October, pp 4–5.

[31] *The Sun* (2010) 'Peter's legacy: Baby P never stood a chance', 27 October, p 8.

[32] Department for Education (DfE) (2012) 'Publication of the two Serious Case Review overview reports – Peter Connelly', updated 12 July 2012 (www.education.gov.uk/a0065483/serious-case-review).

[33] BBC TV London (2012) 'Great Ormond Street: Too important to fail,' 18 April.

[34] Butler, P. (2011) 'Apology for whistle blower at Baby P clinic', *The Guardian*, 15 June, p 15.

[35] Haringey Local Safeguarding Children Board (LSCB) (2008c) *Serious case review 'Child A'*, full report published 26 October 2010, London: Department for Education.

[36] Sibert, J. and Hodes, D. (2008) *Review of child protection practice of Dr Sabah Al-Zayyat*, London: Great Ormond Street Hospital NHS Trust, p 2.

[37] Sibert and Hodes (2008) op cit, p 7.

[38] Sibert and Hodes (2008) op cit, pp 17–18.

[39] Sibert and Hodes (2008) op cit, p 17.

[40] Great Ormond Street Hospital (2011) 'MP asked to withdraw "incorrect and unsubstantiated" allegations', Press release, 22 June.

[41] Gilligan, A. (2011) 'Great Ormond Street tries to lie its way out of trouble', *The Daily Telegraph*, 5 July (http://blogs.telegraph.co.uk/news/andrewgilligan/100095432/great-ormond-street).

[42] Donovan, T. (2011) 'MP tells Great Ormond Street chief to quit over Baby P', BBC News, 9 June (www.bbc.co.uk/news/uk-england-london-13715065).

[43] Donovan, T. (2010) 'Great Ormond Street report on Baby P "not disclosed"', BBC News, 12 April (http://news.bbc.co.uk/1/hi/england/london/8616529.stm).

[44] Great Ormond Street Hospital (2011) op cit.

[45] Donovan (2011) op cit.

[46] Donovan (2010) op cit.

[47] Donovan (2011) op cit.

[48] Donovan, T. (2012) 'Great Ormond Street Hospital "victimising concerned staff"', BBC News, 18 April (www.bbc.co.uk/news/uk-england-london-17733798).

[49] Gilligan (2011) op cit.

[50] Horton, R. (2011) 'The depth of deception?', *The Lancet*, vol 377, p 2068.

[51] Hammond, P. (2010) 'Whistleblowing under Labour', *Private Eye*, 7 April (http://drphilhammond.com/blog/tag/dr-kim-holt).

[52] Featherstone, L. (2011) 'Lynn Featherstone MP fights for children and Dr Kim Holt' (www.doctors4justice.net/2011/07/lynn-featherstone-mp-fights-for.html).

[53] Donovan, T. (2011) 'Baby P hospital chief "should have resigned"', BBC News, 5 July (www.bbc.co.uk/news/uk-england-14022752).

[54] *The Lancet* (2011) 'GOSH consultants express alarm', letter, 9 July, p 123.

[55] Featherstone, L. (2011) 'GOSH continued' (www.lynnefeatherstone.org/2011/06/gosh-continued).

[56] Hammond, P. and Bousfield, A. (2010) 'Shoot the messenger: How NHS whistleblowers are silenced and sacked', *Private Eye Special* (http://drphilhammond.com/blog/wp-content/uploads/2010/07/Shoot_the_Messenger_FINAL).

[57] Allen, V., Fernandez, C. and Bentham, M. (2008) 'At least two doctors believed Baby P had been abused and police WERE told about his injuries ... but still no one would save him', *Daily Mail*, 18 November (www.dailymail.co.uk/news/article-1086862/At-doctors-believed-Baby-P-abused-police-WERE-told-injuries--save-him.html).

[58] Haringey LSCB (2008c) op cit (full report), p 51.

[59] Donovan, T. (2009) 'Police "culpable in Baby P case"', BBC News, 9 April (http://news.bbc.co.uk/1/hi/england/london/7991820.stm).

[60] Donovan (2009) op cit.

[61] Allen, V. and Moult, J. (2009) 'Bungling police missed chance to charge Baby P's mother before his death, says report', *Daily Mail*, 10 April (www.dailymail.co.uk/news/article-1168929/Bungling-police-missed-chance).

[62] Willetts, D. (2009) 'Cops "let Baby P's mum go"', *The Sun*, 11 April (www.thesun.co.uk/sol/homepage/newss/article2371229).

[63] Maier, E. (2009) 'Baby P: One rule for police: one rule for social workers', *Community Care*, 16 April (www.communitycare.co.uk/blogs/social-work-media/2009/04/baby-p-one-rule).

[64] Care Quality Commission (CQC) (2009) *Review of the involvement and action taken by health bodies in relation to the case of Baby P*, May.

[65] Care Quality Commission (CQC) (2009a) 'Care Quality Commission publishes report on the NHS care of Baby Peter', Press release, 13 May.

[66] CQC (2009) op cit, p 35.

[67] CQC (2009) op cit, p 28.

[68] CQC (2009) op cit, p 28.

[69] CQC (2009a) op cit.

[70] CQC (2009) op cit, p 16.

[71] Moore, M. (2009) 'Baby P "failed by NHS staff who saw him 35 times"', *Telegraph*, 13 May (www.telegraph.co.uk/news/uknews/baby-p/5313303/Baby-Peter-failed-by-NHS-staff-who-saw-him-35-times.html).

[72] Ofsted (2009) *Inspection of progress made in the provision of safeguarding services in the London Borough of Haringey*, 3 July, p 3.

[73] Ofsted (2009) op cit, p 4.

FIVE

The story's damaging impact

Chapter One told the story of Peter Connelly's life from March 2006 to his death in August 2007. Chapters Two, Three and Four have recounted how the story of 'Baby P' came to be started and shaped in November 2008, and was sustained. This chapter looks at the impact of the 'Baby P story'. *The Sun*, in particular, majored on the story and made it a campaigning issue. And the story was increasingly not about Peter Connelly or his family, but about a Director of Children's Services, managers and social workers in Haringey. Sharon Shoesmith, Director of Children's Services, along with Maria Ward, a social worker, and Gillie Christou, her manager, became and stayed the focus of a campaign of harassment and hatred over many years.

The Sun's 'Campaign for Justice' 2 December 2008

In what ways was the story of 'Baby P' a media creation? First, because Peter's life and death was horrific; unfortunately, however, this terrible tragedy was only one of many more terrible tragedies of child abuse at that time and since, although the names and stories of most of these other children are not known to the public as they did not attract much attention from the media. It was the editors at *The Sun*, and to a lesser extent other media, that decided to create a campaign and a continuing catalogue of reports about 'Baby P'.

Second, it was also the media, and especially *The Sun*, that decided to focus the 'Baby P story' on Sharon Shoesmith and the Haringey social workers. There was limited coverage and comment about health service managers and practitioners, with the Metropolitan Police and police officers largely absent from the media coverage.

Third, it was the media, and especially *The Sun*, but with contributions from other tabloid newspapers, that made the 'Baby P story' one of anger and hatred directed at childcare professionals who, day after day and year after year, gave their professional lives to helping and protecting children. It was a professional task that was distressing and difficult at the best of times, and which had within it constant tension and threat. Adults who abuse children may be manipulative and cunning; they may also be hostile, violent, threatening, intimidating and dangerous. But the story that was created and told made it more difficult for all social workers, and denied Peter Connelly's social workers and their managers the opportunity to continue to work to help and to protect children. Not only did it end their careers and result in their sackings, but it also led to them and their children and wider families being hunted and threatened in their personal lives.

Why would anyone want to create this hostility and hatred and a climate where safety and lives are threatened, and then report this with no contrition or condemnation? In his biography of Rupert Murdoch, owner of *The Sun* and a champion for Rebekah Brooks, Michael Wolff, who was himself immersed in US newspapers and media, wrote: 'The Murdoch formula – his tabloid magic, his working class insouciance, his badgering and bullying – is for men. The aggressiveness, the girls, the sports, the jokiness, the news – all for men.'[1]

But this is only partly true. The account of the terrible treatment of Peter Connelly engendered a horror that crossed class and gender divides. But how the story was simplified, sensationalised and sustained by making public figures out of people who sought no celebrity – this is the tabloid art form at work, and its purpose is to market a media product. Wolff tells how this tabloid media marketing works, with private lives made public, and those already in the public arena denied any privacy. In particular, he wrote about cash-driven and symbiotic relationships between celebrity seekers and *The Sun*, and as an example reflected on the coverage of Princess Diana and the commercial interests involved:

> *The Sun* is as dismissive of the royal family as any mass-market British publication could ever be. And yet the internal cash flow of News Corp becomes highly dependent on the *Sun's* obsession with Diana, Princess of Wales. If the eighties represent a convergence of publicity seekers and publicity givers, each rewarded by the market for their efforts and their symbiosis, then the relationship of Murdoch and Diana is an apogee of the era. The great, roaring bull market for newspapers in the United Kingdom during the eighties and nineties is fuelled by Diana – and when she dies in 1997, the newspaper business will also start to die.[2]

When Diana died there was an immediate outpouring of public grief, with piles of flowers and teddy bears left outside the gates of Buckingham Palace. Seventeen months after Peter Connelly died, the media coverage led by *The Sun* also resulted in a shrine of flowers, toys and teddy bears being created. The similarity with Princess Diana is startling.[*]

---

[*] In December 2008 and into 2009, as the media storm erupted and continued, there were demonstrations and rallies as the media-inspired public grief and anger about Peter Connelly's death mounted, with the focus heavily on the social workers and their managers. I was asked to speak at one of the rallies. At a meeting with one of the rally organisers I came to understand that although the grief was real, its outlet through vengeance

Note continues over

A demonstration outside Haringey Council offices and a demonstration in Central London, both photographs from *The Sun*

If Diana was the beautiful fairy tale-like princess of the 1980s and 1990s, captured in a relentless following by *The Sun*, then in 2008 *The Sun* created its version of social workers as fairy tale witches and villains. But unlike those who actively seek, or who knowingly move into, the public's gaze, this was not sought or merited by Peter Connelly's social workers and their managers. They did not seek, and had no reason to expect, that they would become commercial fodder, feeding the relentless tabloid market machine.

So is there any good reason, compared to commercial vested interest, which might give justification and a rationale for how *The Sun* and others created and channelled the 'Baby P story'? This chapter reflects on the impact of the 'Baby P story'. What was its impact on those people and personalities around whom the story was structured and who became, to greater or lesser degrees, the foundations and scaffolding for the story that was built? And what was the impact of the 'Baby P story' on children who may need protecting, families who may need assistance and on the policies and practices of different agencies and workers seeking to help and protect children?

> aimed at the social workers was not appropriate or constructive. I could not imagine what I would say at the rally that those attending would want to hear and that they would find acceptable or tolerate. Maybe rather like the two- or three-sentence paragraph quoting a social services manager somewhere late in a lengthy article attacking social workers, it seemed that I was being asked to speak to provide a veneer of fairness and balance. Rightly or wrongly, I decided that my prior commitment that Saturday could not be cancelled.

Unfortunately, not much good has resulted from the 'Baby P story', with lives shattered and arguably children made more vulnerable and less safe. Strangely, when reflecting on the denigration and dismissal of social workers in *The Sun*, the *Daily Mail* and other tabloid papers and media, if there is any good at all that has arisen from the 'Baby P story', it may be for social work and social workers. There may now be an opportunity to have social work more valued and recognised, and for social workers to have more professional space in which to practice. But the evidence for this is thin. More on this later in this chapter.

What has been the impact on the individuals who have reluctantly been characters within the 'Baby P story'? For Peter's sisters, only slightly older than him, not only have they had the horror of living in a household that must have been terrifying and threatening, but there was abuse and neglect by adults and little protection from hazards in a chaotic and increasingly overcrowded household, with seven young children in total and three dogs. As the 'Baby P story' gathered momentum, they needed protection from media intrusion and exposure. As attempts have been made to stabilise and normalise their lives, they themselves are now always at risk of media tracking and story-telling for no good reason other than it might interest the public, even if it is not in the public interest.

This has already happened with one of Peter Connelly's relatives, with a report in the *Mail on Sunday* in November 2008 stating that:

> A close male relative of Baby P was feared to have recruited youngsters in care for a notorious paedophile ring, according to a secret report seen by the *Mail on Sunday*. Although he is not believed to have had any contact with Baby P, his involvement in a child abuse scandal in Islington, North London, in the early Nineties raises questions on the extent of checks on Baby P's background.... The relative was named in reports as a victim and a feared recruiter of children for pimps. In the early Nineties he was put in a children's home....The relative, then a frightened 13-year-old, was under the

control of three pimps – Alan, John and George – who persuaded him with money, drugs and threats to bring other children to them.[3]

This is a report about a 'close male relative' of Peter Connelly who was aged 13 in the 1990s and was living in a children's home in Islington – there is enough in this report to allow him to be readily identified by anyone who knew the Connelly family in the 1990s. At least a decade later, this 'close male relative' found himself the unsuspecting subject of a major story in a tabloid paper. Why? Because he was related to 'Baby P'.

And for Peter's father, grandmother and other relatives, it is known that they continued to be contacted for comments about child abuse even years after Peter had died, comments which were then used to build links between a new child abuse story or issue and the death of Peter, with them quoted as denigrating others, including Tracey Connelly, Steven Barker, Jason Owen and social workers.

Possibly the most notable example was *The Sun* report in May 2009 at the time it launched another petition, following the undoubted success of its 2008 petition demanding the sackings of Sharon Shoesmith and the social workers, with the new petition (unsuccessfully) seeking to have the sentences of Tracey Connelly, Steven Barker and Jason Owen lengthened:

The Sun, 25 May 2009, p 9

34,000 back *Sun* fight for longer sentences. BABY P GRAN SIGNS PETITION.... The distraught woman branded her own daughter 'pure evil' after she and her child-raping boyfriend were jailed over the death of the youngster.... The grandmother said of her daughter: "I am the first in the queue when it comes to getting the sentence increased. She may think I'm a traitor but I will be signing your petition. My daughter is pure evil. I've lost my grandson". [4]

And in August 2009, *The Sun* carried a story with information about Steven Barker and Jason Owen's father. He is quoted as saying, 'Everybody thinks they are monsters and they are. What they did was awful. They deserved to be punished. I don't care what happens to them. They're not mine. I don't want anything to do with them. I don't want people to think I am related to them.' [5] *The Sun* report continued (the full names in the quote and paragraph below were within *The Sun*'s reports but to avoid further identification have not been included here):

Mr P... [changed] his name from Barker two years ago to distance himself from his sons.... Mr P..., 63, said his life was a 'living hell' because of his sons. He said: "I'm scared to go out, my life is in danger. Everyone knows who I am. I have to watch my back. It's a living hell. I can't eat. I can't sleep. I'm terrified. It will only get worse now they are named, the people will really know who I am. It's bad enough as it is. I've tried to explain but people don't want to know, they don't understand. I've been threatened lots of times". Mr P... used to live in North London with the killers' mother J..., who has also changed her name to P... two years ago. But he said after Baby P she had left him. He said, "Would you blame her? She couldn't go out either. She's gone. I don't know where". [6]

What might be surprising here is that *The Sun* reporter was told about the danger and threat to Steven Barker and Jason Owen's parents, and that they had changed their names to seek to protect themselves from this danger. But it still chose to inform the public at large of their new names. Why?

Four months later and the same *Sun* reporter identified and quoted another relative of Steven Barker and Jason Owen, and named her in his report. This time it was their sister, named as S... B.., 'aged 35 ... who left the family home at 11 because of problems with Owen', and who was reported as stating that Owen 'used his bulk to terrorise her, Steven, their younger brother A... and sister K...'.[7] So, the parents and sisters and brothers are each named in *The Sun*. They all may understandably have felt very vulnerable with the continuing tabloid coverage, vigilantism and with personal information being provided about them in the press. Any anonymity they may have sought, including taking the drastic and dramatic action of changing names, had been undermined.

The Sun also identified and marked with a headstone where Peter's ashes were scattered so it can now be sought out and visited, including by those who only know of 'Baby P' as a result of all the media coverage.

The 'Baby P' shrine of flowers, shown in *The Sun*

Peter Connelly's father was also a focus of personal media attention when *The People*, a tabloid newspaper published by Mirror Group Newspapers, wrongly reported that he had been convicted in the

1970s of raping a 14-year-old girl. Referred to in court as 'KC', Peter's father is quoted in a statement in the court proceedings suing for libel as saying:

> I was shocked and upset beyond words. I thought the whole world would think I was a really awful man. I could not believe that such an appalling, untrue statement had been published about me to the whole country. I feel [Mirror Group Newspapers'] whole approach has been to pretend I do not exist, because they did not contact me about the story, to treat me and correspondence on my behalf as an annoyance as not worth their time, and to belittle me and my feelings.[8]

Peter's father's libel case was successful, and he was awarded £75,000 in damages. It was actually Tracey Connelly's father who had been convicted of rape.[9] Not for the first time in reviewing how the story of 'Baby P' has been told is there evidence of sloppy, headline-grabbing journalism, with no concern for accuracy or for the impact on innocent people. But all members of Peter's family may probably now know that they are the possible potential targets of accurate or inaccurate tabloid coverage as they are fringe players in the continuing 'Baby P story', and for no better reason than that they are now in the public's collective memory, and it is easy to catch the public attention with new stories about them.

And for those convicted of causing or allowing Peter's death, they now themselves have a life of fear and threat. It has been reported, for example, that Steven Barker was assaulted while in prison and had his jaw broken, and the *Daily Mirror* reported in 2011 that 'Crossbow cannibal Stephen Griffiths is friends with Baby P killer Steven Barker' and that 'serial killer Griffiths, 41, chats with Steven Barker at meals time on the medical wing at the top security Wakefield Prison'.[10] Wakefield Prison may be top security, but not apparently for information about prisoners being provided to the press.

Tracey Connelly's personal correspondence from prison has also become publicly available and reported by newspapers. In 2010 there was a report in *The Sun* about her seeing her daughters:

> **Outrage over Baby P mum's day with kids.** Baby
> P's mother has astonishingly been allowed to see her
> other children, *The Sun* can reveal. Evil Tracey Connelly,
> caged last May after the 17-month-old lad died of abuse,
> was taken to a meeting in London ... a jail source said
> last night: "It's staggering that she's able to have face-to-
> face contact with her kids while serving a sentence for
> Baby P's death".[11]

There was similar coverage of Karen Matthews, the imprisoned
mother of Shannon Matthews who, she had claimed, was kidnapped
as Karen Matthews apparently sought a reward from the tabloid press
for her daughter's discovery On one occasion when briefly taken
outside the prison, she was photographed wearing a t-shirt with the
face of Marilyn Monroe that then appeared in *The Sun* with the
caption, 'Beauty on the beast'.[12]

But how is this information from within prisons and about
prisoners being made available for reporting in the tabloid press?
One concern that arose through the police investigations into phone
hacking by newspapers is that prison officers, among other public
officials, may have received significant cash payments for passing on
information to the papers.[13]

In August 2011 Jason Owen was released on licence from prison
having served half of his sentence. *The Sun*'s coverage suggests that
the newspaper must have committed considerable resources to the
story about his release.

The Sun prepared the ground for its readers in the days before the
release, with the headline on Tuesday 2 August: 'Baby P killer is free
on Friday'.[14] It included the iconic picture of Peter looking up with
the background of the chequered floor. It also had photographs of
'Peter's evil mum Tracey' and of Jason Owen. In addition there was
a photograph of Sharon Shoesmith, and integrated into its report
was the news that 'Supreme Court judges booted out an appeal by
Education Secretary Michael Gove and her former council employers
against a ruling that she was unfairly sacked'. There was a subheading
to the report about Jason Owen's prison release that stated, 'Double
insult as Shoesmith set for £2.5m'. So, in one report, *The Sun* alerted

its readers to Jason Owen's forthcoming release, gave the date of the release, and also managed to bring Sharon Shoesmith into the story, albeit without having to give too much prominence to the fact that the Supreme Court had ruled in Sharon Shoesmith's favour by not allowing an appeal by the Secretary of State against the Court of Appeal's judgment that she had been 'unfairly sacked'.

Four days later, on Saturday 6 August, *The Sun* published a photograph of Jason Owen and again the iconic photo of Peter Connelly, with the headline, 'Baby P killer is smuggled out of prison'[15] and reported that 'cowardly Owen, 39, left a nick hidden inside a prison van to avoid being photographed.... He will have to live at an approved address and report to a probation officer.' The report's last sentence was 'Bungler Sharon Shoesmith – head of children's services in Haringey, North London, when Peter died – is claiming £2.5 million over her sacking'.

And now the hunt was on to find, identify and photograph Jason Owen. It took a little time, but three weeks later the hunt was successful. On Friday 26 August, *The Sun* published two contemporary photographs of Jason Owen looking at his mobile phone and carrying a plastic shopping bag, and had the headline, 'Baby P killer Jason Owen on the street', with a report that:

> This is killer Jason Owen – back on the street as a free man.... He looked relaxed and fit as he was spotted shopping near his probation hostel at a secret location.... Passers-by had no idea he was one of the three caged for causing the death of baby Peter.... But as Owen bought ice cream, a newspaper and some groceries, he displayed several tell-tale signs of his identity. He showed off his distinctive 'angel wings' tattoo on his left arm. And inked on his right forearm was a large crucifix with the grimly ironic slogan: 'Only God can judge me'. Owen, also a convicted arsonist, crack addict and National Front member, had hoped he would be given plastic surgery and a new identity on his release from London's Wandsworth jail. But instead he has been forced to rely on keeping a low profile to avoid being attacked.[16]

So despite a concern that Owen might be attacked, *The Sun* published two close-up pictures of him, and in case the pictures were not clear enough in identifying him, gave detailed descriptions of his tattoos. Not surprisingly, the following day, *The Sun*'s report was that 'Baby P monster Jason Owen is taken to hideout' and 'The law protects killer Jason Owen ... why didn't it protect baby Peter Connelly'. *The Sun*'s report, by the same reporter as before, noted that:

> Baby P killer Jason Owen was dramatically whisked to a new hideaway yesterday as outrage erupted after *The Sun* revealed he was back on the streets.... Baby Peter's sickened gran last night blasted Britain's legal system for protecting Owen – after it failed to prevent the toddler's horrific death. [The grandmother – whose full name was given in *The Sun*], 61, said: "It makes me angry that Owen is living in a secret location. Why should he be given any protection when my grandson didn't receive any? If it wasn't for *The Sun*, nobody would know where he is or what he was doing".... Owen, 39, had been living at a probation hostel in a secret location.... But yesterday he was moved after *The Sun* published exclusive pictures of him smirking as he strolled down the street among unsuspecting shoppers.[17]

It was a theme of *The Sun*'s reports at this time to claim that they were 'exclusives', that it was *The Sun* that was leading the (successful) hunt for Jason Owen, and that this was a moral campaign for justice. Others might have seen it as potentially enabling vigilante action.

But the hunt was now on again, with the probation service having moved Jason Owen to another secret location to avoid the very real danger of vigilante violence. And in what was a very serious game of cat and mouse, two weeks later, *The Sun* had traced Jason Owen again. The report on 13 September was headed, 'Baby P killer Jason Owen in park'.[18] This time there were four photographs of Jason Owen that not only allowed him to be readily identified, but also probably to anyone who knew the park and the surrounding streets, his location was identifiable. And there was a reminder about the tattoos, albeit 'he kept his distinctive tattoos – including one that reads "Only God can judge me" – hidden under long sleeves', and with a quote from a 'furious relative' saying 'He thinks he can waltz back into society, which just goes to show his arrogance'.

It was not only *The Sun* that covered Jason Owen's release from prison, although it was *The Sun* that claimed exclusive reports on his release and subsequent whereabouts and identified him to others.* However, the *Daily Mirror*[19] and *Daily Mail*,[20] for example, also reported on Jason Owen's release, but with less attention and detail.

The consequences of the 'Baby P story' for Sharon Shoesmith, the managers and social workers in Haringey have been referred to earlier. They were also hunted. The harassment and hatred, and the threat and fear, placed their personal safety and security at significant risk and undermined their physical and mental health. They have been directly and remorselessly targeted by the tabloids, and in particular *The Sun*, and there have been concerns about the safety of other members of their families.

What rationale can there be for a reporter, with no warning and without it being anticipated, to cold contact Sharon Shoesmith's elderly mother in Ireland at the start of the 'Baby P story', and to ask her what she thought about her daughter being involved in the death of a child? What legitimacy or justification is there for those who have threatened to trace and harm the children of the social workers and their managers?[21] Why did *The Sun* show no condemnation or contrition when it reported that some of its readers 'want to take the law into their own hands'?[22] What was *The Sun*'s motivation in seeking to get personal information from its readers about the social workers? Why did any editor or journalist think this harassment, threat and intimidation were responsible rather than reprehensible?

So what was it like to be targeted by *The Sun* and other tabloids? Paparazzi photographers and reporters mounting a vigil for months

---

* It was also *The Sun* that tracked down and had an 'exclusive' full front page and page 5 pictures of Tracey Connelly when she was released from prison in October 2013 (Wells, T. [2013] 'Picture exclusive: Smile of Baby P's evil mum', *The Sun*, 15 November, front page and p 5).

outside homes and peering through windows; being followed and pursued when shopping, walking along the pavement or when necessarily and inevitably having to attend tribunal and court hearings; pictures shown over and over again beside the now iconic photograph of Peter Connelly with captions such as 'the accused'. Family members may be fictitious, allegedly quoted saying they should be sacked. Telephones regularly ringing in the middle of the night with encouragement to commit suicide. Shouted at and threatened when seen by members of the public who recognise them from the tabloid pictures and who have been stimulated to be aggressive and abusive by the tabloid story-telling. And with the threat of violence so real that special arrangements have to be made by the police to create safe rooms, fitting panic alarms and strengthening the perimeter security of properties, with advice from the police to stand back from the edge of underground railway platforms in case some stranger tried to push them onto the electrified track. And then having to change address and home and make other arrangements for the care and safety of their own children. This was the experience of Sharon Shoesmith, Gillie Christou and Maria Ward; not just for days, weeks or months, but for years, the media coverage and tabloid vilification continued relentlessly and with the consequent threat and abuse it spawned. Livelihoods were lost, with no income and no one willing to offer any employment of any sort to those who had become high profile and outcasts.

It is hard to see how this could possibly have been justified, but Rebekah Brooks, *The Sun*'s editor in 2008–09, commented that 'I have spent my journalistic career campaigning for victims of crime'.[23] It is stated in 2012 that, 'as the former chief executive of News International Brooks was one of the most powerful people in the UK, a conduit between Rupert Murdoch's newspaper empire and David Cameron. She was a key figure in persuading Murdoch that *The Sun* should switch from backing Labour to backing the Conservatives at the 2010 election.'[24] Chapter Two has already recounted how *The Sun* and Mr Cameron confronted Mr Brown and Mr Balls about 'Baby P', and how both *The Sun* and Mr Cameron targeted Haringey Council, seeking and demanding that Sharon Shoesmith and the social workers be sacked.

At the time Mrs Brooks described it as a 'campaign for justice'. In a lecture she gave at the London College of Communications in January 2009 it is reported that she said, 'The public outcry was deafening. And we began our fight for justice with a determination to expose the lack of accountability and responsibility for Baby P's brutal death....This is not a modern day witch-hunt but a petition for justice' that put 'morality over political correctness'.[25] But it was seen as a witch hunt, with the Court of Appeal calling it 'scapegoating', and it is difficult to see any relevance for her comment about 'political correctness', although this may have been an opportunistic, albeit irrelevant, tangential comment aimed at liberals and the left.

Mrs Brooks' view of justice, and what is legitimate in pursuing it, is a contested and challengeable view, even if it is accepted that that was her motivation when editor of the *News of the World* and then of *The Sun* in majoring on stories about the abuse and killing of children. However, how these stories were sourced and shaped is increasingly contentious and a cause for concern as they are linked with allegations of phone hacking and other personal intrusions into the lives of grieving parents and the disruption of criminal investigations focused on the real seeking of justice by apprehending and convicting those who were the criminals who killed children.

But maybe even Mrs Brooks and *The Sun* came to the view that it was a headline too far when their November 2008 front page about Haringey Council and its social workers had the caption '**BLOOD ON THEIR HANDS**' in bold dominating the page. It was a phrase previously used about *The Sun* by Earl Spencer at the time his sister, Princess Diana, died when the car in which she travelling in Paris crashed while being chased by paparazzi photographers.[26]

In 2012 I could not, unlike other reports from *The Sun* that have been quoted, find this front page on *The Sun's* website. But it could still be found with some difficulty, referred to within other web pages,[27] and there are comments criticising and complaining about it.[28, 29] There is still, however, on *The Sun's* site, a report dated 14 January 2009 with a picture of Sharon Shoesmith at the time her appeal to Haringey Council against her dismissal was unsuccessful. The report has the headline, 'Shoesmith loses blood money' and

The Sun's infamous front page in November 2008

claims that 'it marks a victory for the *Sun*'s campaign for all social services staff who failed the tragic toddler to be sacked'.[30]

But what of other key people who had roles within the 'Baby P story'? It was commented in May 2009 in the CQC's review of the health service responses to Peter Connelly, that:

> We note that the role of the GP in this case also had some responsibility for the care of Baby P. The GP would have received letters that reported Baby P's attendance at hospital and, as the central medical record holder, the GP may have been able to identify the trend of recurring visits to A and E as a signal of potential abuse. The clinical practice of the GP involved in the Baby P case is currently being investigated by Haringey PCT and the GMC.[31]

In January 2009, at the height of *The Sun* campaign calling for sackings a year-and-a-half after Peter Connelly's death, Dr Ikwueke, Peter Connelly's GP, was suspended by Haringey PCT, and in February 2009 the GMC suspended his registration for 18 months.[32] He subsequently returned in 2011 to his GP practice in Tottenham.[33, 34]

Dr Al-Zayyat, the paediatrician who saw Peter at St Ann's Clinic, did not have her rolling six-monthly contract renewed by Great Ormond Street Hospital NHS Trust, and then attempted to sue for wrongful dismissal.[35] *The Sun* had the headline 'Baby P bungler sues hospital', and commented that:

> The woman doctor who failed to spot Baby P's back was broken is suing for £100,000 after being sacked. Shameless Dr Sabah Al-Zayyat, 52 – who also missed broken ribs suffered by the horrifically abused toddler two days before he died in agony – claims she was unfairly dismissed. Last night London's world-famous Great Ormond Street Hospital which employed the paediatrician vowed to fight the law suit – which is being funded by the **TAXPAYER**.[36]

Dr Al-Zayyat had also been referred to the GMC. The account given in the CQC's 2009 review of the health services received by Peter Connelly shows that she was not, however, referred to the GMC until a year after Peter died and following the Sibert and Hodes review, discussed in Chapter Four, into her practice and into the paediatric services at St Ann's Clinic. When she was first considered by the GMC she was not suspended but allowed to continue working:

> The consultant [Dr Al-Zayyat] was referred to the GMC's Interim Orders Panel on 11 August 2008. The committee imposed conditions on the consultant's registration that allowed her to continue to work as a paediatrician under supervision.
>
> In September 2008, when the trial of the mother of Baby P, her partner and the lodger commenced at the Old Bailey, the consultant was referred back to the

panel for a review of her conditions. The panel made no changes to the conditions at that time.

On 21 November 2008, the GMC's Interim Orders Panel reviewed the case for the third time and decided that it was in the public's interest to suspend the consultant's registration pending the outcome of the investigation into her conduct.[37]

It was only, therefore, at the time when the 'Baby P story' and *The Sun*'s campaign for sackings started in November 2008 that Dr Al-Zayyat and Dr Ikwueke had their registrations suspended by the GMC. *The Sun*'s 'campaign for justice' could be seen to be having an immediate impact. As noted earlier, the same happened for the social workers where disciplinary hearings already concluded with outcomes of warnings were then heard again, with the social workers dismissed.

Dr Al-Zayyat was later, in 2011, granted a 'voluntary erasure' from the GMC's register of doctors after successfully arguing at a judicial review[38] that she should not be subject to a full hearing as she was not well enough to attend. It was reported that she was 'suicidal [and] had suffered panic attacks'[39] and in 2010 she left the UK and returned home to Saudi Arabia.[40] She has not, therefore, been subject to a misconduct hearing or judgment,[41] but is no longer registered as a doctor in the UK.

In 2010, Dr Jane Collins, Chief Executive of Great Ormond Street Hospital NHS Trust, also applied to the GMC to have her name removed from the medical register. It was reported in the *Daily Telegraph* at the time that:

> Jane Collins insisted that her decision to remove her name from the General Medical Council roll was not connected with criticism of her management at the hospital. But the move means she could not be subjected to any future GMC investigation of her handling of the Baby P case. Great Ormond Street was heavily criticised last year by the Health Watchdog the Care Quality Commission into the death of the 17-month-old.... Last

year Dr Kim Holt, a Great Ormond Street consultant who worked at St Ann's, claimed that Baby P would be alive if concerns she had earlier raised about standards of care had been heeded by managers. In a private meeting in June of this year some Great Ormond Street consultants also voiced criticism of patient care and are said to have warned of 'dangerous' skills developing.[42]

Dr Collins explained within *The Daily Telegraph* report that her reason for removing her name from the GMC register was that she had not practised as a doctor for nine years. But the pressure on Dr Collins did not ease with headlines such as 'Doctors demand Great Ormond Street Hospital chief quit',[43] 'Baby Peter clinic "did not heed doctors' concerns"',[44] 'Call for sacking over Great Ormond Street "cover-up" of Baby Peter report'[45] and 'Great Ormond Street hospital issues apology to Baby P whistleblower'.[46] In April 2012 BBC London broadcast a 30-minute television programme titled 'Great Ormond Street too important to fail?' which focused on claims of harassment of whistleblowers, and on the alleged editing and withholding of information from the Peter Connelly serious case reviews.

There is no doubt that Great Ormond Street Hospital is an important national and international centre of excellence for very ill children. Indeed, Mr and Mrs Cameron's disabled son was treated over many years at the hospital, and it was the subject of a very powerful and positive BBC television documentary series in late spring 2012 about the surgical and medical care for children and young people with very complex and life-threatening conditions. It was also a major feature in the tableau about the NHS in the opening ceremony of the summer 2012 London Olympics. But was this internationally famous and much-respected clinical centre of excellence geared up to provide community paediatric and child protection services in a demanding diverse and disadvantaged area of north London?

In May 2012, Great Ormond Street Hospital noted in a press release that 'Dr Jane Collins announces she is leaving Trust after nearly 11 years as Chief Executive' to become Chief Executive of Marie Curie Cancer Care.[47]

Dr Kim Holt was a consultant paediatrician at St Ann's Clinic who, along with colleagues, had raised concerns about capacity and arrangements at the clinic before Dr Al-Zayyat saw Peter Connelly. After several years of not being able to practise, it was reported in 2011 that she had received an apology from Great Ormond Street Hospital for the response she had received as a whistleblower, and that she 'is now understood to have returned to work with a new NHS employer, Whittington Hospital in North London'.[48] (North Whittington Hospital was where Peter Connelly was admitted when he had his injuries in December 2006.) Dr Holt has also been a leading figure in establishing Patients First, an NHS whistleblowers campaign group.

But what about the Metropolitan Police officers who were involved with the Connelly family, or with the management of policing services in Haringey? They are largely unknown to the public except possibly, but very unlikely, Detective Superintendent Caroline Bates of the Child Abuse Investigation Command. She was a senior officer in the Metropolitan Police with responsibility for child protection criminal investigations and fronted up for the police the media coverage in November 2008 when Tracey Connelly, Steven Barker and Jason Owen were each found in the criminal proceedings to have caused or allowed Peter Connelly's death.

It is not known what happened to the police officers who undertook the two criminal investigations before Peter died. They are not named or identified in the official or media reports which consistently used the amorphous and anonymous term 'the police' when referring, albeit only in general terms, to the police officers. However, in a report following the findings of guilt at the criminal trial in November 2008, the BBC noted that 'the police officer investigating the suspected abuse, [*with the name of the police officer given*], said she had also been opposed to Baby P returning to the family home because her investigation had not been completed'.[49]

I am not aware of any information that any police officer has been the subject of any formal disciplinary action at all in relation to Peter Connelly and the Connelly family. This is not, however, an argument for more sackings and dismissals. A thread throughout the

'Baby P story' is that blame and vengeance has overwhelmed learning and commitment. Removing those with experience whenever an unpredicted terrible tragedy occurs does not lead to improvement; instead it leads to a loss of learning, including the learning prompted by the tragedy.

In a book published in 2009 about the 'Baby P story',[50] and essentially telling the story as told within *The Sun* and other tabloid newspapers, a list is given of 'the personnel involved in the Baby P case'. It is a fascinating list. It gives the names of many of the people referred to earlier in this book. But what is most fascinating is, first, the ordering of the list and, second, those who are not named within it.

This list might be seen as a hierarchy of blame as largely presented in the tabloid press. It starts with the perpetrators, and then the family, followed by Haringey Council's children's services managers, councillors and social workers, and finally, the health workers and doctors. No police officers are listed, and no police or NHS managers.

Personnel involved in the Baby P case

Baby P: Peter Connelly, born 1 March 2006, died 3 August 2007

Tracey Connelly: Peter's mother

Steven Barker: Peter's brutal 'stepfather'

Jason Owen: Barker's elder brother, who had changed his surname

[Name given]: Tracey Connelly's mother

[Name given]: Tracey Connelly's natural father

Sharon Shoesmith, Head of Children's Services at Haringey Council

Cecilia Hitchen, Shoesmith's Deputy

George Mehan, Haringey Council Leader

Liz Santry, Haringey Council's Cabinet Member for children and young people

Clive Preece, Haringey Council's Head of Safeguarding Services

Agnes White, social worker

Maria Ward, social worker

Sylvia Henry, social worker

Paulette Thomas, health visitor

[Name given], family friend

Nevres Kemal, former Haringey social worker and whistleblower

Gillie Christou, team manager in Haringey Council children's services

Karolina Jamry, mental health worker

Dr Sabah Al-Zayyat, the doctor who saw Peter two days before he died

Dr Heather Mackinnon, consultant paediatrician concerned by Peter's injuries, who contacted social services

Dr Jerome Ikwueke, GP who saw Peter several times and twice referred him to specialists after becoming concerned

Source: Taken from McShane, J. (2009) *It must never happen again: The lessons learned from the short life and terrible death of Baby P*, London: John Blake, pp 249-50.

This list of people involved with Peter Connelly and the Connelly family reflects the targeting of Haringey Council. But the Metropolitan Police in totality, and NHS managers largely, were absent in the media story-telling, and this is replicated in the listing in the McShane book.

With regard to the Metropolitan Police, basing his comments in 2009 largely on the second serious case review report, John McShane notes that 'the police were only informed and involved at two stages'[51] with Peter Connelly. This is not so, although Mr McShane's comment might be understood in the context of the lack of attention given to the Metropolitan Police in the second serious case review. The first criminal investigation started in December 2006. The second criminal investigation started in June 2007. The investigations were not concluded with decisions taken and communicated until July and August 2007. Throughout a period of eight months up until the time Peter died, therefore, police officers were pursuing their inquiries and investigations into Peter Connelly's injuries.

But although it might be seen that it was the tabloid press, with politicians, and also with the police, that shaped the 'Baby P story', they themselves have had a torrid time since 2008, as partly recounted in Chapter Three. This has included the *Daily Telegraph*-led MPs' expenses scandal, followed by *The Guardian*-led exposure of News International newspaper phone hacking. Rupert Murdoch and his son, James Murdoch, have had their intention to own Sky News thwarted, the *News of the World* has closed down and journalists from the *News of the World* and *The Sun* have been investigated and charged with criminal offences. Rebekah Brooks has been charged with perverting the course of justice, phone hacking and conspiracy to commit misconduct in public office,[52] and has resigned as the UK Chief Executive of News International. It is reported, however, that she has received a £10.8 million 'pay-off' from News International.[53] (On Sharon Shoesmith's salary as Director of Children's Services it would have taken 100 years to earn this amount; for the social workers, it would have taken 300 years.)

So Mrs Brooks was a senior editor and executive central to the concerns about alleged criminal activities and yet was still given a multi-million-pound payment. This is the same Mrs Brooks who led a campaign demanding that no payment or pension be paid to Sharon Shoesmith following her dismissal, even though Ms Shoesmith has never been investigated or charged with any criminal offence. Mrs Brooks' campaign also made much of Sharon Shoesmith having a salary of £110,000 while leading a large children's services department (albeit it was reported her successor was appointed on a salary nearer £200,000 ... probably a necessity to get anyone to take such a high exposure service leadership role in Haringey[54]). Sharon Shoesmith's salary was about the same as the payments being made by *The Sun* to a private investigator to hack phones.[55]

The contamination from the News International scandals has also led to resignations and retirements of a whole tranche of the most senior officers in the Metropolitan Police who were seen to have shown great reluctance to investigate claims of criminal activity by News International and its employees. Top police officers from the Metropolitan Police have been exposed as having very close friendships with News International editors and journalists, and with the Metropolitan Police employing recently retired News International editors and other staff.[56] The lack of distance and discretion between the Metropolitan Police and the News International newspapers has been startling, with comments about 'the scale of corruption, collusion and cover-up between News International, politicians and police'.[57]

And it is not only top Metropolitan Police officers who have been found to have had extensive relationships with editors and others within Rupert Murdoch's newspapers. David Cameron became Prime Minister in 2010 and brought with him Andy Coulson as his Director of Communications. Mr Coulson had previously resigned as editor of *News of the World* following the phone hacking of members of the royal family. Despite this background he was appointed, with limited security checks, to a role at the centre of government and with easy access to secret and confidential information.[58] He has since been charged in relation to criminal offences of corruption and conspiracy.[59]

Mr Cameron is also now known, especially through evidence given at the Leveson Inquiry and discussed in Chapter Two, to have had a personal friendship with Rebekah Brooks, including sending her 'LOL' text messages which, according to Mrs Brooks, he thought meant 'lots of love'. Rebekah Brooks' husband and David Cameron were at Eton College together. They were near-neighbours living at Chipping Norton in the Cotswolds, socialising at weekends and over Christmas.

Mr Gove became Secretary of State for Education, and with a responsibility for child protection, in the Coalition government led by Mr Cameron. He was also within a social network that included the Murdochs and Rebekah Brooks. Indeed, Mr Gove's wife, Sarah Vine, was a columnist with Mr Murdoch's *Times* newspapers. Mr Gove had also been a former reporter for *The Times*, and was a strong advocate for Rupert Murdoch at the Leveson Inquiry.

Mr Balls and Mr Brown, however, were no longer in government following electoral defeat for Labour in 2010, although both remained as MPs. Mr Balls was now Shadow Chancellor of the Exchequer and Mr Brown had no official parliamentary role beyond being an MP. Rebekah Brooks and Mr Cameron had cornered each of them at the time the 'Baby P story' was being shaped and championed by *The Sun*.

Ms Featherstone and Mr Lammy, the two local MPs for Tottenham, remained in Parliament. Ms Featherstone became the Equalities Minister within the Coalition government, and Mr Lammy the Shadow Minister for Higher Education.

So, out of all the key players within the 'Baby P story', it was the politicians who were still in play, including Beverley Hughes, Children's Minister in 2008–09 and a former Lecturer in Social Work. She resigned as a minister in June 2009, and then became a baroness and entered the House of Lords. Newspaper editors, on the other hand, are facing criminal charges, and top police officers have resigned. Their misfortunes may be seen largely as of their own creation. But the same cannot be said for Sharon Shoesmith, the social workers and the social work managers. Their misfortune was to be targeted and traduced by the tabloid press and politicians.

Others that have not flourished during the telling of the 'Baby P story' are two of the three inspectorates (the exception being the national police inspectorate) that had key roles in the hasty joint area review of child protection in Haringey commissioned by Mr Balls in November 2008. For both Ofsted and the Healthcare Commission/

CQC and their chief executives it was a tumultuous, tricky and traumatic time between 2009 and 2012.

As noted earlier, there were concerns about Ofsted's role in November 2008 when, in the eye of the media and political storm, it revised and reversed its assessment of Haringey's children's services and re-rated it from 'good' to 'inadequate'. ADCS and House of Commons Children, Schools and Families Select Committee had major misgivings more generally about Ofsted. This was reflected, for example, in the later headline in February 2010, that 'Directors of children's services remain unconvinced about the quality of Ofsted's workforce and leadership'. This headline was based on a survey with responses from 25 Directors of Children's Services. It was reported that of this small sample 82 per cent said Ofsted inspectors were 'not up to the job' and 72 per cent responded that Christine Gilbert was not the 'right person to lead the watchdog'.[60]

At about the same time, Dame Denise Platt was stated as telling the House of Commons Children, Schools and Families Select Committee that 'not many of the 300 CSCI staff who were transferred to Ofsted were analysts or senior' and that 'CSCI's expertise had been dissipated during the transfer in 2007'.[61] Denise Platt was a former social worker, Director of Social Services, Chief Inspector for Social Services in the Department of Health, and then chair of the Commission for Social Care Inspection (CSCI). In 2007 Ofsted took over the inspection and regulation of children's social care services from CSCI, including child protection.

Speculation increased that Christine Gilbert would stand down from being Ofsted's Chief Executive after the Conservative-led Coalition government came into power in May 2010. It was reported on 21 June, for example, that the 'Ofsted chief will step down early if "helpful" for the new government' and that 'the move follows rumours in national newspapers that education secretary Michael Gove has asked Gilbert to leave before her contract expires in 2011'.[62] But the following day there was a further report that 'Christine Gilbert [was] to remain at Ofsted until next year' and that Barry Shearman, former chair of the Select Committee and who had been critical of Ofsted, said 'Christine Gilbert is a public servant and should be treated with respect. If she has a contract till a certain date she should be allowed to honour that.'[63]

Christine Gilbert did remain as Ofsted's Chief Executive for another year until June 2011,[64] following earlier speculation in December 2010 that:

> Christine Gilbert, the chief inspector of schools, is in talks to leave her job early after coming under pressure from ministers to resign.... In June [2010], Gilbert, who has headed Ofsted since 2006, announced that she would leave when her £200,000-a-year, five-year contract expires at the end of October next year, amid reports that the education secretary, Michael Gove, was keen to replace her [and that she] has been interviewed for the job of group chief executive of the United Learning Trust (ULT), the biggest provider of academy schools, which also runs a chain of private schools.[65]

In 2012 Christine Gilbert was leading Christine Gilbert Associates, 'a small expert company with a passion for education and children's services'.[66] In September 2012 it was announced that she was to become the interim Chief Executive of the London Borough of Brent Council.[67]

By 2012 Cynthia Bower, Chief Executive of the CQC (formed in 2009 from a merger of the Healthcare Commission, Mental Health Act Commission and the adult social care responsibilities of CSCI), had also resigned from her post after concerns about the performance of the CQC. It was a not dissimilar tale to that of Ofsted, with debate about the competence and capacity of the CQC to inspect, register and regulate a wide range of services on a platform that had been built for inspecting hospitals, not social care services. In particular, there were significant concerns, initially exposed in a BBC *Panorama* programme, about the policies, processes, expertise and experience within the CQC to inspect services for people with a learning disability.

At the time of her resignation in 2012 it was noted that:

The head of England's NHS regulator, Cynthia Bower, has resigned after growing criticism that the watchdog was not fit for purpose. Bower, chief executive of the Care Quality Commission, announced that she is quitting her £195,000-a-year post after four increasingly difficult years at the helm. Concern over the watchdog grew in the Department of Health last year after organisations including care home operators and the NHS Confederation, which represents hospitals, voiced their fears that their establishments were not being policed properly by the CQC. A Whitehall source said: 'Ministers had been assured that the CQC's house was in order. But each time they opened a door, skeletons fell out.'[68]

The suggestion that every time a door was opened which had been inspected by the hospital watchdog a skeleton fell out may be a little too graphic, if very visual. But within four years of the 'Baby P story' being launched in November 2008, two of the major national inspectorates, Ofsted and the CQC, had damaged reputations, inspired little confidence from those inspected, and their chief executives had left. Yet these were the inspectorates that, in their present or previous incarnations, were central to delivering the hasty but damning report to Mr Balls in November 2008 which led to him immediately removing Sharon Shoesmith from her role as Haringey's Director of Children's Services.

But what happened to all those national reports commissioned by Mr Balls in late 2008 – the Laming review, the CQC review of the NHS and child protection, and the Social Work Task Force? And to this list can be added the Kennedy review of child health services, the pre-'Baby P' review of social work commissioned by Tim Loughton when Shadow Minister of State for Children, and the Munro review on social work and child protection. What was the impact of these reports, largely, but not all, spawned or influenced by the 'Baby P story'?

It was the Laming review[69] that was quickly undertaken and then published first, in March 2009. Lord Laming had previously led the Victoria Climbié Inquiry that reported in January 2003.[70] Victoria Climbié lived towards the end of her life and died, aged eight, in Tottenham less than half a mile from where Peter Connelly later lived and died. She was killed by her great-aunt and the great-aunt's boyfriend, having suffered severe chronic neglect and gross physical abuse over a period of many months. She died in February 2000 having spent the winter months 'living and sleeping in a bath in an unheated bathroom, bound hand and foot inside a bin bag, lying in her own urine and faeces'.[71]

In the Victoria Climbié Inquiry report Lord Laming was critical of all the agencies that had contact with Victoria and her great-aunt, including social services departments in Ealing, Brent and Haringey, health services including Central Middlesex Hospital and North Middlesex Hospital (where Peter Connelly was later a patient) and the Metropolitan Police. Laming commented in 2003:

> Not one of the agencies empowered by Parliament to protect children in positions similar to Victoria's – funded from the public purse – emerge from this Inquiry with much credit. The suffering and death of Victoria was a gross failure of the system and was inexcusable. It is clear to me that the agencies with responsibility for Victoria gave a low priority to the task of protecting children. They were under-funded, inadequately staffed and poorly led. Even so, there was plenty of evidence to show that scarce resources were not put to good use. Bad practice can be expensive.[72]

Lord Laming made comments that might also be seen as relevant five years later, to Peter Connelly:

> The most senior police officer to give evidence from the MPS [Metropolitan Police Service] was Deputy

Assistant Commissioner William Griffiths. He said of the investigation carried out by the Haringey Child Protection Team, 'In the A to Z of an investigation, that investigation did not get to B.' Therefore, I conclude that, despite the Children Act 1989 having been in force for just a decade, the standard of investigation into criminal offences against children may not be as rigorous as the investigation of similar crimes against adults.

... [And] it seems that the basic discipline of medical evaluation, covering history-taking, examination, arriving at a differential diagnosis, and monitoring the outcome, was not put in practice in Victoria's case ... I found it hard to understand why established good medical practice, that would have undoubtedly helped clarify the complexities in Victoria's case, was not followed at the Central Middlesex Hospital and the North Middlesex Hospital.[73]

The comparisons concerning Victoria Climbié and Peter Connelly are complex. First, there were still lessons to be learned about the urgency and attention to be given to the criminal investigations of injuries to children. Second, time and resources were still an issue. And third, it was still social workers who experienced the brunt of suspensions and disciplinary actions.

But there were also differences. There was a considerable contrast between the engagement with Peter Connelly by social workers and health workers compared to the much more limited engagement with Victoria Climbié. Peter Connelly was not a child neglected by social services. With all the benefit of hindsight and knowing what is now known, different decisions would have been taken, but Peter was not unseen, and many resources were mobilised to seek to improve and oversee his care.

In his 2003 Inquiry report Lord Laming had 108 recommendations.[74] There were 17 'general' recommendations that related in part to the establishment of new national and local infrastructures for monitoring and managing partnership working across agencies. Local safeguarding children boards could be seen to have their roots here. There were 46 'social care' recommendations; many were quite specific about management oversight of practice and information sharing and recording. There were 27 'healthcare' recommendations about child protection decision-making and medical examinations and assessments where there were concerns about deliberate harm to children. And there were 18 'police' recommendations about ensuring proper investigations were carried out, and giving greater priority to child protection.

One of the recommendations for the police was that 'the police [should] carry out completely, and exclusively, any criminal investigation elements in a case of a suspected injury or harm to a child, including the evidential interview with the child victim. This will remove any confusion about which agency takes the "lead" or is responsible for certain actions.'[75] This was an attempt by Lord Laming to be clear that it was the responsibility of the police, and of the police only, to undertake the criminal investigation. For the flawed two investigations before Peter died it is, therefore, clear that the responsibility was with the Metropolitan Police.

But the more general impact of this recommendation was to undermine what had been the well-established practice of joint investigations between police officers and social workers. If this practice was still in place when Peter Connelly was injured, it may be that there would not have been the delay and drift in the investigations. The investigations would not have been totally dependent on police officers, and the first investigation may not have been disrupted without anyone recognising that this was an unintended and unexpected consequence of one police officer changing role.

But what was not in the 2003 Laming recommendations were the abolition of social services departments and the advent of children's services within local councils by merging together leadership and management arrangements that had been separate for education and schools and for social work and social care. Indeed, 23 of the Laming recommendations were specifically and directly addressed to 'Directors of Social Services', a statutory role and function within local government about to be ended by the then Labour government.

It has been frequently claimed that it was Lord Laming's Climbié Inquiry report and recommendations that led to the *Every Child Matters* Green Paper, and then to the Children Act 2004. Indeed, the then Prime Minister, Mr Blair, in his foreword to the Green Paper, published alongside the government's response to the Laming Inquiry, specifically referred to the death of Victoria Climbié. But it is not true that it was the Laming Inquiry that primarily resulted in the Green Paper. The proposals in the White Paper, and the new arrangements required by the 2004 Act, were based on the long-standing commitment and intention of government ministers to tackle social exclusion by bringing services together.[76] Margaret Hodge was the Children's Minister in the early 2000s, and as Leader of Islington Council in the 1980s she had introduced the general management of a wide range of services, including child protection social work, which would be integrated within local decentralised and devolved neighbourhood teams. It was an imaginative concept to break down departmental and professional barriers and to focus on communities. In Islington in the 1980s the council lost the local specialist management and supervision of crucial and complex children's social work. The 2004 Act was to achieve the same nationally for the top management of children's social work.

One immediate consequence in the mid-2000s was that each local authority was required to appoint a Director of Children's Services. Most councils brought together their education departments and children's social work and social care services which had previously been within social services departments. These had largely been led by Directors of Social Services who had been social workers and knew about social work and child protection. In carving up and allocating the new top management roles within local councils, former Directors of Education became the new Directors of Children's Services and the Directors of Social Services became the new Directors of Adult Social Services.

So at a stroke the top management experience and expertise built up during careers of children's social work practice and management was largely dissipated and destroyed. This was not unlike the initial loss of children's social work and social care experience and expertise when Ofsted took over responsibility for children's social care, including child protection, from CSCI. National and local leadership of children's social care and social work was now largely with top managers and professionals with a professional grounding in education, schools and teaching. This did not go without later comment:

> Child deaths and non-accidental injuries are rising and, because of monstrous Government tinkering with long-established child protection systems, there will be many other Baby Ps. For example, due to an insane Government diktat of 2004, education and social services have merged and are now treated alike as 'children's services'. Councils are meant to act as if one child's need to learn and write, and another terrified child's desperate need to evade being sold into a killer paedophile ring, can be met by the same department. Former teacher Shoesmith had no specialist training in child protection, yet was placed in charge of it in Haringey, as well as education, on a £100,000 salary. Her replacement is also a former council education head. So there's no change there, then.[77]

Rather less dramatic and less personalised was the letter in *The Guardian* from a former Director of Social Services:

> I retired as director of social services and head of children and families for a London borough in April 2007, precisely because I knew I would not make a good director of children's services. Sure, I could do as well as anyone with regard to assessing need, and safeguarding and parenting the most vulnerable children but I was not equipped to drive up schools standards and close the yawning academic gap that still persists nationally.
>
> Logically there can only be one dominant culture in any one organisation. A culture in which a highly regulated, directly managed and targeted service will thrive is entirely at odds with that necessary for the

coordination of universal services for which the service leader has no direct authority over most of their people or cash.

The mindsets needed are simply different and no amount of training or experience can change that.[78]

Sharon Shoesmith has been a champion for social workers, as represented in a piece she wrote in *The Guardian* in July 2010 where she noted, 'I can only imagine how difficult the last 18 months has been for social workers all over the country.... I pay tribute to the perseverance and commitment of social workers in the face of some of the most hostile public reaction I think the country has ever seen'.[79] She has also been recognised as a successful and respected leader, with much support and praise, as noted earlier by headteachers across Haringey. But she and Haringey Council had had to work within, and Lord Laming in 2009 had to review, a system and structure for local authority children's services and child protection social work introduced in 2004 that was not what Lord Laming had actually recommended. So what did he find and what did he conclude through his review?

Laming had six main recommendations for government:

1. The Secretaries of State for Health, Justice, the Home Office and Children, Schools and Families must collaborate in setting strategic priorities for the protection of children and young people for each of the key frontline services and ensure sufficient resources in place to deliver these priorities.
2. The Government must immediately inject greater energy and drive into the implementation of change and support local improvement by establishing a powerful National Delivery Unit to report directly to Cabinet through the Families, Children and Young People Sub-Committee.
3. The Secretary of State for Children, Schools and Families must immediately address the inadequacy of the training and supply of frontline social workers.

4. The Secretary of State for Health must immediately address the wariness of staff throughout the health services to engage with child protection work.
5. The Home Secretary must urgently address the adequacy of the resources devoted to police child protection teams.
6. The Secretary of State for Justice should take immediate action to shorten the time taken in court processes.[80]

What Lord Laming found and reported on in his brief 2009 review was a child protection system which was under considerable pressure, with 60,000 children in the care of local councils, 29,000 with child protection plans and, for the then most recent data collected in 2005, 235,000 children 'in need' and requiring and receiving support from local authorities.[81]

He also noted, as commented on above, that 'the creation of Children's Services Departments has meant that a large proportion of DCSs [Directors of Children's Services] do not have first-hand experience of frontline social work', and recommended that 'all Directors of Children's Services who do not have direct experience or background in safeguarding and child protection must appoint a senior manager within their team with the necessary skills and experience'.[82] Haringey Council already had this arrangement in place from the time it established its children's services department in the mid-2000s.

But what about the pressures within child protection services? First, social work:

> Frontline social workers and social work managers are under an immense amount of pressure. Low staff morale, poor supervision, high case-loads, under-resourcing and inadequate training each contribute to high levels of stress and recruitment and retention difficulties. Many social workers feel the size of the task in protecting children and young people from harm is insurmountable and this increases the risk of harm. Social work and, in particular, child protection work is felt to be a 'Cinderella' service within other parts of the children's workforce. It is

noticeable that education has received substantially more investment over the last decade. Public vilification of social workers has a negative effect on staff and has serious implications for the effectiveness, status and morale of the children's workforce. There has been a long-time appetite in the media to portray social workers in ways that are negative and undermining.... However, without highly motivated and confident social workers the reality is that more children will be exposed to harm.[83]

The pressure and media issues were not only noted to be relevant for social workers but also had an impact on child health services:

The number of health visitors has dropped by 10% in the last three years and case-loads are significantly higher than the recommended 300 families or 400 children, with 40% of health visitors handling case-loads of over 500 children and 20% over 1,000 children. 69.2% of health visitors say that they no longer have the resources to respond to the needs of the most vulnerable children.[84]
... Evidence to this report suggested that paediatricians are sometimes reluctant to become involved in child protection work.[85]

And for the police:

Concerns about the resourcing of child protection teams exist within a large number of police forces, particularly since other issues [for example, international terrorism was a major concern at this time] have taken on greater national significance. Although not general, there is clearly an issue that, in a number of forces, child protection work is accorded low status and does not attract the most able and experienced police officers. Some forces that contributed to this report also described high vacancy rates within child protection teams and others have seen significant reductions in posts in the years since the initial response to Victoria Climbié.[86]

The concerns about pressure and morale and about recruitment and retention across child protection services, with some key professionals seeking to avoid child protection work altogether, is a disturbing picture of the state of child protection in England after the initial media fury in November 2008 about 'Baby P'. It is also a damning indictment of the impact of the media frenzy, with workers anxious about being tabloid and then public targets. Child protection is difficult and distressing work. Following the abuse and threat to social workers and others generated by how the 'Baby P story' was shaped and targeted, it had become even more difficult and anxiety-provoking. Lord Laming bravely captured this picture in his report.

The Sun's report on the Laming review was headed 'Now Just Do It':

> A DESPAIRING peer who probed the Baby P tragedy recommended 58 ways to keep kids safer yesterday – and told child protection staff: "Now just do it!"....And nearly 250,000 kids are at risk because child protection networks are a shambles ... In a shocking condemnation, the peer found staff plagued by low morale, poor supervision, under-funding and inadequate training ... and he said staff were obsessed with form-filling, box ticking and meeting targets – at the expense of protecting children.... Lord Laming called on council executives to take responsibility for blunders. It was a barb aimed at Sharon Shoesmith, the social services chief at London's Haringey Council....[87]

There was no reference to Sharon Shoesmith in Lord Laming's report, but *The Sun* still found the opportunity to continue its harassment. Beside this report in *The Sun* was a column by Deidre Sanders, subtitled the 'Sun Agony Aunt'. It was, not surprisingly, relatively sympathetic to social workers. Why so? Deidre Sanders had been appointed by Mr Balls as a member of the Social Work Task Force which he had set up to improve social work and its status. What was a surprise to many social workers and others was that Mr Balls had thought it appropriate to appoint a columnist from *The Sun* to improve the profile of social work and its public standing. In her column Deidre Sanders asked *Sun* readers to send her their views and experiences. Having been bombarded by *The Sun* with a diet of blame and shame targeted at social workers, it is hard to imagine that a balanced response was likely to be received.

The government's response[88] to the Laming review was published two months later, in May 2009. There was a ministerial foreword from Mr Balls, which was possibly surprising in its tone and content considering his actions of targeting Haringey Council with the subsequent sackings of Sharon Shoesmith and the social workers. Mr Balls wrote:

> This country has one of the best child protection systems in the world. Every day, thousands of people at the front-line – social workers, teachers, police officers, doctors, nurses and others – work tirelessly to support children and young people and help keep them safe. But good practice is not yet standard practice – and we should not rest until it is.[89]

In essence, the government largely accepted Lord Laming's recommendations in full. Among its commitments was the introduction of a new leadership programme for Directors of Children's Services, a specialist child abuse investigators' development programme for the police, the development and enhancement of health visiting services and action with the courts to reduce delays in care proceedings.

But the major thrust of the government's response was for social work, and included confirmation of the importance of the Social Work Task Force Mr Balls had initiated in December 2008. There was also the introduction of a Social Work Transformation Fund of £57.8 million on top of £73 million previously announced, noting that 'it is clear that the recruitment and retention of children and families' social workers are issues of key concern, and particularly severe in local authorities'.[90] The money was to be spent to assist former social workers to return to social work, for a recruitment scheme to encourage graduates to train as social workers, a programme for newly qualified social workers, and to encourage experienced social workers to remain in practitioner roles through an advanced social work practitioner status.

The Social Work Task Force reported in November 2009.[91] It was chaired by Moira Gibb, a much respected former social worker, Director of Social Services, and in 2009, Chief Executive of Camden Borough Council (which shared a boundary with Haringey). The Task Force commented that:

> Good social work ... depends on confident, effective frontline professionals. These professionals depend, in turn, on a system of high quality training, regulation and leadership behind them.... When social workers have confidence in their own skills, purpose and identity, and in the system in place to back them up, they have a huge amount to offer.... At present, however, social work in England too often falls short of these basic conditions. Weaknesses in recruitment, retention, frontline resources, training, leadership, public understanding and other factors all compound one another.[92]

It was also noted that:

> Social workers have spelled out to the Task Force how deeply concerned they are by the way their profession is reported in the media.... They have expressed their anger at how social workers often appear singled out for blame in the aftermath of a child's death.... The public image of the profession therefore seems unremittingly negative, with damaging consequences for recruitment, morale and public perceptions.[93]

The Task Force sought to address these issues within its 15 recommendations, with a new College of Social Work to be created to lead on a programme of action on the public understanding of social work. Other recommendations focused on social worker education and training and improved supervision and management of social workers, with standards to be set for employers so that there was clarity as to what social workers should expect to allow them to practise well.

As with the Laming review recommendations, the Social Work Task Force recommendations were largely accepted by the government, and a Social Work Reform Board was established, also chaired by Moira Gibb, to deliver on the recommendations. It worked on a framework of professional standards for social workers and standards for employers. It commented on the systems, procedures and processes – the bureaucracy – which was overwhelming social work practice and taking up much of the time of social workers, procedures and bureaucracy that had built up incrementally over time, often as a consequence of the recommendations of inquiries into the deaths of children. The Reform Board noted that social workers were saying 'that in order to improve services they need more time to spend working directly with families'.[94]

This theme was picked up in a further report. This time it was based on a review, not commissioned by the Labour government, but in June 2010, by the new Conservative-led Coalition government. It should not have been too much of a surprise that the new government initiated this further review. In opposition, in October 2007, soon after the death of Peter Connelly but unrelated to it, and well before the media frenzy started in November 2008, it published a report of a Commission chaired by Tim Loughton, Shadow Minister for Children. David Cameron, as the then new leader of the Conservative Party, noted in his foreword to the Commission's report that it was part of a wide-ranging programme of research by the Conservative Party to inform its policy reviews as it prepared its manifesto for the next election. Mr Cameron wrote:

Social workers, particularly those dealing with child
protection cases, are at the sharp end ... often dealing
with very difficult and damaged families. They have a
key role to play in early intervention to keep families
together wherever possible, and in meeting the needs of
vulnerable children who are taken into care when their
safety is put at risk.[95]

The 2007 report of the Conservative Party's Commission was called
No more blame game: The future for children's social workers, a title Mr
Cameron and Mr Gove subsequently failed to live up to when *The
Sun* launched its 'justice for Baby P' campaign in November 2008.

The 2007 Commission had a membership that included
experienced Directors of Social Services and managers, the recently
retired Head of the British Association for Adoption and Fostering
(BAAF), a leading Professor of Social Work, along with a senior
local authority councillor and a professional journalist who had
been editor of *Community Care* magazine. It was a non-party political
membership with considerable experience and expertise and chaired
by a Conservative MP who was and continued to be a champion
for social work. Like the later Social Work Task Force, it looked at
the education and training of social workers, their recruitment and
retention and their management and work priorities. But it started
by looking at the public image of social workers, noting:

Social workers often receive a disproportionate share
of the blame in highly publicised cases even though a
team of professionals from health, education and police
is usually involved, and major decisions are made by the
courts. This singling out of social workers for blame was
commented on in much of the evidence we received as
contributing to the negative image. The social worker's
negative image is highlighted in the media coverage of
cases where failures are reported and successes rarely.[96]

The Commission's report then quotes evidence it received from
Helen Grant, a family court lawyer:

———

The media relies upon simplified and generalised tabloid sensationalism to sell papers and grab audiences. The resulting demonization of individuals positively undermines the vocation and disincentivises quality individuals becoming involved.[97]

This message, and the Commission's conclusions, were presumably not recalled by Mr Cameron when he was an early contributor to *The Sun*'s 'Baby P story' only a year later with the blaming, bullying and battering of social workers in Haringey.

But another area of concern identified by the Commission was about the 'bureaucracy and administration' overwhelming social workers:

Nearly all respondents stated that while they could see the need for accountability through careful record keeping, it was taking a disproportionate amount of social worker's time. The [General Social Care Council] wrote that some social workers are spending at least 60–70% of their time on administrative work as opposed to client contact. Much of this time is spent filling in forms to ensure accountability rather than working with the family.[98]

So with the Conservative Party's Commission in 2007 coming up with these conclusions it should not be too surprising that, when it came into government in 2010, the new review it then initiated should pick up on and address these issues. It should be even less surprising when the person appointed to undertake the review was Professor Eileen Munro from the LSE. A former social worker, she had a number of published books and academic papers that focused on how blaming and bureaucracy had a negative impact on social work practice,[99, 100] and wrote a piece in November 2009 headlined, 'Beyond the blame culture':

Both public opinion and formal investigations conclude that children are harmed or killed because people

working in child protection are stupid, malicious, lazy
or incompetent. (There is surely, as Sharon Shoesmith
knows, deep and lasting anger.) Why is this assumed?
Surely it is reasonable to believe that people who
choose to work in this demanding field want to help
children, rather than allow them to be hurt.... We know
that protection broke down in the cases of Baby Peter,
Victoria Climbié and others whose names are still
veiled. But we have failed to ask the right questions in
response – not "How could they get it so wrong?", but
rather: "How can we build a system that is more likely
to get it right?"[101]

The Munro review's final report[102] on child protection was published
in May 2011, almost four years after Peter Connelly had died, and
two-and-a-half years after *The Sun* launched its then still continuing
'Baby P campaign for justice'. Its recommendations, which again
were largely accepted by the government,[103] focused on cutting
bureaucracy and procedures, cutting data collection and performance
indicators on timescales that stifled and distorted professional practice,
and instead creating a system that facilitated learning, with more
space for social work practice, and for more time to be spent in direct
contact and work with children and families. It also recommended
more early intervention rather than later crisis work with families.
Munro soon became concerned, however, about how government
policies and funding cuts were undermining early intervention with
families, and leading to more families getting into difficulty.[104]

But there is something strange and quite unusual here. What has
invariably happened over the past 60 years is that from time to time
there is, albeit often short-term, media, public and political attention
given to a death of a child. Most children who are killed attract little
media or public attention, but every so often a child is killed and it
becomes a matter of national concern. What usually then happens
is that there is new legislation and more procedures and statutory
guidance to be followed by social workers and others to try to
stop it happening again. The killing of Dennis O'Neill was seen to
lead to the Children Act 1948, the death of Maria Colwell to the

Children Act 1975 and Adoption Act 1976, the Cleveland Inquiry to the Children Act 1989, and the death of Victoria Climbié to the Children Act 2004. So why did the death of Peter Connelly not lead to major new children's legislation but instead to a commitment to reduce procedures, guidance and bureaucracy?

The answer is that each of the child deaths noted above contributed to and were used as a rationale for changes that were already being developed and that fitted the political context and plans already in place.[105] So it was in the late 2000s, when there was a move away from the over-prescription and over-elaboration of performance management systems that had built up under the Labour government as it sought to modernise public services through increased performance monitoring and management by central government.[106]

Oliver Letwin, who led on the Conservative Party's policy development in the late 2000s, is reported to have made specific comments in January 2009 at the height of the 'Baby P' media frenzy about how the 'death of Baby P highlights failure in regulation':

> Labour's obsession with the wrong sort of regulation may have contributed to the death of Baby P, the Conservative Party's policy chief, Oliver Letwin, suggested today. In a speech ... Letwin made a distinction between rule-based regulation, which he criticised, and judgement-based regulation, which he backed. He said that children's services in Haringey – heavily criticised in the Baby P case – were a prime example of the failed rule-based regulation. "They receive just after the horrific death of Baby P a commendable Ofsted report.... Processes were in order. Everything requiring to be done under (rule-based regulation) had been done. The baby was dead – ah yes, a tragic error. But the regulation had been observed".... Fans of rule-based regulation have a 'touching faith' that it would deliver results but it was inappropriate when applied to complex activities, Letwin said. "Every time there is a call for something to be regulated, the Labour government leaps into the

fray – with new rule-based regulation that specifies more processes that must or must not be followed".[107]

Unfortunately, however, the Coalition government's rhetoric about reducing central prescription ran parallel, as noted above by Professor Munro, with significant and severe cuts in public expenditure, leaving local councils and their employees such as social workers the freedom, but also the responsibility, only to reduce help for families and to have to ration their own time more heavily.

So did the 'Baby P campaign for justice' launched in November 2008 make it safer for children? Hardly. First, it became more difficult to recruit and retain social workers within child protection services. This was not only true for Haringey Council and but for other councils too. Second, the number of referrals to social workers from schools, health visitors and others about possible abuse and neglect of children escalated. Third, when the Conservative-led Coalition government was elected with *The Sun's* support in 2010, the new government pursued an aggressive policy of rapidly reducing public expenditure, including reducing the funding to local councils with responsibility to care for and protect children. It also reduced funding for services to help families in difficulty by, for example, cutting the money for the Sure Start programme. And it hit the poorest children and families hardest by severely cutting welfare and housing benefits. Under the new Coalition government it is likely that the Connelly family would have experienced more poverty and greater housing difficulties, with less help and less social work supervision and oversight.

So, the 'Baby P story' contributed to, and was a primary creator of, the 'perfect storm' of recruitment and retention difficulties for child protection social workers at a time of increasing workloads. These were in part a consequence of other professionals and agencies referring more children to social workers, and also of Coalition government policies that will have led to increasing numbers of families and children stressed, in poverty and with less help and assistance available. Is this what was intended by Mrs Brooks and *The Sun* and by Mr Cameron? Surely not, but it was an easily anticipated and predictable consequence of their actions and behaviour. This did not go without comment, including from Sharon Shoesmith:

> Children's social care depends upon a delicate balance of the competence and confidence of front-line staff, and their teamwork; the supply of foster parents and adoptive parents; the availability of good residential placements; and the funds available, because social care cannot be demand-led – and therein lies the serious problem. As 2008 closed, we saw that balance collapse. Then, one in 200 children were in care: now the figure is one in 150. One in 400 children were subject to a child protection plan: now it's one in 200. This is the so-called 'Baby P effect'. But in my mind it was more due to the reaction of politicians and other senior leaders – were they really so naive?[108]

Others also anticipated and commented on this 'Baby P effect' generated by parts of the press and politicians:

> When Baby Peter died, the repercussions went far beyond the jailing of his brutal family. The hidden victims of the aftermath are still feeling its impact across Britain. More children than ever are being taken into care and social workers are demonised yet again.... One result of the Baby P case has been a 40 per cent increase in the children taken into care.... The numbers with child protection plans have also increased. But there has been no corresponding rise in the number of social workers, children's homes, foster places or adoptive families. Nor in the number of Cafcass [Children and Family Court Advisory and Support Service] workers who act for the children in the Family Court. Nor is there an increase in the number of judges who hear their cases.[109]

> This frenzy of hatred is a disaster for children at risk.... There will always be catastrophic failure, but one case

blasted out of all proportion can undo years of good. David Lammy, the MP for the Haringey constituency of Tottenham, wonders how his borough will ever attract new social workers with *The Sun* waiting to tell them they have blood on their hands. If too few are found and more children suffer, *The Sun* is unlikely to own up to blood on its hands.[110]

And this is exactly the difficulty that arose in Haringey and elsewhere. More work for social workers, increased difficulty in recruiting and retaining social workers to do the work, and with the new Director of Children's Services in Haringey in January 2009 asking other London boroughs, which were also under great pressure, to 'lend it social workers to ease a recruitment crisis triggered by the case of "Baby P"'[111] in the context of 'care figures in Haringey soar[ing]'.[112] But this was not a difficulty confined to Haringey or to London with a Local Government Association survey reported in May 2009 finding that '57% of councils in England have found recruiting social workers more difficult in the past six months', with 13 per cent of children's social work posts unfilled.[113]

Even in October 2012, four years after the November 2008 start of the 'Baby P story', there were continuing difficulties in recruiting and retaining social workers to work at the sharp end of child protection, and this was still being related back to 'Baby P':

> The [social work] sector is still reeling from the Baby P tragedy, which undermined public confidence and damaged recruitment and retention of staff. Many departments have shortages and there are about 1,350 vacancies in child protection work.[114]

The proposed solution, as noted in *The Times* article and in a column[115] by Lord Adonis, a Labour peer who had himself been in care, was a Social Work First fast-track programme to entice new graduates from the best universities and with the best academic grades to become children's social workers. A similar programme was reported to have been successful in attracting the brightest graduates into teaching, called Teach First. This recognised the intellectual capacity required to make difficult judgements based on collating and appraising the information available at the time decisions had to be taken.

In a paper[116] published at almost the same time as the Social Work First programme was launched, I had argued that the intellectual capacity and competence required of social workers needed to be given emphasis and a greater profile. But I disagree with the assertion made by Lord Adonis that 'there is serious demoralisation in the [social work] profession after failings in the Baby P case and in the grooming of girls in Rochdale and Rotherham', the latter being much in the news in October 2012. Any demoralisation is more likely to be as a consequence of the harassment and hatred directed at social workers.

What was surprising was the speed of impact of the 'Baby P story' and *The Sun*'s campaign targeting social workers. The number of care cases in the courts, according to Cafcass figures,[117] jumped from 482 in September 2008 and 496 in October 2008 to 716 in December 2008 as *The Sun*'s 'Baby P story' and campaign quickly started to bite. In January–March 2009 the figures were 663/657/739. In 2008 the figures for these months had been 514/502/536. This was a staggering increase during the period December 2008 to March 2009, and an increase that occurred very quickly.

It was also an increase that was sustained, unlike other peaks following major child protection stories which, as with the stories themselves, were more short-lived. For example, Cafcass undertook a review in 2012 of care proceedings applications to courts. It called its study *Three weeks in November ... three years on*,[118] a reference back to the three weeks in November 2008 when the 'Baby P story' was launched by the press. The figures below, taken from Cafcass reports, show how immediately, and then how sustained, the increases in care applications to courts from November 2008 were.

Care applications to courts[119]					
	2007/08	2008/09	2009/10	2010/11	2011/12
Total applications	6,323	6,488	8,832	9,204	10,218
% increase from 2007/08	–	2.6	39.7	45.6	61.6
% increase from previous year	–	2.6	36.1	4.2	11.0
Rate of applications per 10,000 children	5.8	5.9	8.0	8.3	9.2

As shown, this surge of increased court applications continued into 2009/10, and has continued to increase since then, but at a slower rate. Is this good news for children who need protecting? Here are two different views from April 2012 commenting on the same figures, and each relating comments back to 'Baby P':

> It shows that as a result of intensive work on behalf of children, court applications on behalf of children are being made in a more timely way than in 2008, and at an earlier stage of local authority contact with a family. In particular, neglect cases are being acted on more quickly, in terms of making court applications than was the case prior to the Peter Connelly case. (Anthony Douglas, Chief Executive of Cafcass)[120]

> Since Haringey Council failed to prevent the tragic death of Baby P, the number of children being taken into care has accelerated. Figures released yesterday by the Children and Family Court Advisory Service [Cafcass] showed that care applications have arisen by 10 per cent since last year, to a record of 10,199. I struggle to believe that every single one of these children would be better off in care than with their families. (Camilla Cavendish)[121]

Camilla Cavendish, writing in *The Times* in 2012, fits within the script of only targeting Haringey Council with comments about failings in relation to 'Baby P', but her concern about the increased numbers of care proceedings in the courts was, at the early height of the 'Baby P story' in November 2008, also recognised by Cafcass Chief Executive, Anthony Douglas:

> Whilst it is too early to be definitive, we may already be seeing a 'Baby P' effect in a reported increase in applications to court by local authorities to protect children in many parts of England, and in more cautious decision-making about contact applications in some cases. This is hardly surprising. Negative publicity usually leads to institutional risk aversion. This may be, if confirmed, good news for those children who need protection, and bad news for others who need more contact with a wide range of family members, not less.[122]

And this is the dilemma every day for social workers and for doctors, other health workers and the police ... and then ultimately to be decided by the courts ... is it best for *this* child with what is known at *this* time that the child stays within their family or best to remove the child from the family?

However, although there was without a doubt a significant and immediate escalation of child protection workloads following the initial media telling of the 'Baby P story', some of the trends were already upwards, but they escalated and then continued to increase post-'Baby P', and have now reached particularly high levels. Colin Green, Director of Children's Services in Coventry (who in 2013 was the target of hostile and vengeful comments by parts of the media following the death of Daniel Pelka, a four-year-old abused in Coventry by his mother and her new partner) and previously a leading child protection specialist in the DCSF, commented that:

> The number of children with child protections plans has increased from 25,000 in 2004/05 to 42,300 in 2010/11. This is an increase of 63%. The numbers of referrals to children's social care have increased in the same period, from 552,000 to 613,000, and the numbers of initial assessments from 293,000 to 441,000, an increase of 34%.[123] At the sharpest end of child protection work,

the evidence points to more need, as figures for children subject to care proceedings have risen more than 40% since 2008/09 and continue to rise.[124] I do not think that we can just see this as an effect of the Peter Connelly case. The rise started before the case attracted widespread public attention, and unlike the rises in activity following other high profile cases such as Victoria Climbié this rise has been sustained: the latest figures from Cafcass indicate that over two years later the level of activity is still rising.[125]

However, even if the rise in child protection workloads was not only due to the media creation and coverage of the 'Baby P story', there is a wide acceptance that this story-telling, with its personalised harassment and threats to those working within child protection services, has had an impact that continues.

In 2012, four years after it had led on the 'Baby P story', *The Sun* was itself expressing shock at what it headlined as 'The Baby P effect':

Shocking figures show a record number of applications from local councils to take children into care in the past 12 months. They exceeded 10,000 for the first time in the year to the end of March.... This is a 10.8 per cent increase from the previous 12 months, when there were 9,202 applications. And there has been a massive leap since 2008–2009, when there were 6,488. The reason is being put down to a so-called "Baby P effect", following a tightening of procedures since the sickening death of 17-month-old Peter Connelly, who died in 2007 after suffering more than 50 injuries. Following his death *The Sun* launched a campaign to ensure the tragedy was never repeated. The case provoked a storm of criticism of police, social workers and health professionals.... But while applications to take children into care have risen, there is a shortage of foster carers to meet the demand.[126]

There is, however, a subtle change in this report in *The Sun* compared to its reports during the previous four years. It mentions criticism of the police, and it mentions the police even before social workers. Had the previously very warm relationship between *The Sun*'s editors and reporters and top and other officers in the Metropolitan Police felt a chill? Might this have been a consequence of the Leveson Inquiry and the phone hacking scandal, with News International editors and journalists, including Rebekah Brooks, facing criminal trials? But *The Sun* still managed to integrate a picture of Sharon Shoesmith alongside a photograph of 'Baby P's' grave into its report.

The changing stance of *The Sun* was commented on by Roy Greenslade, a long time ago a former deputy chief sub-editor with *The Sun* and in 2012 a Professor of Journalism, who noted that:

> The paper has shifted from heaping all the blame on to the council's social services department to include others.... The latest formulation is a further refinement as the paper moves away from its single-minded and narrow-minded assault on a single department and named individuals. But the damage was done at the time because Shoesmith was controversially dismissed following the intervention of the then children's secretary Ed Balls. Several of her colleagues were also traduced due to *The Sun*'s hue and cry.[127]

But *The Sun*'s 'damage' went much further than the sackings of Sharon Shoesmith and the social workers. It destabilised a child protection system which had been finely tuned over 50 years since the death of Maria Colwell and the Colwell Inquiry in the early 1970s, albeit a system where the burgeoning procedure manual had led to the clogging up of the engine as the oil of professional judgement and wisdom was drained from it.

The damage, as reported in the press, included:

* 'Public opinion of social workers worsens after "Baby P"', based on a telephone survey of 1,005 adults in which 'two out of five

people say their opinion of social workers has got worse since the tragic case of Baby P'.[128]

- 'Health visitors quit Haringey after Baby P case: the number of health visitors in Haringey has almost halved in the wake of the Baby P tragedy.'[129]
- '... the continuing increase in care applications by England's local authorities following the Baby P case could cause a "catastrophe" in children's services unless central and local government put in place joined-up strategies to deal with its impact. That is the warning from the British Association for Adoption and Fostering....'[130]
- 'ADCS reveals extent of strain on child protection ... while councils have seen an average 21% rise in most safeguarding work activities [between the end of 2007 to the end of 2009], there has only been a 10% increase in staff working in this area.'[131]
- 'Councils struggle to find social workers.... Council chiefs fear that after the Baby P debacle the situation will only worsen, with potential recruits put off by the bad publicity surrounding the Haringey case.'[132]
- 'Nottinghamshire Council has spent £1.5m on agency social worker teams because it does not have enough permanent staff to handle a jump in child protection referrals since Baby P.'[133]
- 'Social workers lack time to work with children.'[134]
- '£100m bill as social workers intervene more readily post-Baby P. Children's services departments could be faced with extra costs of hundreds of thousands of pounds a year if the surge in child protection orders continues.'[135]

And increase they did, with higher costs, higher workloads, no commensurate increase in workers, and with a care system creaking under exceptional numbers and pressure, and all in the context of less public support. Sir Roger Singleton, former Chief Executive of Barnardo's, who was appointed in March 2009 as the government's Chief Adviser on the Safety of Children following the post-'Baby P' Laming review of child protection in England, explicitly warned Mr Balls and the government about the impact of increasing child protection workloads, especially in the context of cuts in public expenditure that would reduce the capacity to handle the increases in workload:

> Singleton, in his first annual report to parliament, leaves no one in any doubt of the extreme demands and pressures facing child protection services in the wake of Baby Peter. Over the past year, safeguarding has become more 'complex and pressurised', he notes. The number of youngsters being put on the child protection register or taken into care has risen dramatically. There are huge and possibly unrealistic public expectations about what safeguarding can achieve. What are not increasing are child protection budgets, he says, and they may even start shrinking: cuts to safeguarding services will be 'firmly in the offing' when councils, NHS trusts and police forces start to look for savings.[136]

But, as above, with Camilla Cavendish in *The Times*, not everyone thought increasing numbers of children in care was bound to be a good idea. The *Daily Mail* continued to follow its damned-if-you-do-damned-if-you-don't targeting of social workers about removing or leaving children with their families, with headlines such as 'In hiding, the mother accused of abuse for cuddling her child'.[137] And the then new Head of Family Courts, Lord Justice Wall, is reported in *The Guardian* to have been 'shocked by social workers who split families',[138] or even more dramatically with the headline in the *Metro* of 'The "Stalinist" workers who grab children'.[139] More measured, Christina Blacklaws, a solicitor specialising in children and families work, was quoted by the BBC as saying 'I am worried that local authorities may now be overly cautious, potentially removing children who could safely stay at home with support, rather than face another Baby Peter situation'.[140]

There were, therefore, concerns that there may have been too much of a swing towards assertive and defensive practice, with children removed from their families inappropriately, albeit when a child is then found to have been abused there is still a media-in-waiting ready to pounce on the professionals who had not taken action to seek to get the courts to place the child in care.

Another concern was about all the changes being generated by the government across public services, and how this was destabilising child protection services. There was increasing complexity and competition and fragmentation and fragility.[141] This related to the greater independence and autonomy being given to schools, but focused particularly on the NHS. For example, the Royal College of General Practice, the Royal College of Nursing and the Royal College of Midwifery each expressed concerns about increasing competition rather than collaboration, and the damaging and destructive impact of further reorganisation.[142]

Concerns about the potential negative impact from changes in the NHS were all the more significant when it had already been found that many health services were not doing well in contributing to the safety and protection of children. Following the start of the telling of the 'Baby P story' in November 2008, Alan Johnson, Secretary of State for Health, ordered a national review into child protection and the NHS. The CQC reported in July 2009, and Cynthia Bowers, its Chief Executive, is reported to have said:

> It is clear that safeguarding has not been as high on the agenda of [NHS] trust boards as it should have been.... In some cases NHS staff have not been given the support they need in terms of training and clear procedures for handling concerns. If that were to change, it would be an appropriate legacy for Baby Peter.[143]

The CQC found that only 54 per cent of eligible NHS staff had received basic child protection training. It was found that there were concerns nationally for three groups of staff who would have been particularly significant for Peter Connelly when he had his NHS contacts, with only 58 per cent of A&E staff having had adequate child protection training, only 35 per cent of GPs known to have had relevant child protection training, and a fifth of NHS trusts employing health visitors where each health visitor had caseloads of more than 500 children, well above the upper recommended limit of 400.[144]

Over a year later, in September 2010, there was a further national report about NHS services for children. The report was by Professor Sir Ian Kennedy and it generated a headline in *The Sun* of 'NHS IS FAILING KIDS SAYS BABY P PROF'. *The Sun* report continued with:

> Prompted by the death of Baby P, the Government-commissioned report warns that kids get 'low priority'. Standards of care 'are often mediocre or worse' and GPs have too little paediatric training – with many cases palmed off on hospital A and E units.... Sir Ian, ex-boss of the NHS regulator, slams the collection and sharing of information on kids 'as a mess', saying it led to the 'horror story' of Baby P.[145]

One of the consequences of the Kennedy report was that work was undertaken to prepare new guidance on child protection for doctors. The General Medical Council issued this guidance in 2012 with a report that the GMC 'calls on doctors to raise their child protection concerns without delay [and] doctors will be expected to communicate effectively and work with social workers and other professionals and must cooperate fully with child protection procedures'.[146]

So what might it be like for someone such as Peter Connelly and his family after the structuring and telling of the 'Baby P story' by *The Sun* and others? Would the impact of the story and government policies five years on from Peter Connelly's death have made it any safer for children like Peter?

With what was known to police officers, social workers, doctors, other health workers and teachers prior to Peter's death it is still uncertain, and maybe even unlikely, that there was evidence for a successful application to court for Peter to be removed from his mother. This would be so even with the number of care applications having increased in Haringey by 211 per cent between 2008 and 2009,[147] a rate of increase even higher than the national increase, and not surprising bearing in mind how threatened by media attention Haringey Council and its social workers would have been.

There are concerns that under the 2012 Cameron-led Coalition government a family like the Connellys would have experienced more difficulties, with less help and supervision. Professor Eileen Munro, author of the government's review report on child protection and social work, was quoted, in an article headed '"Terrifying" welfare reforms will drive up care referrals, warns Munro', as saying:

> Some of the political statements on what [the Coalition government] might do with welfare are quite terrifying ... the idea of stopping child benefit after three children, for example. Do you stop feeding the others? It doesn't seem helpful. There are plenty who go on being good parents, but those who are under great stress are more likely to be abusive parents.[148]

It is unlikely that the Connelly family would have fitted within the Coalition government's Troubled Families programme as they would not have met a number of the anti-social indicators that determine access to the programme. They were not seen as causing a nuisance locally, and there were no complaints from neighbours or others about them or the care being received by the children.

Although more children have child protection plans, more children are the subject of care proceedings in the court, and more children are looked-after and in the care of councils, there has been no similar increase in the number of social workers. Councils are still reported to have high thresholds[149] for the allocation of children to social workers and before initiating care proceedings in the courts. This is bound to be the reality when the government is cutting back its funding to councils and deterring them from raising local council tax. Councils' care costs have already risen significantly, with it stated that 'the Local Government Association has estimated that [the increase in care applications and children in care in 2009 alone] will have cost the taxpayer an additional £226m. This includes £39m in court costs and £187m spent on looking after children in local authority care.'[150]

Compared to other families where there were more immediate child protection concerns, although there were concerns about neglect and at least two sets of injuries to Peter, there had been no identified serious severe injury to the children, no known sexual abuse, no domestic violence or other violent behaviour by adults, no reported anti-social behaviour or criminality, and no recognised significant drug and alcohol misuse. None of these factors were known to be serious or extreme in the Connelly household before Peter died.

As Robert Tapsfield, Chief Executive of the Fostering Network, wrote in August 2010, soon after the new Coalition government was elected, the '[care] system is in a dire state – and the Government's cuts will make it worse',[151] and it is not likely that it would now be safer for Peter.

And what of a child like Peter as he grew older? One of the bravest comments running alongside and with a different message from *The Sun's* 'Baby P' story line, where little Peter Connelly was presented as angelic and innocent, which would have been true for a 17-month-old toddler, was by Martin Narey, former Head of the Prison Service, then Chief Executive of Barnardo's and the government's champion on adoption when Mr Gove was heavily promoting adoption. It was a message that linked the innocent and angelic Peter with the depiction of two evil and vile 10- and 11-year-old brothers in Edlington, Doncaster, who had viciously assaulted two other boys:

> It saddens me that the probability is that, had Baby P survived, given his own deprivation, he might have been unruly by the time he had reached the age of 13 or 14. At which point, he would have become feral, a parasite, a yob, helping to infest our streets.... Until we recognise that offending might in part be linked to levels of poverty in the UK – levels which should shame a country with our affluence – we have to be resigned to that offending continuing.[152]

Now here is a potential 'campaign for justice' that could have been championed by *The Sun*. It could have sought to influence

Mr Cameron and government policy to tackle disadvantage and deprivation experienced by an increasing number of children in the UK, and with a campaign that more also be invested in those crucial services and workers who 24/7 and 365 days a year are committed to protecting children. But it is not the campaign *The Sun* chose to run.

Notes

[1] Wolff, M. (2008) *The man who owns the news: Inside the secret world of Rupert Murdoch*, New York: Broadway Books, p 206.

[2] Wolff (2008) op cit, p 178.

[3] Fairweather, E. (2008) 'Revealed: How a close male relative of Baby P is linked to a big paedophile network', *Mail on Sunday*, 16 November (www.dailymail.co.uk/news/article-1086200/Revealed-How-Close-Male-Relative).

[4] France, A. (2009) 'Baby P gran signs petition', *The Sun*, 25 May, p 9.

[5] Wells, T. (2009) 'Jason Owen: Baby P's "uncle" and one of his killers', *The Sun*, 11 August (www.thesun.co.uk/sol/homepage/news/2581059/Jason-Owen-Baby-Ps-uncle-and-one-of-his-killers.html).

[6] Wells (2009) op cit.

[7] Wells, T. (2009) 'Baby P fined Jason Owen's sister claims he is a "vile thug"', *The Sun*, 2 November (www.thesun.co.uk/sol/homepage/news/2708852/Baby-P-fiend-Jason-Owens-sister-claims-he-is-a-vile-thug).

[8] BBC News London (2012) 'Baby P's father sues *The People* for libel', 27 February (www.bbc.co.uk/news/uk-england-london-17181065).

[9] Halliday, J. (2012) 'Baby P's father gets £75,000 damages in *People* libel case', *The Guardian*, 5 March (www.theguardian.com/media/2012/mar/05/baby-p-father-people-libel-case).

[10] *Daily Mirror* (2011) 'Crossbow cannibal Stephen Griffiths friends with Baby P killer Steven Barker', 8 August (www.mirror.co.uk/news/uk-news/crossbow-cannibal-stephen-griffiths-friends-146360).

[11] Wells, T. (2010) 'Outrage over Baby P mum's day with kids', *The Sun*, 15 May (www.thesun.co.uk/sol/homepage/news/2974074/Outrage-over-Baby-P-mums-day-with-kids.html).

[12] Wells, T. (2012) 'Shannon mum's Monroe t-shirt: Beauty on the beast', *The Sun*, 9 May, p 5.

[13] Halliday, J. (2012) 'Operation Elveden police arrest prison officers over alleged payments', *The Guardian*, 11 September (www.guardian.co.uk/uk/2012/sep/11/operation-elveden-police-arrest-prison-officer).

[14] Schofield, K. (2011) 'Baby P killer is free on Friday', *The Sun*, 2 August (www.thesun.co.uk/sol/news/homepage/nes/3729798/One-of-the-evil-trio-jailed-over-Baby-Ps-death-will-walk-free-on-Friday).

[15] Keay, J. (2011) 'Baby P killer is smuggled out of prison', *The Sun*, 6 August (www.thesun.co.uk/sol/homepage/news/3737009/Baby-P-killer-Jason-Owen-is-smuggled-out-of-jail-after-serving-just-over-2-years-of-his-sentence.html).

[16] Wells, T. (2011) 'Baby P killer Jason Owen on the street', *The Sun*, 26 August (www.thesun.co.uk/sol/homepage/news/3776075/Baby-P-killer-Jason-Owen-on-the-street.html).

[17] Peake, A. and Wells, T. (2011) 'Law protects killer Jason Owen ... why didn't it protect Peter Connelly?', *The Sun*, 27 August (www.thesun.co.uk/sol/homepage/news/3778476/Law-protects-killer-Jason-Owen-why-didnt-it-protect-baby-Peter-Connelly.html).

[18] Peake. A. (2011) 'Baby P killer Jason Owen in park', *The Sun*, 13 September (www.thesun.co.uk/sol/homepage/news/3812871/Baby-P-killer-Jason-Owen-in-park.html).

[19] *Daily Mirror* (2011) 'Baby P killer Jason Owen freed after three years', 6 August (www.mirror.co.uk/news/uk-news/baby-p-killer-jason-owen-184364).

[20] Greenwood, C. (2011) 'Monster who killed Baby P: Jason Owen is free to walk the streets after just two years', *Daily Mail*, 26 August (www.dailymail.co.uk/news/article-2030473/Anger-Baby-Ps-family-lodger-jailed-death-freed-walk-streets-just-years.html).

[21] Edemariam, A. (2009) '"When a dead child is known to us, that's the biggest horror. We knew the size of that"', *The Guardian*, 6 February (www.theguardian.com/society/2009/feb/06/sharon-shoesmith-haringey-interview).

[22] Nasdir, N. (2008) 'Baby P: Will you fight for justice?', *The Sun*, 17 November (www.thesun.co.uk/sol/homepage/mysun/1927507/Baby-P-Will-you-fight-for-justice.html).

[23] Sabbagh, D. and Dodd, V. (2012) 'Eight face hacking charges: Coulson and Brooks among those accused', *The Guardian*, 25 July, p 2.

[24] Sabbagh and Dodd (2012) op cit, p 2.

[25] Ahmed, M. (2009) 'Wade denies "witch hunt" of social worker', *Community Care*, 27 January (www.communitycare.co.uk/Articles/27/01/2009/110558).

[26] Chippindale, P. and Horrie, C. (1999) *Stick it up your punter: The uncut story of The Sun newspaper*, London: Simon & Schuster, p 482.

[27] Claude (2008) 'Wake up from your slumbers', 21 November (http://wakeupfromyourslumber.com/node/9248).

[28] Ahmed (2009) op cit.

[29] Butler, P. (2009) 'Sharon Shoesmith emails reveal extent of media and political storm', *The Guardian*, 7 October (www.guardian.co.uk/society/2009/oct/07/baby-p-sharon-shoesmith-emails).

[30] Willetts, D. and O'Shea, G. (2009) 'Shoesmith loses blood money', *The Sun*, 14 January (www.thesun.co.uk/sol/homepage/news/2124605/Baby-P-boss-Sharon-Shoesmith).

[31] Care Quality Commission (CQC) (2009) *Review of the involvement and action taken by health bodies in relation to the case of Baby P*, May, p 17.

[32] CQC (2009) op cit, p 13.

[33] Goodchild, S. (2011) 'GP who bungled Baby P case set to be reinstated', *Evening Standard*, 15 July, p 12.

[34] BBC News (2011) 'Baby P doctor Jerome Ikwueke can return to work', 21 July (www.bbc.co.uk/news/uk-england-london-14236950).

[35] *The Guardian* (2009) 'Baby doctor sues hospital over her dismissal', 19 June (www.theguardian.com/society/2009/jun/19/babyp-doctor-sues-hospital).

[36] Pascoe-Watson, G. (2009) 'Baby P bungler sues hospital', *The Sun*, 19 June (www.thesun.co.uk/sol/homepage/news/2490512/Baby-P-bungler-Dr-Sabah-Al-Zayyat-sues-hospital.html).

[37] CQC (2009) op cit, p 13.

[38] *Daily Mail* (2011) 'Baby P doctor struck off after failing to spot abused boy had broken back', 11 February (www.dailymail.co.uk/news/article-1356068/Baby-P-doctor-struck-failing-spot-abused-boy-broken-back.html).

[39] BBC News London (2011) 'Baby P doctor removed from medical register by GMC', 11 February (www.bbc.co.uk/news/uk-england-london-12429911).

[40] Field Fisher Waterhouse (2011) *R (on the application of Sabah Al-Zayyat) v General Medical Council* – Queen's Bench Division (Administrative Court) – 25 November 2010, Public and Regulatory Law Alert (www.ffw.com/publications/all/alerts/prg-alert-january-2011).

[41] Dyer, C. (2011) 'Baby P doctor is allowed to remove herself from medical register', *British Medical Journal*, 14 February (www.bmj.com/content/342/bmj.d1015.extract).

[42] Bingham, J. (2010) 'Great Ormond Street chief removes her name from medical register', *The Telegraph*, 23 August (www.telegraph.co.uk/news/uknews/baby-p/7958705/Great-Ormond-Street-chief-removes-name-from-medical-register.html).

[43] BBC News London (2010) 'Doctors demand Great Ormond Street Hospital chief quit', 6 June (www.bbc.co.uk/news/10249547).

[44] BBC News London (2010) 'Baby Peter clinic "did not heed doctors" concerns', 30 June (www.bbc.co.uk/news/10468747).

[45] Butler, P. (2011) 'Call for sacking over Great Ormond Street "cover-up" of Baby Peter report', 9 June, *Guardian Society* (www.theguardian.com/society/2011/jun/09/great-ormond-street-baby-peter-report).

[46] Butler, P. (2011) 'Great Ormond Street hospital issues apology to Baby P whistleblower', 14 June, *Guardian Society* (www.theguardian.com/society/2011/jun/14/baby-peter-whistleblower-great-ormond-street-apologises).

[47] Great Ormond Street Hospital (2012) 'Dr Jane Collins announces she is leaving Trust after nearly 11 years as Chief Executive', Press release, 28 May (www.gosh.nhs.uk/news/press-releases/2012-press-release-archive/dr-jane-collins-announces-she-is-leaving-trust-after-nearly-11-years-as-chief-executive).

[48] Butler (2011) op cit, 14 June.

[49] Murphy, J. (2008) 'A short life of misery and pain', BBC News, 11 November (http://news.bbc.co.uk/1/hi/uk/7708398.stm).

[50] McShane, J. (2009) *It must never happen again: The lessons learned from the short life and terrible death of Baby P*, London: John Blake, pp 249-50.

[51] McShane (2009) op cit, p 192.

[52] Dodd, V. and Rushe, D. (2012) 'Rebekah Brooks and Andy Coulson to face fresh charges', *The Guardian*, 20 November (www.guardian.co.uk/media/2012/nov/20/rebekah-brooks-andy-coulson-face-charges).

[53] BBC News (2012) 'Rebekah Brooks receives £10.8m News International payoff', 12 December (www.bbc.co.uk/news/business-20705535).

[54] Wilson, G. (2008) 'New Haringey chief gets £200K', *The Sun*, 13 December (www.thesun.co.uk/sol/news/2034777).

[55] BBC News (2012) 'Profile: Glenn Mulcaire', 24 July (www.bbc.co.uk/news/uk-14080775).

[56] Jukes, P. (2012) *The fall of the House of Murdoch: Fourteen days that ended a media dynasty*, London: Unbound.

[57] Milne, S. (2012) *The revenge of history: The battle for the 21st century*, London: Verso, p 238.

[58] Boothy, R. (2012) 'Andy Coulson is likely to have attended sensitive meetings, No 10 admits', *The Guardian*, 9 May (www.guardian.co.uk/media/2012/may/09/andy-coulson-sensitive-meetings-no-10).

[59] O'Hare, S. (2012) 'Rebekah Brooks and Andy Coulson appear in court accused of making corrupt payments to public officials', *Daily Mail*, 6 December (www.dailymail.co.uk/news/article-2243991/Rebekah-Brooks-Andy-Coulson-appear-court-accused-making-corrupt-payments-public-officials.html).

[60] Higgs, L. (2010) 'Service chiefs lack faith in Ofsted', *Children and Young People Now Daily Bulletin*, 2 February (www.cypnow.co.uk/bulletins/Daily-Bulletin/news/980885).

[61] Garboden, M. (2010) 'Denise Platt highlights flaws in transfer from CSCI to Ofsted', *Community Care*, 20 January (www.communitycare.co.uk/Articles/2010/01/20/113605/denise-platt-highlights).

[62] Garboden, M. (2010) 'Ofsted chief will step down early if "helpful" for the new government', *Community Care*, 21 June (www.communitycare.co.uk/Articles/2010/06/21/114761/ofsted-chief-will-step-down).

[63] Lepper, J. (2010) 'Christine Gilbert to remain at Ofsted until next year', *Children and Young People Now Daily Bulletin*, 22 June (www.cypnow.co.uk/Daily-Bulletin/news/1011510).

[64] Department for Education (DfE) (2011) 'Michael Gove formally accepts the resignation of Christine Gilbert, Her Majesty's Chief Inspector', 6 April (www.education.gov.uk/inthenews/a0076494).

[65] Curtis, P. (2010) 'Ofsted head Christine Gilbert in talks to leave early to join academy sponsor', *The Guardian*, 9 December (www.guardian.co.uk/education/2010/dec/08/ofsted-gilbert-leave-academy-sponsor).

[66] Allen, K. (2012) 'Academisation, academisation, academisation', 5 April (www.leftfootforward.org/2012/04/acemies-commission).

[67] Brent Council (2012) 'Brent Council appoints interim chief executive', Press release (www.brent.gov.uk/pressreleases.nsf/News/LBB-1872).

[68] Campbell, D. (2012) 'NHS watchdog chief Cynthia Bower resigns', *The Guardian*, 23 February (www.guardian.co.uk/society/2012/feb/23/nhs-watchdog-cynthia-bowers-resigns).

[69] Lord Laming (2009) *The protection of children in England: A progress report*, House of Commons, 12 March, Norwich: The Stationery Office.

[70] Lord Laming (2003) *The Victoria Climbié Inquiry*, Norwich: The Stationery Office.

[71] Lord Laming (2003) op cit, p 1.

[72] Lord Laming (2003) op cit, p 4.

[73] Lord Laming (2003) op cit, p 4.

[74] Lord Laming (2003) op cit, pp 371-83.

[75] Lord Laming (2003) op cit, pp 318, 382.

[76] Jones, R. (2009) 'Children Acts 1948–2008: the drivers for legislative change in England over 60 years', *Journal of Children's Services*, December, vol 4, no 4, pp 39-52.

[77] Fairweather, E. (2009) 'Council chief's continuing ignorance of child killers is breathtaking', *Daily Mail*, 7 February (www.dailymail.co.uk/debate/article-1138744/EILEEN-FAIRWEATHER).

[78] Fallon, P. (2009) 'Different strokes', Letter, *Guardian Society*, 21 January, p 4.

[79] Shoesmith, S. (2010) 'The real Baby P effect', *The Guardian*, 7 July, p 24.

[80] Lord Laming (2009) op cit, pp 4-6.

[81] Lord Laming (2009) op cit, p 13.

[82] Lord Laming (2009) op cit, p 20.

[83] Lord Laming (2009) op cit, pp 44-5.

[84] Lord Laming (2009) op cit, pp 57-8.

[85] Lord Laming (2009) op cit, p 59.

[86] Lord Laming (2009) op cit, p 60.

[87] Wooding, D. (2009) 'Now just do it', *The Sun*, 13 March (www.thesun.co.uk/sol/homepage/news/2317263/Now-just-do-it).

[88] Department for Children, Schools and Families (DCSF) (2009) *The protection of children in England: Action plan: The government's response to Lord Laming*, Cm 7589, May, Norwich: The Stationery Office.

[89] Balls, E. (2009) 'Ministerial foreword', in DCSF, op cit, p 1.

[90] DCSF (2009) op cit, p 25.

[91] Social Work Task Force (2009) *Building a safe, confident future: The final report of the Social Work Task Force*, November, London: Department for Children, Schools and Families.

[92] Social Work Task Force (2009) op cit, pp 5-6.

[93] Social Work Task Force (2009) op cit, p 48.

[94] Social Work Reform Board (2010) *Building a safe and confident future: One year on*, London: Department for Children, Schools and Families, December, p 5.

[95] Conservative Party Commission on Social Workers (2007) *No more blame game: The future for children's social workers*, London: The Conservative Party.

[96] Conservative Party Commission on Social Workers (2007) op cit, p 18.

[97] Helen Grant, quoted in Conservative Party Commission on Social Workers (2007), op cit, p 18.

[98] Conservative Party Commission on Social Workers (2007), op cit, p 43.

[99] Munro, E. (2004) 'The impact of child abuse inquiries since 1990', in N. Stanley and J. Manthorpe (eds) *The sage of inquiry*, London: Routledge, pp 75-91.

[100] Munro, E. (2005) 'A systems approach to investigating child abuse deaths', *British Journal of Social Work*, vol 35, no 4, pp 531-46.

[101] Munro, E. (2009) 'Beyond the blame culture', *The Guardian*, 3 November (www.theguardian.com/commentisfree/2009/nov/03/serious-case-review-child-protection).

[102] Munro, E. (2011) *The Munro review of child protection: Final report: A child-centred system*, Cm 8062, May, London: Department for Education.

[103] Department for Education (DfE) (2011) *A child-centred system: The government's response to the Munro Review of child protection*, July.

[104] Higgs, L. (2012) '"Terrifying" welfare reforms will drive up care referrals, warns Munro', *Children and Young People Now*, 6 July (www.cypnow.co.uk/cyp/news/1073834).

[105] Jones. R. (2009) 'Children Acts 1948–2008: The drivers for legislative change in England over 60 years', *Journal of Children's Services*, December, vol 4, no 4, pp 39-52.

[106] Barber, M. (2007) *Instruction to deliver: Fighting to transform Britain's public services*, London: Methuen.

[107] Sparrow, A. (2009) 'Death of Baby P highlights failure of regulation says Letwin', *The Guardian*, 27 January (www.guardian.co.uk/politics/2009/jan/27/baby-p-oliver-letwin).

[108] Shoesmith, S. (2010) 'The real Baby P effect', *The Guardian*, 7 July, p 21.

[109] Graef, R. (2010) 'Baby P: the new victims', *Radio Times*, 3 October, p 9.

[110] Toynbee, P. (2008) 'This frenzy of hatred is a disaster for children at risk', *The Guardian*, 18 November (www.theguardian.com/commentisfree/2008/nov/18/comment-social-services-child-protection).

[111] Curtis, P. (2009) 'Baby P council issues urgent appeal for staff', *The Guardian*, 26 January (www.theguardian.com/society/2009/jan/26/haringey-social-workers-baby-p).

[112] Mahadevan, J. (2009) 'Care figures soar in Haringey', *Children and Young People Now*, 24 September (www.cypnow.co.uk/bulletins/Daily-Bulletin/news/940161).

[113] Lombard, D. (2009) 'LGA survey finds mounting recruitment and retention problems', *Community Care*, 5 May (www.communitycare.co.uk/Articles/Article.aspx?liAryticleIFD=111471).

[114] Bennett, R. (2012) 'Best graduates to be sent into frontline social work', *The Times*, 4 October, p 6.

[115] Adonis, A. (2012) 'Social work needs a Teach First revolution', *The Times*, 4 October, p 26.

[116] Jones, R. (2012) 'The best of times; the worst of times: Social work and its moment', *British Journal of Social Work*, published online 8 October (doi: 10.1093/bjsw/bcs157).

[117] Children and Family Court Advisory Support Service (Cafcass) (2009) 'Cafcass care demand', Press release, 8 May.

[118] Children and Family Court Advisory Support Service (Cafcass) (2012) *Three weeks in November … three years on …*, Cafcass care application study 2012, London: Cafcass.

[119] Cafcass (2012) op cit, p 2.

[120] Cafcass (2012) op cit, p ii.

[121] Cavendish, C. (2012) 'The shocking tale of a mother seeking help', *The Times*, 12 April, p 21.

[122] Douglas, A. (2008) 'Baby P's legacy must be better status for children's social workers', *The Guardian*, 23 November (www.theguardian.com/society/2008/nov/23/baby-p-child-protection).

[123] Department for Education (DfE) and Department for Business Innovation and Skills (BIS) (2011) *Referrals, assessments and children who were the subject of a child protection plan* (2010/2011 Children in Need Census), provisional, Statistical First Release, London: DfE.

[124] Children and Family Court Advisory Support Service (Cafcass) (2011) *August 2011 care statistics*, London: Cafcass.

[125] Green, C. (2012) 'Early intervention', in M. Blyth and E. Solomon (eds) *Effective safeguarding for children and young people: What next after Munro?*, Bristol: Policy Press, p 11.

[126] Jackson, K., Sloan, A. and Jones, A. (2012) 'The Baby P effect', *The Sun*, 12 April (www.thesun.co.uk/sol/homepage/features/4251974/The-Baby-P-Effect.html).

[127] Greenslade, R. (2012) 'The Sun changes its stance, yet again, over the Baby P case', *The Guardian*, 2 August (www.theguardian.com/media/greenslade/2012/aug/02/sun-baby-p).

[128] Smith, R. (2009) 'Public opinion of social workers worsens after Baby P', *Children and Young People Now*, 25 March (www.cypnow.co.uk/cyp/news/1039007/public-opinion-social-workers-worsens-baby-p).

[129] Puffet, N. (2009) 'Health visitors quit Haringey after Baby P case', *Children and Young People Now*, 21 May (www.cypnow.co.uk/cyp/news/1037665/health-visitors-quit-haringey-baby-p).

[130] *Community Care* (2009) 'Warning of "catastrophe" in children's services if trends continues', 20 October (www.communitycare.co.uk/Articles/2009/10/20/112907).

[131] Garboden, M. (2010) 'ADCS reveals extent of strain on child protection', *Community Care*, 20 April (www.communitycare.co.uk/Articles/2010/04/20/114327).

[132] Sherman, J. (2008) 'Councils struggle to find social workers', *The Times*, 10 December, p 5.

[133] McGregor, K. (2010) 'Nottinghamshire spent £1.5m on agency social workers', *Community Care*, 25 June (www.communitycare.co.uk/Articles/2010/06/25/114808).

[134] Mahadevan, J. (2012) 'Social workers lack time to work with children', *Children and Young People Now*, 2 February (www.cypnow.co.uk/Social_Care/article/1115377).

---

[135] Dunton, J. (2009) 'Protection orders hit new high', *Local Government Chronicle*, 14 May, p 3.

[136] Butler, P. (2010) 'Balls sent clear warning on child protection funding', *The Guardian*, 17 March (www.guardian.co.uk/society/joepublic/2010/mar/17/child-protection-funding).

[137] Kisiel, R. (2010) 'In hiding, the mother accused of abuse for cuddling her child', *Daily Mail*, 27 April, p 25.

[138] Butler, P. (2010) 'Judge shocked by social workers who split families', *The Guardian*, 13 April, p 4.

[139] McGuinness, R. (2010) 'The "Stalinist" workers who grab children', *Metro*, 13 April, p 5.

[140] BBC (2012) 'Why is the number of children in care rising?', 9 February (http://news.bbc.co.uk/today/hi/today/newsid_9694000/9694564.stm).

[141] Toynbee, P. and Walker, D. (2012) *Dogma and disarray: Cameron at half-time*, London: Granta Books.

[142] Lepper, J. (2011) 'Midwives fear NHS reforms will destabilise care for mothers and babies', *Children and Young People Now*, 9 May (www.cypnow.co.uk/bulletin/cypnow_daily/article/1068948).

[143] Bowcott, O. (2009) 'Many NHS staff not trained to spot abuse, Baby P report finds', *The Guardian*, 16 July (www.guardian.co.uk/society/2009/jul/16/baby-p-child-protection-nhs).

[144] Bowcott (2009) op cit.

[145] Hartley, C. (2010) 'NHS is failing kids says Baby P prof', *The Sun*, 17 September, p 31.

[146] Donovan, T. (2012) 'GMC launches new child protection guidance for doctors', *Community Care*, 10 July (www.communitycare.co.uk/2012/07/10/gmc-launches-new-child-protection-guidance-for-doctors).

[147] Mahadevan, J. (2009) 'Care figures soar in Haringey', *Children and Young People Now*, 24 September (www.cypnow.co.uk/bulletins/Daily-Bulletin/news/940161).

[148] Higgs, L. (2012) '"Terrifying" welfare reforms will drive up care referrals, warns Munro', *Children and Young People Now*, 6 July (www.cypnow.co.uk/print_article/cyp/news/1073834).

[149] McGregor, K. (2012) 'Thresholds for accepting child protection referrals "too high"', *Community Care*, 27 July (www.communitycare.co.uk/Articles/27/07/2012/118408/Thresholds-for-accepting-child-protection-referrals).

[150] Cassidy, S. (2010) 'Response to Baby P "has pushed foster care network to the brink"', *The Independent*, 5 August (www.independent.co.uk/news/uk/home-news/response-to-baby-p-has-pushed-foster-care-network-to-the-brink-2043647.html).

[151] Tapsfield, R. (2010) 'System is in a dire state – and the Government's cuts will make it worse', *The Independent*, 5 August (www.independent.co.uk/voices/commentators/robert-tapsfield-system-is-in-a-dire-state-ndash-and-the-governments-cuts-will-make-it-worse-2043648.html).

[152] Narey, M., quoted in F. Attewill (2008) 'Upbringing "could have turned Baby P feral"', *Metro*, 27 November, p 9.

SIX

The continuing legacy of the 'Baby P story'

It should never be forgotten that the 'Baby P story' starts with the terrible tortured life and death of a little boy, where the adults within his home who should have been caring for him were instead callous, cruel and criminal. Peter Connelly touched the hearts of a nation. The angelic photograph of an innocent child, now dead, stirred shock and grief that rippled out far beyond those who ever knew or met Peter.

But the 'Baby P story' came not to focus on Peter and those who abused him or allowed him to be abused, but on those who daily gave their working lives to protecting and caring for children. They knew Peter. How much more distressing then for them when Peter was killed and found to have been horrifically abused. Their commitment to children, and their distress and devastation when they found out that Peter had died, was never acknowledged or given account in the telling of the story of 'Baby P'.

Instead there was an alliance of press, police and politicians that shaped a story which focused on and targeted a Director of Children's Services and social workers. The decisions and actions of the social workers and their managers were interrogated and interpreted with all the benefits of hindsight, and then conclusions were drawn which set them up to be blamed and shamed, and with vilification and vengeance they were then threatened and terrorised.

Even those who might have been potentially sympathetic to the social workers and their managers came to make passing comments based on the assumption that the dominant story line was accurate. For example, in his book *Chavs*, attacking the demonisation of the working class by politicians and the media, Owen Jones had a comment about 'Baby P' that referred only to Haringey Council and 'the systemic failures of the local council's child protection agencies'.[1] This scripting of the story served several purposes. First, it allowed *The Sun* newspaper and its editor, Rebekah Brooks, to claim a moral high ground by presenting the hatred and harassment it generated and targeted at Sharon Shoesmith, Director of Children's Services, and the social workers as a 'campaign for justice'. It probably also helped with the paper's profile, promotion and profits. Second, the omissions especially in the first criminal investigation went largely unrecognised and untold. The police became of minimal interest, on the margins of the story. Third, the story was promoted and opportunistically used by Mr Cameron and other politicians in opposition to attack Mr Brown and the Labour government and the Labour council in Haringey.

The Sun's shaping and capturing of the 'Baby P story'

But others then came to feed the story as well, adding ammunition to the abuse directed at Haringey's Director of Children's Services and social workers. A powerful tabloid newspaper, with its powerful owner Rupert Murdoch, and with its editor having access to and influence with both the police and politicians, was able to brag, bluster and bully. Within little more than a month, at the end of 2008 it congratulated itself on achieving its ambitions of getting Sharon Shoesmith sacked, the social workers suspended and then sacked, and a GP and paediatrician also suspended. Mr Balls, as Secretary of State for Children, delivered what *The Sun* wanted, with national inspectorates providing the fuel for his actions. But it was *The Sun* that took the credit that its campaign of vengeance had got its victims. The social workers and their managers had become captured in what Professor Harry Ferguson, in his historical review of child protection, called 'scandal politics'.[2]

So did the story end there? No, the tracking and tailing of Sharon Shoesmith and the social workers continued year after year. And it was *The Sun* that was most active in keeping the 'Baby P story' running, a story that it had shaped and largely captured and claimed as its own. The flurry of reviews and reports commissioned by Mr Balls in November and December 2008 provided fodder for the story whenever they were completed and then published.

It was now a story in which the police had almost completely disappeared from view, and the NHS was absent or marginal. It became a story not about Peter and those who killed him, but largely, as the story became even more simplified and targeted, about three people – a Director of Children's Services, one social work manager and one social worker – Sharon Shoesmith, Gillie Christou and Maria Ward. Who would have anticipated prior to November 2008 that these three, who had been head down, day-by-day, providing services to protect and care for hundreds of children, and were recognised and respected for their care and commitment, would, 17 months after Peter Connelly's death, have become public figures, threatened and tormented, with the public hatred whipped up by a press and politicians with their own motivations and missions.

And the significance of *The Sun* and Mr Cameron's calls for the sackings in November 2008 should not be underestimated. Haringey Council had already concluded after Peter Connelly died that there were no grounds to suspend or sack its Director of Children's Services, managers or social workers. Local NHS organisations had not seen it as appropriate to sack or suspend any doctors or other health workers.

The police, it seems, undertook no formal inquiries at all into the conduct of its police officers. Yet following the press and political calls for sackings a year-and-a-half after Peter's death, quick action was taken by Haringey Council to sack a whole management line of senior staff and social workers; two leading councillors also got caught up in the flak and resigned, and a paediatrician and GP were suspended. But *none* of those, who four years later have had their cases considered by their professional registration bodies, have had their licence to practice terminated by the GSCC or the GMC, and the one challenge to the sackings that went to the High Court's Court of Appeal concluded that Sharon Shoesmith had been scapegoated and wrongfully dismissed.

But was this all exceptional and unique? Not quite. There is now a long history in the UK of the press allocating blame and shame when a child is abused and killed, with the resulting threat and fear focused on social workers. This is a hit-and-miss process as it is not known in advance which child's abuse and death will attract media interest. It is also not known which will then become long-running stories, with names recognised well into the future. Peter Connelly has become one such name, although much more known and remembered as 'Baby P'. Victoria Climbié is another. But the first was Maria Colwell.

Maria Colwell died in Brighton in 1973. The subsequent public inquiry was the first time an individual social worker was to experience the full force of media attention and denigration. What happened has recently been recounted in a book reflecting back 40 years to the inquiry:

> Diana Lees' [the local authority social worker's] cross-examination began with a warning aimed directly at her from Mr Mildon [Counsel for the Inquiry] that has resonated with a folk horror through social work: "What I am going to do is to suggest that Maria's death occurred because of the failure to seize an opportunity which occurred in April, 1972, and that you were primarily responsible"[3].... At the Maria Colwell public inquiry in 1973 'lawyers routinely referred to [social

workers and health visitors as] "defendants" and even the chair referred to "the defence'"[4].... Press photographers were already gathered to record [Diana Lees'] arrival, as they were to take photographs of her arriving and leaving from every session.... Then during the lunch interval, matters deteriorated further. The *Daily Mirror* (6 November 1973) reported that, 'Fury erupted at an inquiry yesterday over the heart-rending ordeal of tug-of-love girl Maria Colwell....When 29 year old Miss Lees left during the lunch break, she was followed by thirty women who booed and chanted, "Liar" and "Get out!"'. The police escorted her for 100 yards before the crowd broke up.' *The Sun* (6 November 1973), on the same day, told readers that, 'A crowd of booing, fist-waving people chased social worker Diana Lees along a street yesterday after she gave evidence at the Maria Colwell inquiry.... Even as Miss Lees gave her evidence, there were cries of abuse from the public gallery.' At the end of the day, a crowd of 20 people, almost all women, was waiting again. Police surrounded Miss Lees as she hurried to a waiting taxi.... Nor were reports of this sort confined to the mass circulation newspapers. *The Times, Telegraph* and *The Guardian* all covered events in similar detail. Soon, the *Daily Express* (14 November 1973), among others, was bringing readers up to date with new details that verged on the surreal. Under the headline 'Maria social worker gets bodyguard', it reported: 'Social worker Diana Lees, the woman at the centre of the storm over the death of seven-year old Maria Colwell, has been provided with a squad of bodyguards. The move follows harassment from the public, threats and "vile letters". The squad, set up by East Sussex Social Services Department, includes ex-Brighton police superintendent, Alan Probyn, and 16st former Nigerian police chief, Leonard Oliver. They chauffeur Miss Lees to and from the Inquiry into Maria's death, and take her away at lunch. Miss Lees, 29, has been booed and shouted at during her six days of evidence.

—

Yesterday she dashed through the public gallery when the inquiry adjourned. She was escorted downstairs by Mr Oliver and swiftly entered a car with its engine running'.... Miss Lees continued to give evidence over five consecutive days, with 25 hours of cross-examination. She faced some of the most challenging questioning in the whole Inquiry. Gradually, however, her composure wore down both the Inquiry and the gallery.[5]

The impact of the Maria Colwell inquiry and the targeting of the social worker was long-standing. For example, almost 20 years later, in 1990, it was noted that:

Social work had to develop a thick skin to cope with the seemingly unending succession of child-care tragedies.... There were three reasons for the profound emotional impact of the Colwell case on the profession. First, it was the first such case and the face of Maria Colwell stared prominently at readers of every daily paper. Secondly, it was dealt with by a full-scale public inquiry, with the consequence that the social worker most directly involved had to push her way into the hearing through a crowd of jeering, abusive onlookers. Thirdly, it marked the end of the honeymoon period when the effectiveness of social work as a means of changing human behaviour had been taken as axiomatic.[6]

The same author, Terry Bamford, a former social worker and Director of Social Services, has noted elsewhere that 'the unfortunate social worker in the case was treated by the public as if she had struck the blows which killed Maria'.[7] There are strong similarities, 40 years later, with the harassment targeted at Peter Connelly's social workers.

The shaping and telling of the 'Baby P story' was, therefore, not totally unusual or unique in the attention and anger it directed almost exclusively at social workers. It also was not unique in that it resulted from a coming together of a triumvirate of press, police and politicians, and even more specifically, *The Sun* and Conservative politicians.

As this book was being prepared there were two stories which reflected on the past relationships between the press, police and politicians. One was about the Leveson Inquiry (see Chapter Three) into press and media behaviour. The other was about the Hillsborough disaster in 1989 when 96 Liverpool football supporters died. The fans themselves were blamed for the deaths, but subsequent inquiries found that a decision taken by a police officer in the heat of the moment resulted in a crowd becoming a crush. This was then compounded in its error and impact by senior and other officers in South Yorkshire Police conjuring up a story to deflect responsibility for the tragedy away from a decision by the police commander to a story that blamed the fans.

The story that was created was then peddled and promoted by a Conservative MP, with Mrs Thatcher as Prime Minister also drawn into supporting the police, and with *The Sun* majoring on the story with its total support for the police, declaring in a headline splashed across its front page that the prefabricated police story was 'THE TRUTH'. It was not until 23 years later, after yet another inquiry into the disaster, that *The Sun* had another full front page, this time with the heading, 'THE REAL TRUTH: Cops smeared Liverpool fans to deflect blame', with it stated that 'An independent report showed police tried to cover up catastrophic failings by disgracefully smearing Liverpool football fans, pinning the blame on them and falsifying reports'.[8]

The editor of *The Sun* who, despite what were stated to have been misgivings from other journalists at the time,[9] decided on 'The Truth' headline, and with *The Sun*'s subsequent reporting vociferous in denigrating and damning the Liverpool football supporters, was Kelvin Mackenzie. This was the same Kelvin Mackenzie who, although no longer editor, had a column in *The Sun* on 16 November 2008 headed 'Idiots who betrayed Baby P must go now'.[10]

But this coming together of *The Sun*, the police and Conservative politicians, again in South Yorkshire, had also led to another major story, a story that has again been found to have been distorted in its telling. It was a story about miners attacking South Yorkshire Police at the time of the miners' strike in 1984–85. The miners were demonstrating against the decisions facilitated by the government, led by Mrs Thatcher, that allowed the mass closure of coal mines and the subsequent collapse of communities. Once more there was a coming together of the police, press and politicians[11] in mistelling the story. The miners were

---

* I have had a personal, although a comparatively minor, professional experience of being the target of a story created between a senior police officer, a Conservative MP and a tabloid paper (*Mail on Sunday*). In 1994 a police superintendent briefed a Conservative MP who briefed the *Mail on Sunday* about a 14-year-old boy who was involved in much petty crime, was in care and where social workers had arranged for him to spend two weeks at Easter with his grandmother who now lived and worked as a waitress in Spain. It was a sensible decision to get him away over a school holiday period from his delinquent friends. It was also low cost and meant he spent time with one of the few members of his family who cared for him and was a positive influence. The *Mail on Sunday* spent three weeks secretly preparing the story – including sending a reporter to Spain to doorstep the grandmother. I was the Director of Social Services and received a phone call at 4pm on a Friday, just as local offices were closing. By chance I was in my office. The reporter said the story probably would not be used but did I have anything to say about it? Not surprisingly, I knew nothing about it – I was heading up a service delivered from over 120 centres, with more than 3,000 staff, over 400 children in care and 200 children with child protection plans, receiving 21,000 new referrals about children, disabled adults and older people each year, and with total expenditure at 2012 costs of about £250 million – but got a quick briefing and gave my positive and supportive comments about the actions taken by the social workers. I then had calls from friends on Sunday morning – had I seen the *Mail on Sunday*? There was a full-page spread with a photo of me obtained from a local paper with the caption 'Council official who authorised boy's trip' cut beside a finger-wagging police chief superintendent in full uniform, with the headline 'Spanish holiday for a criminal aged 14: *Mail on Sunday* investigation into a case that should concern us all' (Gordon, A., Holliday, R. and Barton, F. [1993] 'Spanish holiday for a criminal aged 14', *Mail on Sunday*, 22 August, p 3). This became the 'Costa Kid' story and was covered on national television, radio and across the print press, and ran for over six months. It generated much abusive and threatening correspondence and telephone calls from across the UK, and even from elsewhere in Europe, America, the Far East and Australasia, to my office and home, directed personally at me. Paparazzi photographers and reporters camped outside the boy's foster home. He became notorious and a celebrity within his peer group and had a reputation to maintain. His delinquency escalated and he had to be placed in very expensive secure accommodation, and was later in prison.

---

presented as the transgressors and aggressors, whereas it was actually the police who were later found to have been violent and to have assaulted the demonstrators.[12] Thirty-nine miners were subsequently paid £425,000 by South Yorkshire Police following claims of assault, malicious prosecution and wrongful arrest.* [13]

There is NO suggestion or allegation being made that any police officer committed any offence, or any misconduct, in relation to Peter Connelly or the shaping and telling of the 'Baby P story'. But it was the police who initially briefed the press, mitigating and minimising their own omissions in the first criminal investigation, and claiming in the press that they wanted Peter removed from his mother, which had the consequence of focusing concerns on the Haringey social workers.

Although not primarily related to the 'Baby P story', the interlinkages between the press, police and politicians in London became more fully known through the Leveson Inquiry. What is now known is that at the time the 'Baby P story' was first being shaped and promoted, there were close links between *The Sun*, its editor Rebekah Brooks and other News International journalists and employees, with the Metropolitan Police, Mr Cameron and other politicians.

But how was it that these close relationships were formed and with the media, in this case *The Sun*, having so much influence? There does seem to have been an interdependence suiting each party's purpose, with a parasitical partnership spanning power and privilege. And it is not necessary to be a conspiracy theorist to see the connections. It is now well known through the Leveson Inquiry that there were frequent business and social contacts spanning the senior executives of News International, senior officers in the Metropolitan Police and senior politicians. Mr Gove, for example, was a former journalist with *The Times*, and his wife continued as a *Times* columnist. He had also shared dinners with Mr Murdoch and others at the top of News International.

Possibly most surprising was that Mr Cameron, when he became Prime Minister, appointed Mr Coulson, who Mr Cameron described as a friend and who had resigned as editor of the *News of the World* following criminal prosecutions for phone hacking by those who had worked for the paper, as his Director of Communications.

There is relevance here in a statement from Mr Cameron about employing Mr Coulson that contrasts with Mr Cameron's call in *The Sun* in 2008 that social workers be sacked. It is reported that:

> Cameron also distanced himself further from Andy Coulson, his recent guest at Chequers, and who only a week earlier [in July 2011] had been his friend. He told the House of Commons that if it turned out he had been misled [*by Mr Coulson about his knowledge of phone hacking at the News of the World when Mr Coulson was editor*], he would have to offer a 'profound apology'. He said: 'With 20:20 hindsight and all that has followed, I would not have offered him the job [*as Mr Cameron's Director of Communications*], and I expect that he would not have taken it. But you do not make decisions in hindsight; you make them in the present. You live and learn and, believe me, I have learnt'.[14]

It was not only Mr Cameron who used the argument that what was now being judged was all with the benefit of hindsight. Sir Paul Stephenson, who had been Commissioner of the Metropolitan Police, made the same claim when he was speaking about the police appointing Neil Wallis to provide public relations advice. Mr Wallis had worked at *The Sun*, and in 2003 became deputy editor of the *News of the World* and its executive editor in 2008. He retired in July 2009 and soon after in October was contracted by the Metropolitan Police.[15] When he appeared before the House of Commons Media and Culture Select Committee, Sir Paul Stephenson was asked if he had been consulted before Mr Wallis was recruited by his police force to advise on public relations. Sir Paul replied:

> Yes, I was. Just let me say with the benefit of what we know now, I am quite happy to put it on the record that I regret that we went into that contract. I clearly regret it because it is embarrassing.[16]

So a Commissioner of the Metropolitan Police and Mr Cameron both had argued that decisions taken in the past were only now being found to be flawed or contentious because they were being looked at with the benefit of hindsight. This is not the stance and sentiment, however, applied by Mr Cameron and *The Sun* to Sharon Shoesmith and the social workers. There was to be no allowance or benefit of hindsight for them.

But it was not only senior Conservative politicians who were woven into the network of privilege and power and who had personal as well as professional relationships that spanned the press and politics. Mr Brown's immediate predecessor as Labour Prime Minister, Mr Blair, was reported to be godfather to one of Rupert Murdoch's children.[17] There were also other friendships with Mrs Brooks. Mr Brown, with his wife Sarah, had attended the wedding of Rebekah Brooks to Mr Brooks (as had Mr Cameron and his wife, the then Shadow Chancellor George Osborne and Rupert Murdoch) in June 2009 in the midst of the continuing 'Baby P' coverage.[18] Sarah Brown was described by Rebekah Brooks as a 'good friend' who had, in 2008, organised a 40th birthday party for Mrs Brooks, and with Rupert Murdoch's daughter and wife also present, at the Prime Minister's country retreat at Chequers, the 'so-called "slumber/pyjama party"'.[19] And Mr Straw, a senior minister in the Labour government, gave evidence at the Leveson Inquiry that:

> During my period as Justice Secretary I would often travel to London on Monday morning from the West Oxford station Charlbury. Mrs Rebekah Brooks used to use the same train. After a while, we made arrangements to meet up and sit together for the journey ... we'd talk about what was in the papers, what was – we'd gossip about personalities, that sort of thing.[20]

Mr Jay, Counsel to the Leveson Inquiry, noted in his evidence to the Inquiry that Mr Straw had stated that his train journeys with Mrs Brooks stopped in September 2009 when she became Chief Executive of News International. This presumably means that Mr Straw and Mrs Brooks were travelling on the train together and 'gossiping about personalities' and 'about what was in the papers' in 2008 and 2009, when Mrs Brooks was editor of *The Sun* and was leading the 'justice for Baby P campaign' and Mr Straw was Justice Secretary.

The links and relationships between the Metropolitan Police and News International and its newspapers, which included *The Sun*, *News of the World*, *The Times* and *The Sunday Times*, were also extensive, with much of this becoming known through the Leveson Inquiry and the investigations into phone hacking. The Metropolitan Police, for example, employed former News International editors and journalists to assist with media and reputation management, and had also received advice and assistance from current News International senior employees.

The linkages between the Metropolitan Police and News International were summarised in Tom Watson and Martin Hickman's book based on the phone hacking investigations and the Leveson Inquiry:

A series of personal and professional friendships had connected Britain's biggest news group and its biggest police force. The chief reporter of its Sunday newspapers, Neville Thurbeck, was being slipped criminal records by the police, while its news editor interpreted for criminal inquiries. Its quality daily, *The Times*, had employed Andy Hayman [*a retired senior Metropolitan Police officer*] after he headed the failed hacking inquiry in 2006 (where he voiced his opinion that there had been only a 'handful' of victims). And one of News International's most senior executives, Neil 'Wolfman' Wallis, had long been friends with Dick Federico, who ran the [Metropolitan Police] media unit, John Yates, [the senior police officer] who reviewed the failed [phone hacking] inquiry, and the Commissioner, Sir Paul Stephenson – who had all complained to *The Guardian* about its coverage. Wallis had then been employed by Scotland Yard at exactly the same time it was maintaining that the original inquiry had been a success. All the while, News International journalists had been bribing Met officers for tips, leaks and telephone numbers.[21]

It was within this web of power and privilege, weaving together in particular the press and politicians, that Sharon Shoesmith and the social workers found themselves trapped and ensnared. In 2008, when the 'Baby P story' started to be shaped and told, it was Rupert Murdoch, Rebekah Brooks and *The Sun* that might be seen to have been at the centre of the web. Their influence and impact was considerable, and it has been commented that, for a long time, both Conservative and Labour politicians had been fearful of and unwilling to challenge or offend Rupert Murdoch and the editors of *The Sun*, with accounts of their influence running through political diaries of, among others, Chris Mullin,[22, 23] Alistair Campbell[24] and Tony Blair,[25] and through political commentaries.[26, 27, 28, 29, 30]

In looking back over the years New Labour was in government, years which included 2008 and beyond, when the 'Baby P story' was first told, Polly Toynbee and David Walker commented: 'Try governing calmly, let alone progressively, amid [the bias of the national press with its] catcalls, bullying and daily bile',[31] and specifically in relation to 'Baby P' they wrote:

> Inquiries and trials after the 2007 murder of Baby P (Peter Connelly) caused an outrage against social workers, as if they were the killers. Even allowing for the cynical manipulation of sentiment by *The Sun* and such papers, popular anger was remarkable in its ferocity.[32]

And possibly surprising, considering his closeness to Rupert Murdoch, Tony Blair, in a farewell speech as he stood down as Prime Minster, spoke of the media as 'feral beasts' hunting in packs and that 'it is not enough for someone to have made an error. It has to be venal.'[33]

So might it be any different in the future? In September 2012 a survey of public perceptions of trust of different professions and occupations was reported. It was undertaken for *Which?*, the consumer organisation. At the *bottom* of the trust league table were journalists and politicians, each with only 7 per cent of those surveyed saying that journalists and politicians could be trusted. Civil servants scored 25 per cent, above bankers (11 per cent), but below accountants (29 per cent). Those at the *top* of the trust table were all public servants delivering services, with teachers (69 per cent), doctors (80 per cent) and nurses (82 per cent) all getting high trust scores.[34]

As this book is written, Rebekah Brooks, Andy Coulson and other News International journalists are facing criminal trials with allegations that range from phone hacking to perverting the course of justice. If found guilty, they could be imprisoned. It was reported that 21 journalists from *The Sun* alone had been arrested.[35] In 2012 a senior police officer in the Metropolitan Police was charged with breaching the Official Secrets Act as part of the Operation Elveden investigations into alleged inappropriate payments by journalists to police and other public servants.[36] James Murdoch, Rupert Murdoch's son and assumed heir apparent, has left the UK and resigned from key Murdoch media roles he held in the UK, having been quizzed and questioned twice by the House of Commons Media Select Committee about the behaviours and actions of News International. The Leveson Inquiry into the behaviour of the press and wider media has now reported with recommendations made about strengthening future press regulation.[*]

But it is not clear and convincing, nor persuasive and promising, that the Coalition government or any government will seek to constrain and contain the media's excesses and exploitation.[37] In shaping and sustaining the 'Baby P story', threat and fear were unleashed by the media, with vilification and vengeance targeted at

---

[*] Amid all the reflection on and reviews of the relationships between the press, politicians and the police there was a contemporary story which brought all the protagonists into the same story – 'Plebgate' – where there were allegations – initially in *The Sun* – that police officers had contentiously claimed a government minister called them 'plebs', and that their police logs of the incident had been provided to the press (Wheatcroft, G. [2013] 'Plebgate: why did so many of us believe the police over Andrew Mitchell?', *The Guardian*, 15 October, www.theguardian.com/commentisfree/2013/oct/15/plebgate-why-believe-police-andrew-mitchell).

those who undertook the demanding, difficult and distressing work of protecting children. Will this happen again?

Social workers and others have to stand up and confront everyday bullies and bigots who are disturbed and dangerous, who abuse and assault children, and who are excited and exhilarated by their experience and exploitation of power. It remains to be seen whether politicians will have the same commitment and courage in the future to confront the media rather than being fearful of the bullies and then feeding into the bullying themselves.

Notes

[1] Jones, O. (2011) *Chavs: The demonisation of the working class*, London: Verso, p 23.

[2] Ferguson, H. (2004) *Protecting children in time*, Basingstoke: Palgrave Macmillan.

[3] Butler, I. and Drakeford, M. (2011) *Social work on trial: The Colwell Inquiry and the state of welfare*, Bristol: Policy Press, p 123.

[4] Butler and Drakeford (2011) op cit, p 100.

[5] Butler and Drakeford (2011) op cit, pp 113-14.

[6] Bamford, T. (1990) *The future of social work*, Basingstoke: Macmillan, p 4.

[7] Bamford, T. (1982) *Managing social work*, London: Tavistock, p 19.

[8] Moriarty, R. (2012) '23 years after Hillsborough THE REAL TRUTH', *The Sun*, 13 September, front page.

[9] Chippindale, P. and Horrie, C. (1999) *Stick it up your punter: The uncut story of The Sun newspaper*, London: Simon & Schuster, pp 331-53, 405-11.

[10] Mackenzie, K. (2008) 'Idiots who betrayed Baby P must go now', *The Sun*, 16 November (www.thesun.co.uk/sol/homepage/news/1924847/Kelvin-Mackenzie-Idiots-who-betrayed-Baby-P-must-go-now.html).

[11] Conn, D. (2012) 'From Orgreave to Hillsborough: One police force, two disgraces', *The Guardian*, 13 April, pp 1, 16-17.

[12] Jackson, B. and Warde, T. (undated) *The battle for Orgreave*, Brighton: Vanson Wardle Productions Ltd.

[13] Conn (2012) op cit.

[14] Watson, T. and Hickman, M. (2012) *Dial M for Murdoch: News Corporation and the corruption of Britain*, London: Allen Lane, pp 259-60.

[15] Sabbagh, D. and Baird, D. (2012) 'Leveson Inquiry: Neil Wallis appears', *The Guardian*, 2 April (www.guardian.co.uk/media/2012/apr/02/leveson-inquiry-neil-wallis-live).

[16] Lisner, J. (2012) *The rise and fall of the Murdoch empire*, London: John Blake, p 146.

[17] Lisner (2012) op cit, p 164.

[18] Johnson, A. and Bell, M. (2009) 'Celebrity wedding: The Sun and the stars', *The Independent*, 19 June (www.independent.co.uk/news/people/news/celebrity-wedding-the-sun-the-stars).

[19] Leveson Inquiry (2012) (www.levesoninquiry.org.uk/wp-content/uploads/2012/05/Second-Witness-Statement-of-Rebekah-Brooks).

[20] Leveson Inquiry (2012) (www.levesoninquiry.org.uk/wp-content/uploads/2012/05/Transcript-of-Morning -Hearing-16-May-2012).

[21] Watson and Hickman (2012) op cit, pp 235-6.

[22] Mullin, C. (2011) *A walk-on part: Diaries 1994–1999*, London: Profile Books.

[23] Mullin, C. (2011) *Decline and fall: Diaries 2005–2010*, London: Profile Books.

[24] Campbell, A. (2007) *The Blair years*, London: Random House.

[25] Blair, T. (2011) *A journey*, London: Arrow Books.

[26] Seldon, A. (2007) *Blair unbound*, London: Simon & Schuster.

[27] Seldon, A. and Lodge, G. (2010) *Brown at 10*, London: Biteback Publishing.

[28] Rawnsley, A. (2010) *The end of the party*, London: Penguin.

[29] Beckett, F. and Hencke, D. (2004) *The Blairs and their court*, London: Aurum.

[30] Jenkins, S. (2007) *Thatcher and sons: A revolution in three acts*, London: Penguin.

[31] Toynbee, P. and Walker, D. (2010) *The verdict: Did Labour change Britain?*, London: Granta, p 8.

[32] Toynbee and Walker (2010) op cit, p 151.

[33] Blair, T. (2007) 'Blair on the media', BBC News, 12 June (http://news.bbc.co.uk/1/hi/uk_politics/6744581.stm).

[34] Hosking, P. (2012) 'They're worse than all those cowboy builders, but what can you do?', *The Times*, 19 September, pp 40-1.

[35] Hickman, M. (2012) 'The 21st journalist from *The Sun* is arrested', *The Independent*, 21 September, p 9.

[36] Halliday, J. (2012) 'Detective charged with NoW leak', *The Guardian*, 2 October, p 4.

[37] Doward, J. (2012) 'Top celebrities turn on PM for "betrayal" over phone hacking', *The Observer*, 7 October, front page.

Appendix: Key reviews and reports

Reviews directly relating to 'Baby P' case

First serious case review (SCR) report (commissioned August 2007)

Haringey Local Safeguarding Children Board (2008) *Serious case review 'Child A'*, Executive Summary, November, London: Department for Education (DfE) [DfE (2012) 'Publication of the two Serious Case Review overview reports – Peter Connelly', updated 12 July 2012 (www.education.gov.uk/a0065483/serious-case-review)].

Sibert and Hodes review report (commissioned January 2008)

Sibert, J. and Hodes, D. (2008) *Review of child protection practice of Dr Sabah Al-Zayyat*, London: Great Ormond Street Hospital NHS Trust.

Individual management review prepared on behalf of NHS London (commissioned December 2008)

Lowton, A. and Bos, S. (2009) *An individual management review into the care of PC on behalf of NHS London*, February, London: Verita.

Second serious case review (SCR) report (commissioned December 2008)

Haringey Local Safeguarding Children Board (2009) *Serious case review 'Child A'*, Executive Summary, May; full report published 26 October 2010, London: Department for Education.

Care Quality Commission (CQC) Review of NHS involvement with Peter Connelly (commissioned December 2008)

CQC (2009) *Review of the involvement and action taken by health bodies in relation to the case of Baby P*, May, London: Care Quality Commission.

Reviews relating Haringey Children's Services

Haringey Joint Area Review (2006) *London Borough of Haringey Children's Services Authority Area, Joint Area Review*, London, Ofsted.

Ofsted (2007) *2007 Annual performance assessment of services for children and young people in the London Borough of Haringey*, 26 November, London: Ofsted.

Haringey Joint Area Review (commissioned November 2008)

Ofsted, Healthcare Commission and Her Majesty's Inspectorate of Constabulary (2008) *Joint area review: Haringey Children's Services Authority Area*, November.

Haringey further Joint Area Review (commissioned December 2008)

Ofsted (2009) *Inspection of progress made in the provision of safeguarding services in the London Borough of Haringey*, 3 July.

Other serious case review reports

Maria Colwell

Department of Health and Social Security (1974) *Report of the Inquiry into the care and supervision provided in relation to Maria Colwell*, London: HMSO.

Victoria Climbié

Lord Laming (2003) *The Victoria Climbié Inquiry*, Norwich: The Stationery Office.

Other relevant reports

Conservative Party Commission on Social Workers (2007) *No more blame game: The future for children's social workers*, London: The Conservative Party.

Lord Laming (2009) *The protection of children in England: A progress report*, House of Commons, Norwich: The Stationery Office.

Social Work Task Force (2009) *Building a safe, confident future: The final report of the Social Work Task Force*, November, London: Department for Children, Schools and Families.

Department for Children, Schools and Families (DCSF) (2010) *Working together to safeguard children: A guide to inter-agency working to safeguard and promote the welfare of children*, Nottingham: DCSF Publications.

Kennedy, I. (2010) *Getting it right for children and young people: Overcoming cultural barriers in the NHS so as to meet their needs*, September (https://www.gov. uk/government/uploads/system/uploads/attachment_data/file/216282/ dh_119446.pdf).

Singleton, R. (2010) *The Chief Adviser on the Safety of Children: First Annual Report to Parliament*, March, London: Office of the Chief Adviser on the Safety of Children (http://webarchive.nationalarchives.gov.uk/20130401151715/ https://www.education.gov.uk/publications/eOrderingDownload/DCSF-00310-2010.PDF).

Social Work Reform Board (2010) *Building a safe and confident future: One year on*, December, London: Department for Children, Schools and Families.

Munro, E. (2011) *The Munro review of child protection: Final report: A child-centred system*, Cm 8062, May, London: Department for Education.

Department of Culture, Media and Sport (2012) *Leveson Inquiry: Culture, practices and ethics of the press* (www.levesoninquiry.org.uk/about/the-report).

Postscript

The publication of this book, which was largely written in 2012 and completed in 2013, has been delayed until after the end of the trial of editors, reporters and others who worked for, or have been associated with those who worked for, the *News of the World* and *The Sun* newspapers, on charges of phone hacking and related offences. The trial was held at the Royal Courts of Justice in London from October 2013 until June 2014. This postscript gives an update noting the outcomes of the trial.

It is reported that at the trial 'Mrs Brooks said "balance went right out of the window" in attacks on social work leader Sharon Shoesmith after the death of Peter Connelly – known as "Baby P"'[1] and that 'Brooks admitted that posting a photographer outside Shoesmith's home was "cruel, harsh and over the top"'.[2] It is also reported:

> Brooks described the Sun's Bonkers Bruno Locked Up headline in 2003 about the boxer Frank Bruno's mental illness as a terrible mistake and said a headline following the death of the serial killer Harold Shipman was in bad taste. 'The speed of decisions at the Sun often causes lapses of judgement', Brooks told the jury.[3]

There is nothing in this book which would disagree with Mrs Brooks' 2014 statement that 'balance went right out of the window' in *The Sun*'s attacks on Sharon Shoesmith (and social workers). It is hard to see, however, that this was a lapse of judgement caused by the 'speed of decisions' as the attacks and vilification continued year after year.

There are also accounts in this book of other stories, in addition to the death of Peter Connelly, of child deaths and about paedophiles. It is now known that some of these stories were, at least in part, based on phones being hacked. At the trial Mrs Brooks, Mr Coulson and Mr Kuttner, all former editors of the *News of the World*, denied knowing that phones had been hacked. It was seen as a defence that senior managers did not know what was happening in the organisation they were leading. The same defence was never allowed or accepted by *The Sun* and Mrs Brooks for the managers of children's services' lack of knowledge of the actions of social workers, however wrongly denigrated in the newspaper.

It is stated that a further defence within the trial was that Mrs Brooks' husband 'hid pornography from the police because he feared embarrassing details would be leaked to the press' and that 'he said he thought "Rebekah's relationship with the police changed", and spoke of her being removed from what he described as a "confidentiality club"'.[4] There are concerns noted within this book that would support Mr Brooks' fears that information might be provided to the press and other media by the police, and in the past maybe this was assisted by *The Sun*, and Mrs Brooks, being part of a 'confidentiality club'.

There was one further aspect of the trial that has a particular affinity with this book. In a report of Mrs Brooks' counsel's summing-up towards the end of the trial it is stated that 'Rebekah Brooks has been subjected to a "witch-hunt" comparable to a medieval trial in the phone-hacking case, the Old Bailey was told yesterday'.[5] It is what has been described as the 'witch-hunt' targeted at Sharon Shoesmith and social workers that is recounted in much of this book.

Notes

[1] BBC News UK (2014) 'Phone-hacking trial: Brooks "agreed payments to officials"', 27 February (www.bbc.co.uk/news/uk-26365524?print=true).

[2] Halliday, J. and O'Carroll, L. (2014) 'Brooks regrets "cruel and harsh"' attack on Clare Short over Sun page 3', 27 February (www.theguardian.com/uk-news/2014/feb/27/brooks-regrets-page-3-attack-clare-short-phone-hacking-trial).

[3] Halliday, J. and O'Carroll, L. (2014) 'Rebekah Brooks "authorised half a dozen payments to public officials"', 27 February (www.theguardian.com/uk-news/2014/feb/27/rebekah-brooks-authorised-payments-public-officials).

4 BBC News UK (2014) 'Phone-hacking trial: Charlie Brooks "feared porn leak"', 31 March (www.bbc.co.uk/news/uk-26816628).

5 O'Carroll, L. (2014) 'Brooks subjected to witch-hunt during trial, defence claims', *The Guardian*, 22 May, p 19.

THE TRIAL VERDICTS

Defendant	Charge(s)	Outcome
Rebekah Brooks – former editor of *NOTW* and *The Sun*, and former chief executive officer of News International	Conspiracy to hack phones Conspiring with others to commit misconduct in public office (x2) Conspiring with others to pervert the course of justice (x2)	Not guilty Not guilty Not guilty
Andy Coulson – former editor of *NOTW*, and former director of communications for David Cameron	Conspiracy to hack phones Conspiring with others to commit misconduct in public office (x2)	Guilty No verdict
Charlie Brooks – husband of Rebekah Brooks	Conspiring to pervert the course of justice	Not guilty
Stuart Kuttner – former managing editor of *NOTW*	Conspiracy to hack phones	Not guilty
Ian Edmundson – former *NOTW* assistant news editor	Conspiracy to hack phones	Not guilty
Cheryl Carter – former personal assistant to Mrs Brooks	Conspiring to pervert the course of justice	Not guilty
Mark Hanna – former head of security for News International	Conspiring to pervert the course of justice	Not guilty
Clive Goodman – former *NOTW* royal correspondent	Conspiring to commit misconduct in public office by offering money to public officials for information	No verdict
Greg Miskiw – former *NOTW* news editor	Conspiracy to hack phones – pleaded guilty at earlier stage of proceedings	Guilty
Neville Thurlbeck – former *NOTW* journalist	Conspiracy to hack phones – pleaded guilty at earlier stage of proceedings	Guilty
James Weatherup – former *NOTW* news editor	Conspiracy to hack phones – pleaded guilty at earlier stage of proceedings	Guilty

Index